GEREON KARL GOLDMANN, O.F.M.

THE SHADOW
OF
HIS WINGS

Translated by
Benedict Leutenegger

IGNATIUS PRESS   SAN FRANCISCO

Original edition of *The Shadow of His Wings*
© 1964, Franciscan Herald Press, Chicago
With ecclesiastical approval
All rights reserved
New edition printed by permission

The Appendix is an excerpt taken from *Against the Current:
Thrilling Experiences of the Ragpicker of Tokyo,
Father Gereon Goldmann*, by Joseph Seitz
Translated from the German by Sister Mary Cherubina Madl, O.P.
Published by the Sisters of St. Francis, Savannah, Missouri
With ecclesiastical approval
Reprinted by permission of the Sisters of St. Francis

Cover art by Christopher J. Pelicano
Cover design by Roxanne Mei Lum

© 2000 Ignatius Press, San Francisco
All rights reserved
Reprinted in 2008
ISBN 978-0-89870-774-8 (PB)
ISBN 978-1-68149-555-2 (EBOOK)
Library of Congress catalogue number 99–75401
Printed in the United States of America ∞

THE SHADOW OF HIS WINGS

CONTENTS

When I became prisoner by the French, they allways wrote on the different papers „Member of the SS!". They told me until the last day of prisoner life (in Constantine (Algér)): You are for us a SS - Nazi"!

In the often discussions in the Camp of Ksar es Souk: I allways spoke clearly, read I have been a member of the SS, — to show these people, read I knew more than them about the Nazis.

I had in this time the uniform of a Feldwebel in the Wehrmacht! All could see, read I was not more SS!

Chapter 1

CHILDHOOD GRACES, GATHERING CLOUDS

On the surface, it would seem amazing that I ever became a priest. Although my parents were deeply religious and steadfast in maintaining not only an atmosphere of piety but the actuality of it as well, my early youth was such that only God could have made me a priest!

My father was born in Fulda, a city that for centuries was called the stronghold of the Catholic faith in Germany. Its patron is St. Boniface, the Apostle of Germany, whose remains are interred under the baroque cathedral. Mother was born in North Germany in Hümmling, a district also known for the strength of its faith. Grandfather from Mother's side was a doctor, and on Father's side of the family there is evidence through many generations of a leaning toward the practice of medicine. Although Father was not a physician for humans, his practice of veterinary medicine in a district primarily devoted to agriculture and animals was surely as important to the people as if he had doctored them directly.

In 1919, three years after I was born, Father brought his family back to Fulda from the little town of Ziegenhain in Hessen, where I had been born while Father was in military service at the western front.

This return to Fulda was the beginning of a bright and mostly happy youth. Father traveled much of the time in pursuit of his profession. His prosperity can be traced over the years in the transportation changes that good fortune and hard work brought about: first, he went on a bicycle, then in a horse-drawn wagon; next, it was an incredible and noisy motorcycle, which announced his coming up and down the mountainside. The last vehicle to carry my father on his rounds was an automobile. Aptly designated "Wanderer" by its manufacturers, it was large enough for all the children— there were now seven boys, with, unhappily, no girls. We were eager passengers with Father on his excursions into the mountains, where Father inspected the flocks of sheep that throve there.

As sons of a veterinarian, we were particularly interested in anything that lived and moved. The barns of the farmers my father served were places of rich-smelling mystery, dark but friendly, having many secret corners and out-of-the-way places for boys to hide and amuse themselves.

The open fields were our collecting grounds, for we could not resist anything that moved. Remembering his own boyhood, Father gave smiling, if secret, approval to our collecting of birds, cats, young dogs, snakes, fish, salamanders, squirrels, and whatever else we could catch, with one exception. We were forbidden to molest or try to catch or even to touch a fawn, for although our deer were so tame that they were almost pets, they were nevertheless wild creatures who could not long survive captivity. We were permitted to leave feed for them in bad winters, but that was all.

Beyond this, however, the boxes and cages we created for the animals were almost constantly full, over Mother's horrified protests. If the animals had not been sufficient to try Mother's great patience, I think the stone collections would

*Dr. Karl Goldmann, Sr.,
veterinarian of Fulda.*

*An early photograph of Margareth
Goldmann, who taught her son to
defend the helpless.*

*Born October 10, 1916,
young Karl Goldmann
was twelve years old
when this photograph
was taken.*

have done the trick. I realize, now, what a chore it must have been to have a houseful of male children close enough together in age for the older ones to lead the younger ones into all kinds of devilment, full of imagination and healthy good spirits. Having no daughters to comfort or to help her, Mother did a really remarkable job. She was not the nagging kind, however, so when she found that we were so intent on filling the house with stones and pets, she permitted the building of cages for the animals and supervised the building of cabinets for each of us, with locks and name plates.

In addition to our other numerous trips with Father, we boys made twice yearly trips alone to the surrounding villages with the bills, hoping to collect and bring home some money. It was exciting, being allowed such responsibility, and we invented many dangers for ourselves to make it even more so. We dreamed that there were robbers hiding in the woods, waiting to spring out and seize us and take our money—perhaps even to kidnap us and make us robbers too!

In time, we learned which farmers would welcome us with a bite to eat; which ones would chase us if we attempted, as who would not, to sample the sweet apples practically falling from their well-loaded trees.

We entertained ourselves by reciting in loud voices bits of Latin phrases and even some French and Greek, which we had learned in school. We really did it to impress those who heard us, unknowing and uncaring that it served the useful purpose of improving our speech and mastery of foreign languages. I imagine if someone had pointed out to us that we were benefiting from the practice, we would have dropped it immediately.

There were plenty of tricks and much mischief in us too, such as inquiring the distance to a certain town from everyone we passed and then laughing uncontrollably while we compared the variant answers we received. We loved to address the plainspoken, honest farmers in a foreign language to see their reactions; but when they caught on to the fact that we were laughing at them and mocking them, a grand chase was instituted, which usually ended with one or more of us having boxed ears or smarting backsides.

Sometimes friends from the local Marian sodality, which our family had joined upon returning to Fulda, would accompany us on these trips. On those occasions, we would spend the night in the open, sleeping in tents or in friendly barns.

In school, the teachers were strict, but since we were fairly bright and talented, we managed to get along without much difficulty. Even with a lot of homework, our wits provided us with good grades and entirely too much free time. From time to time complaints would catch up with us from many sources; our cat-loving aunts, who lived in the city, would make pointed references to boys who stoned cats; the police would be forced to complain that "someone" could not let the doorbells along the street alone; or the gas man would unaccountably find the street lights going out behind him as fast as he would get them lighted in the dusk.

Meanwhile, our religious training was not neglected. Every Saturday I received the sacrament of Penance, and, heaven knows, I had sufficient reason for penitence. Our chaplain had his hands full with me. My father called me a devil in the house and an angel on the street, because I knew how to make a good impression in public, but at home I was so very different.

Our home life was marked by a deep faith and a true piety. Father and Mother were models of Catholic parents, without being the least sanctimonious about it. Every week brought Holy Mass, Communion, and the sacrament of Penance; the

When Margareth died in 1924, Sister Solana May told young Karl, "I will take the place of your mother." She was to carry out her promise in a remarkable way. Sister is shown with Karl (far right) and three other altar boys whom she trained.

feasts of the ecclesiastical year were duly and fully celebrated, with all of the beautiful traditions preserved and perpetuated. There were pilgrimages, especially to our Lady's mountain. Although the services there seemed to be terribly tiresome, with the long solemn High Mass and the friars' choir, they were made more palatable to us by the fried sausages traditionally served after the ceremonies.

I remember how happy I was to be a Catholic: the cemetery visits on Good Friday; the wonderful cribs at Christmastime; the pilgrimages; the devotions; the happy freedom. And most of all, I remember the Christian principles we learned through the example set by our parents, who actually did what others only said was right. Throughout the year, Father would receive many letters from the missions. These he kept until the close of the year, when each letter was answered with a donation, according to how our fortunes had prospered that year.

Father offered a ride to anyone he met on the street. When he met a beggar, he stopped to give him something or to offer him a ride. I suppose that the gypsies were among the few people for whom Father had little sympathy. For reasons that were not clear to me, he seemed also to have little use for the Lutherans or the Jews.

I found it difficult to understand, for I liked the Jews. On Jewish feast days, we always received presents or cakes from them; they always had money. One of our favorite pranks was to entice the children to go beyond the allowed distance on their Sabbath. Often we succeeded, with dire results for them. That is, until Father learned of it. When he did, we were given a severe lesson in the dispensary, with a rod as the chief teaching aid. At such times, we would pad the seats of our pants, hoping that this would spare us some of the sting. When the first one punished began to cry, we would all set up a howl, so that eventually the blows would become softer and softer, and the last one in line for punishment hardly felt the stick at all. We tried to make sure that the last one in the current punishment would be the first in line for the next time; but this didn't always work, especially after Father began to be aware that there was something going on.

Our religious training was somewhat strict, we felt, as was our schooling. In the school, Herr Hagemann found it necessary to bend me over the chair almost daily. We considered it the right of the student to tease the teacher but were prepared for the "reward" that came with playing tricks. In spite of this, we learned. Even in school, the example of our parents had a most profound effect on us. They taught us never to leave a weaker person unprotected; to take care of the sick and the weak; to console the underdogs and lift them up, if possible.

My mother was a truly amazing person, with a wealth of understanding and sympathy. Her kitchen was often occupied by some troubled wife from the countryside who had come to ask her advice. The women would sit with mother in the kitchen, pouring out their troubles, weeping, and then leaving consoled and refreshed in body and soul. Mother was the one who taught me to defend the little and the weak, especially since I was quite big and strong. I brought home many a bloody nose as proud evidence of my battles on behalf of schoolmates who were being bedeviled by the bigger boys.

At the age of eight, I began to experience, even if I did not fully appreciate, the grace of God in serving Mass. I served at the convent of the English Ladies, whose convent and school were opposite each other. Every morning, for nearly six years, I walked to the convent a little before five o'clock and prepared to serve. There were times when I was just too tired to

A music-loving band of hikers, the Marian Sodality of Fulda was one of the many outdoor groups that attracted Karl. He is shown here (front, right) in 1929.

The Institut St. Mariae der Englischen Fräulein (Convent of the English Ladies), Fulda, where Karl served as an altar boy from 1924 until 1931.

get out of bed to go and serve Mass. I would then punch myself in the nose until blood flowed freely and then return to bed. Without revealing the source of it, I could in all truth tell Sister Sacristan that a nosebleed had kept me from my duties.

For the most part, I arrived at the convent fifteen minutes before the Mass. Sister Sacristan would give me a pious book to read. Now, the fact that I had arrived bodily did not mean that my attention had come with me, or that I did not wish I were still asleep. More than once during Mass the Missal fell from the stand when it was my turn to carry it. The Latin was beyond me at first, and only the first and last words came through loud and clear when it was my turn.

Then one day a truly exciting thing happened, which changed the very course of my life, not dramatically and in a split second, as in fiction, but slowly, over the years. Since I was accustomed to go to Communion regularly, I went to confession every week. I saw the Franciscan fathers every morning, and they invited me into their friary. There they jokingly promised me that if I would serve them I could join their community, and I would get sweet pears every day. Many years later, when I became a member of the order, I discovered this was only a pious fib.

One day a Franciscan came from Japan and gave us a lecture. He also preached a sermon in the parish church about the wonderful land of the Orient. It excited my imagination as nothing had ever done before. After Mass, I went to the sacristy and asked him to take me along when he returned to Japan. He laughed and said I was too small. That made me indignant; for, at nine, I was the tallest boy in the class and inordinately proud of my stature. My secret dream was to grow even faster and become taller than my two older brothers, for then I would get the new clothes first and they would have to wear the hand-me-downs that were now my unhappy, though far from ragged, lot.

I protested to the Franciscan priest that I was surely tall enough for Japan.

"But what will your parents say about it?" he inquired. I assured him that there were six other children at home. I would simply go with him and Mother would never miss me with her work and all the other boys.

He laughed, but kindly, and said, "That still would not do, I'm afraid. I cannot steal a boy—that would be a sin. But if you really want to go to Japan, I know a much safer way."

"Please tell me, Father!"

"Say one Hail Mary every day for that intention, and some day you will get to Japan. Will you promise that?"

That was not difficult, so I gave my promise and began to say a Hail Mary every night. I discovered on the very first night that this was not as easy as it seemed at first blush, for I fell asleep while praying. Disgusted with myself, the next night I said three, one for the one missed the first night, one for the present night, and one in case perhaps the Blessed Virgin Mary was as disgusted with me as I was with myself.

After that, it was much easier, and I can't recall that I ever again forgot or fell asleep. This was my first really independent step on the long road that finally led to the priesthood.

My mother died when the oldest of my brothers was twelve and the youngest one year old. She went to God while we were living in Fulda. Her burial on a rainy October day was the darkest day of my youth. Father was absolutely stricken; he stood at the grave motionless, without a tear. Many hundreds of people attended the burial, mostly farmers' wives from the villages around Fulda who had been attracted to Mother's kindness, her thoughtfulness, and the reputation she gained over the years for honest wisdom. It was a funeral procession of grateful people who many times had shared both their tears and their produce with Mother over a cup of steaming coffee.

After Mother's death, Sister Solana May, the sacristan, said: "I will take the place of your mother." But she did not tell me how she proposed to do it. Later, I learned that her superior granted her permission to pray for me that I might become a Franciscan priest. She had heard me express this wish many times since the visit of the missionary. She also asked the more than two hundred Sisters of her community to pray for this intention; she calculated correctly that I would need twenty years to complete the required studies, and she promised before the Blessed Sacrament that she would pray twenty years for me so that our Lord would make me a Franciscan priest.

I knew nothing of Sister Solana's plan as I continued to serve Mass. In spite of my desire to go to Japan as a Franciscan, in spite of the nightly Hail Marys to this intention, in spite of my daily exposure to the Mass, and in spite of the prayers of my Mother before she died and the admonitions of my Father, I had a bad reputation in the city.

I was the leader of a group of boys who were just too wild and rude for the good burghers of Fulda. Attending Mass and receiving Holy Communion brought about no improvement whatever. I think perhaps I was wild, rather than bad—but, whatever the basis of my behavior, I drove my elders to distraction. At times my father thought I had swallowed a devil, which he honestly and earnestly tried to drive out of me. If the devil had resided in the seat of my pants, his efforts would have been effective; but he could not reach my heart with the bamboo stick. My flesh was so impressed with its sting that I rubbed the bamboo with onions, causing it to break—which of course brought about further unavailing applications.

I continued to be incorrigible until my mother's death. Even though I was subdued by her loss, and for a time swore that I would try to be good, youngsters forget easily. A good elderly housekeeper tried to keep us in check. Fräulein Nolte had only one fault—she was Lutheran and hence would some day go to hell, however devoutly she prayed. She did not make the sign of the cross, and she failed to go to church every Sunday. If that were not evidence enough, she said "Mary" and not "Holy Mary", and thus must surely have been predestined to damnation. I told her this often, but she paid no attention to me.

After Fräulein Nolte came to care for us, we became most pious, playing Mass in the house. We made an altar with all the furnishings, including a chalice, which we filled with fruit juice. At times we would hold a procession through the rooms of the three-story house. Dressed in brilliant robes, we sang very loudly, chanting and praying and singing loudest when we were nearest poor Fräulein Nolte. We thought this would let her know what we thought of her, but she remained calm and friendly and cared for us bad boys as if she had been sent from heaven, as indeed she may have been. How we harassed her, and how ashamed we were when her unfailing patience made us see that we were going too far, making a mockery of the most sacred and solemn elements of our lives, simply to show a harmless, friendly old lady that we thought she was damned because she did not share our faith! I am happy now at the thought that I shall be permitted to meet her in heaven. I can express my thanks to her and ask her forgiveness.

Four years after Mother's death, Father married our mother's youngest sister. Though she could never take our own mother's place, we had known her a long time and were used to her, and we grew to love her in a short time. The addition of three more boys and, at last, two girls completed the family picture and made for a bustling household, constantly in motion.

Soon after Father's second marriage, we moved to Cologne, where our father became what he had always called himself—"a man of importance". Changing schools was not difficult, since the school at Fulda had been both outstanding and demanding, and we had no trouble in adapting to the new teachers.

We joined the *Bund Neudeutschland* and spent an unforgettable five years under the direction of the Jesuit Fathers. The *Bund* provided for young boys an unaffected Christian education, with lectures, homework, song and play, trips, camping, and training in taking care of the poor, the suffering, and the distressed. The priests who directed this youth group were ideally suited for it, being young, vigorous intellectuals who could live with us as if they, too, were still boys. We felt that they understood us.

As time passed, and Germany came under the dark spell of Adolph Hitler, the Christian youth group and the Hitler youth group became more and more antagonistic. We engaged in what eventually became battles—real fights where blood was shed and gashes received from knives. We carried our scars like badges of martyrdom. When the police arrested and imprisoned us, we felt it was part of the adventure. It was not that we were really aware of the moral danger or the politics of the worsening situation in our country; we simply opposed the Nazis as our natural enemies, considering ourselves soldiers for Christ, around whom our whole education and lives centered.

Soon, however, things changed. When we had to attend a school where the director was a fervent Nazi, the terrible realization of what was threatening our country began to come alive to us. Because the Catholic youth were good

In September 1926, Karl served in a work camp of the
Arbeitsdienst on the Lüneberger Heath. For the first time
he learned what life was to be like in de-Christianized
Germany. Karl's height makes him stand out from his
fellow-workers.

Among the work Karl did was
ditch-digging, part of a flood-
control project.

This work was not
spectacularly successful, as
this view of the camp
barracks shows.

students, we were not expelled when we engaged in verbal battles with the school director that left him white with rage. But we were in danger, all of us.

Finally, we were arrested. In court, we declared loudly that *we* were the new Germans, not the Nazis, and that the only way to save Germany was through Jesus Christ. The situation rapidly grew worse, and in 1934 the work of the Catholic youth groups was proscribed. Despite that, we were ready to brave anything to prove that we were men, that we were Christians, that we were worthy of our aspirations; so the outlawing of our meetings and our work served only to send most of us "hiking", as we called it in those days. If the police caught us on the road on the way to one of our assignments, they sent us home with only our shirt and pants.

In one trial before the juvenile court, the director shouted at me: "You will be expelled! You are a blot on the good name of the school!" And yet we were granted amnesty again.

We went deeper into the Black Forest on our bicycles, carrying out our Christian missions. When they tried to prevent us from leaving the city, we hid ourselves under piles of cabbages that were waiting in the market to be shipped out. Anything to continue with our work!

The most important things to us, still, were the religious discussions, the weekly community Mass, which we never missed, the retreats and days of recollection, and the feast days. To us, the whole year was a religious feast.

On the feast of the Most Blessed Trinity, the whole of the *Bund Neudeutschland*—all of us harassed Catholic youth— gathered together. After the religious services in the cathedral, the Hitler Youth and the SS were called out to engage us in a street fight. They were thousands strong, and blood flowed; more than one of us had to be carried home.

Under the circumstances, we had little time for studies; but

I still passed the examination, although my mark was lowered in order to reprimand me for being a leader of the Catholic youth. The work of our group seemed far more necessary and important to me than academic studies. After graduation, we were sent to a work camp in the Lüneburger Heath, an assignment I freely chose. Up to this time, I had grown up in the protected surroundings of school; and despite our battles with the Hitler Youth, we were mostly innocent of the real ways of the world. I was astounded when I saw what the average man in the camp was like. It was inconceivable to me that men could think and say and do such things. What surprised me was that the most depraved among them were the so-called leaders; the camp physician was one of the first in giving out detailed instructions to newcomers in every sort of vice. These men not only rejected Christianity and the Catholic Church, but they rejected their own humanity as well.

What a joy and relief it was on Sundays to bicycle the fifteen or so miles to the Catholic mission church where we could participate with grateful heart in the Mass and receive Holy Communion to give us strength to continue for another week! Life in that terrible place was difficult, but in later years the experience proved to be good schooling.

At last, in the fall of 1936, I was able to carry out the plan I had secretly entertained of entering the Franciscan Order. My father did not especially care for this; he felt that if I must become a priest, the least I could do was to enter a seminary where I might become a diocesan priest, perhaps even a bishop! Why choose the Franciscans?

But my mind was made up. With his blessing, I quietly entered the Franciscan novitiate in Salmuenster Bad Soden; then I studied at Gorheim-Sigmaringen and Fulda, where in the summer of 1939 I finished my studies in philosophy.

Divine Providence saw to it that I got a solid education in philosophy and all my scientific studies, so that when the time of trial and endurance arrived, I was ready.

On the day after the final examination in philosophy, the orders came to report for induction into the army. I was twenty-two years old, and, fledgling priest or no, I became a soldier, not by choice, but on command. The unhappy war had begun.

In October 1936, Karl became a novice at the Franciscan novitiate at Gorheim.

From Gorheim, he was sent back to Fulda, where he studied philosophy for two years. This photograph shows the entrance to the Frauenberg cloister.

On August 28, 1939, these young Franciscan seminarians were notified that they were to be inducted into the army. Karl (Frater Gereon to his brothers in St. Francis) is in the third row, third from the right.

Two days later, the students for the priesthood were members of Hitler's Wehrmacht, raw recruits assigned to the cavalry.

Seven weeks of rugged basic training proved the mettle of the "sedentary" young seminarians. Shortly after this picture was taken in September 1939, Karl Goldmann volunteered to go to the eastern front.

Sent to desolate country near the Polish border, the men dubbed their base "Camp Earthworm". Here Goldmann marches head and shoulders above his comrades in the communications platoon of the SS, to which he was assigned.

Chapter 2

THE BROWN MAN

On the last day of August 1939, some two hundred young theologians, students all, arrived at the Fulda barracks with thousands of other young German recruits. We were assigned to a cavalry division and turned over to non-commissioned officers for training. Some of our group were Franciscans, others came from different religious orders; all were equally looked down upon by the officers and non-coms who had our training in their hands.

They were determined to prove to us once and for all that, because we were seminarians and therefore undoubtedly led soft, sedentary lives, we were less than human and could not survive the rigors of military training. They spent hours devising ways of proving to us our inferiority, and they were enraged to learn, over the seven weeks of our basic training, that we were not only in superb physical condition but that our religious background had given us the spiritual strength to withstand their repeated onslaughts on our faith, our morality, and our goals.

In their off-duty hours, the non-coms spent their time regaling one another with tales of drinking bouts and exaggerated anecdotes of their prowess with women; but we quietly continued our education by reading what books on philosophy and other related subjects we could obtain.

We were given the most fractious horses to ride; the most odious duties fell to us; and, worst of all, we were deliberately given duty on every Sunday but one of those first seven weeks to keep us from Mass and from Communion. But we were young and strong enough to endure since we knew the basic training period must soon end. We clung together—not frightened, as they thought, but because we knew that our strength lay in our faith and our unity in Christ.

When we were finally able to leave the camp, all two hundred of us rushed to a nearby monastery where we received Holy Communion to give us strength for the coming days and weeks.

When our basic training period was over, the officers were astonished that none of the seminarians had dropped out or been dropped; they could not understand the source of our ability to withstand the harsh treatment we had received. We began to think that life there in the camp on the home front must be far worse than it was on the battle lines; and so it was that I, with ten other students, volunteered to go to the eastern front. It was not so much from a desire to fight as it was a deep need to get away from the stagnant, evil air of the barracks.

After two days of traveling under secret orders, we came at last, in a torrential rain, to a lonely section of the Polish border. We found a barren camp set in a barren land, called by the evocative name of "Earthworm". We were hungry, but there was nothing to eat but some thin soup that did absolutely nothing to satisfy our hunger or our thirst. We looked for and found the canteen, hoping to find something to eat. We were surprised to find there a great variety of uniforms: some members of the *Wehrmacht*, like ourselves; some corporals in the blue uniform of policemen; many non-coms of a higher rank; and some SS officers in their black uniforms. When the drinks we ordered did not come, we helped ourselves; but we did not return to the table we had vacated. We ran full tilt into a group of twenty men who were earnestly discussing the pope and the Catholic Church, saying that the pope was the greatest warmonger of all history and that this war had as its final goal the abolition of the pope and all priests who called themselves followers of Christ. "The Christians are worse than the Jews", they said, denouncing all that was holy and sacred to us.

I shall never forget what an effort it was for us to keep our mouths shut in the face of all this. To bite our tongues while the saints were reviled and the Mother of God was irreverently spoken of was almost too much for our blood pressure.

Finally, I said to one of the officers who was laughing loudest, "Forgive me for speaking, sir, since I am a newcomer and not yet part of this group. But were you aware that the leaders of the Reich have signed a Concordat with the Catholic Church? Did you know that Christianity is one of the religions Germany is pledged to protect?"

At first they were speechless. Then the officer asked, "What do you mean?"

I answered calmly, on sure ground, "Surely you are aware of the risk you are taking by thus expressing, in the presence of so many witnesses, sentiments that are so exactly opposite those of the government and the Führer?"

"Do you think that you know the mind of the Führer?" he demanded.

"Of course, in this instance. May I respectfully remind you, sir, that he has made his mind quite clear in his public speeches and by the signing of the Concordat that whoever attacks the Christian religion undermines what the Führer himself has set down as a foundation for the German government! He himself has declared that it must be protected."

There was nothing more they could say to this, of course, since I spoke the truth.

Finally, one of them asked if I were a "black" man or a "brown" one—with the black standing for the priests and the brown for the Nazis. I could hardly keep my face straight as I replied firmly, "I am a brown man."

This surprised them. "When did you become a member?" they asked, meaning, of course, a member of the party.

I answered that I joined the browns in 1936.

"Where?"

"In the monastery of the Franciscans in Fulda. They have worn brown habits for six hundred years, far longer, you will agree, than the other browns have been in existence."

The result was an uproar of fury and laughter. I knew, of course, and so did my companions, that this sort of impudence could get me in trouble; but my politics and my faith were in deep conflict with the goals of the Nazis, and to remain silent in the midst of such hatred was more than I could stand. I really do not believe that I was any more courageous than my comrades—simply more outspoken by nature, and perhaps a little more foolhardy!

Reprisals were not long in coming. First thing the next morning, during drill, the young officer who commanded our group shouted, "Where are the priests?"

No one moved. We did not feel that we must answer that question, since none of us was in actuality a priest.

Then he cried out, "Let the priests step forward!" We did not budge.

Finally, one of the men who had heard us the night before pointed to two of us. The officer bellowed, "Didn't you hear me say the priests should step forward?"

In a loud voice, I said, "I am not a priest! I am a student of theology. Applying the term 'priest' to me is an insult to the Catholic Church and our Christian nation." All were silent.

The young lieutenant, younger even than I, turned white and screamed at me and the other seminarian who had been pointed out to him: "Up a tree—quick, march!" Promptly, tongues in cheek, we obeyed the command and climbed the nearest tree. We found comfortable perches on handy cross-branches and peered down. Somehow, our expressions did not seem to the lieutenant to be suitable; we were not contrite, but triumphant, and so once again he gave a command: "Sing a hymn!"

With all the dignity at our command, considering our perch, we loudly sang the *Te Deum*—in Latin, of course. The poor lieutenant understood only his army German and roared, "What was that? I ordered you to sing a church song!"

"But, lieutenant," I replied loudly, so that the others, who were standing around showing various emotions at this spectacle, could hear, "that was a church song. We are sorry that you do not understand it. But, of course, the language of the church is Latin or Greek or Hebrew. Those who do not understand these languages cannot, unfortunately, understand the songs of the church."

Laughter echoed along the entire front ranks drawn up beneath us. The young officer was made to look ridiculous, and, pressing our advantage, we began again to sing the *Te Deum*.

When the lieutenant yelled, "Stop! Descend!" we pretended that we didn't hear him but remained in our tree, still singing, the sonorous and beautiful music rolling out across the parade ground. Fortunately, we both had good lungs.

When we finally came down, he began his attempt at revenge, which included every ridiculous or difficult command

Partially obscured by the antenna of his equipment, Goldmann and a fellow seminarian learn radio operation in the field.

In the winter, despite the fact that the seminarians were exhausted from drilling, they went to a Catholic church in nearby Bürschen for prayer and meditation. Of the eleven seminarians in Goldmann's platoon, the only one to give up his faith was the man who refused to pray each evening.

he could come up with. While trying to put us through our paces and exhaust and show us up at the same time, he succeeded only in appearing even more ridiculous, for our years in the camps had made us hard and strong. We took to the army drill as if we had been made of iron.

At last, when we had had enough, we followed his command to run east into the forest by running so fast and so far that we lost the sound of his voice. At the end of two hours, we had plunged completely through the forest, laughing all the while at the lieutenant's misfortune in having us for recruits. We surmised, correctly, that eventually they would have to come and search for us. We sat idly on the edge of the road at the other side of the forest, and, sure enough, after a while an auto came along.

When we were publicly scolded for "not using our heads and realizing we should have stopped at some point", we reminded him that we had been told again and again as recruits, "Leave the thinking to the officers or to the horses; they have bigger heads."

Again, the company was dissolved in laughter, and the luckless lieutenant could only threaten us. To our secret amusement, we learned later that a large number of the non-coms were pleased to see their conceited lieutenant taken down a few notches. Of course, he was not through with us. There are many ways of tormenting a soldier, and he used them all with vigor. The result was that we showed ourselves to be pretty good soldiers. Finding nothing in our military performance that he could use as a weapon against us, he was at his wits' end.

Then he made another mistake. He began coming to us in the evenings, while we were cleaning our weapons or our uniforms, and trying to convince us how foolish it was to be Christian. He brought with him as part of his mental equipment a few slogans and clichés that he had managed to retain in his empty head from his Nazi schooling. We came to the battle with nine years of classical education and two years of intensive philosophy, of which he knew nothing. It began to amuse us, especially when the other officers and some of the non-coms joined in the discussions—which often lasted until midnight. For us, it was an excellent opportunity to prove not only the soundness of the ideas we had had drummed into us by our education, but also to prove our faith. Nothing could crack the solid front of truth that was ours by virtue of the Cause we served.

Our lives began to adopt a rugged regimentation, brought about partly, and made much rougher, by our insistence that we were right in this running argument that seemed never to end. Our days were spent in eight or more hours of physical training on the ice and snow of a frozen lake between Burschen and Finsterwald. With our background, there was no possibility of our breaking down under this kind of pressure. In the evenings, tired though we were from the day's exertions, we forced ourselves to go to a nearby Catholic church to refresh and strengthen our spirits for the coming debates in the barracks. We knew that somehow we had to win; we knew how important it was for us always to maintain the battle for souls. War or no war, army or no army, in spite of harassment, bullying, ridicule, and pressure, we could not let down our guard before these men. Perhaps even one among them would come to see the truth we served; if that were so, we would be well rewarded.

Only one of the eleven seminarians in our group gave up his faith; and he was the single one who didn't go with us to the church in the evening for meditation and prayer. He was also the only one who did not return to the seminary after the war—with the exception of the many who were killed in Russia.

Chapter 3

"PRIESTLINGS"

The next three years turned out to be among the most interesting in my life.

There was, for example, the matter of our army oath. The night before, we learned that the form of attestation was without the name of God. At once it was clear to us that we could not go along with such an odd promise and consider it an oath. The next morning two regiments stood at attention, a few seminarians in the right wing of the first line. The general came and gave an explanation of the meaning of the oath to the flag. Then all stood still, and an officer recited the formula of the oath, in which it was affirmed that we swore by the honor of German blood to defend the Fatherland. We seminarians did not stir as the thousand soldiers raised their arms to repeat the words of the oath, which was no oath. The general noticed that we did not join the others; and later we were called and asked why we did not take the oath. We answered that an oath is made in the name of God and if his name is not mentioned one is not held by it. We knew we were taking a strong stand, but we had agreed not to give in where there was a question of fundamentals.

We wondered, of course, what the general's reaction to

this bit of daring would be. He was silent for a while, and in amazement he asked us what our former occupation had been. When we told him, he seemed puzzled, wondering how it was that the army got us.

The next morning, we were called before our commanding officer and told that we had a choice of either remaining with the army or going instead into the SS.

We were thunderstruck. I said, "But, *Herr Oberst!* What about the oath? You have heard our protest, I am sure."

He replied, "That will be no problem."

He called in another officer, who administered the old-fashioned military oath, which in another time had had the name of God in it. It was that simple!

"Now. As members of the SS police division, you men will be free to fulfill your religious obligations; you will not be bothered in any way."

"Sir?" I asked, still puzzled by this turn of events.

"Yes, Goldmann?"

"Forgive my asking what may seem an impertinent question, but why would the SS elite guard want us, when the *Wehrmacht* has no use for us—and, in fact, has ridiculed us every step of the way?"

"You men are educated, intelligent, and loyal. Your fuss over the taking of what was to you a false oath gave us assurance that you would not break your oath if it were given in a way that was meaningful to you. The SS is a far higher order than the general run of the army, and we need all the brains and loyalty we can get. This is going to be a difficult war, and it is only through the genuine, reasoning cooperation of men such as yourselves that we will accomplish our ends."

For the second time that day, I was rendered speechless.

The high command had decided to set up a bureau of information, and to that end all the seminarians in the SS were trained as radio officers. This, of course, was far easier than life in the army had been, and we found ourselves with a good deal of leisure time, which we spent in practicing or in reading. We also had Sundays off.

That suited us, for we could now attend Mass. We were warmly received by the priests of the parish and by their parishioners; we returned to the camp each Sunday night refreshed both in body and in spirit.

Things went on in pretty much the same fashion, with occasional skirmishes with the overzealous Nazi non-coms, but, all in all, fairly peaceful. We performed our duties, attended church, and participated in the interminable discussions that still took place almost nightly in the barracks. I came to realize that I personally would not wish to leave the SS or the army even if my release should come tomorrow. I felt that perhaps this was a great opportunity for bringing blessings to these arid men, letting them see that, regardless of the circumstances, men of God were given strength and power to overcome many things, while men without God must know only emptiness, even in the midst of apparent plenty.

On Christmas Eve, there was a celebration, not a Christian one, but a pagan German *Julfest*. We were all together and had to sing some trash about the night of the clear stars and other sad substitutes for the true Christmas message. But our thoughts were elsewhere; we thought of the Christmas tree, the crib, the carols at home. The food was good, and we were given wine, but that was nothing to us.

Around nine o'clock, a one-armed major, a veteran of the First World War, entered with the adjutant. We had heard that a special order from the leader of the SS was to be read, but we had no deep interest in it.

The room was cleared of all but SS men, for the message was secret and directed only to us. The adjutant read from a yellow slip of paper:

"Men, this is the Christmas order from Himmler himself. You must pay close attention. He says:

" 'Our glorious victory over Poland, great though it was, has cost the blood of many thousands of the best Germans. Thousands of our splendid youth will never return. Many families are without a father; many brides are without a groom; many maidens must now live without their intended spouses.

" 'This is a heavy loss for German blood. No victory is anything if the blood stream, the precious stream of the holy and divine German blood, be not renewed and increased.

" 'It is the mission of the SS, the elite company, to present the Führer with the gift of new blood, to beget children in whom the divine stream will flow on for all eternity.

" 'All members of the SS are bound in duty to present the Führer with children. Many eager maidens will be waiting for the man who will help them to give the Führer a child.

" 'A leave of absence is herewith granted to all members of the SS for the purpose of carrying out this glorious mission. The state will assume all costs; and, in addition, will pay the SS members who fulfill this mission a reward of 1,000 marks for every child.' "

Silence reigned; no one spoke. The major asked, "Who is ready to start such a furlough?"

There was no answer; the men just sat there and let their faces show their thoughts.

Then came the question: "Where are the seminarians?" We stood, and I was asked directly what I thought of the command.

"Sir," I replied, "as a soldier I am not allowed to have personal opinions—or to express them."

"So you approve of the command? What do you plan to do?"

My face began to turn red as I answered, "Whether I approve or not, I am not allowed to express myself. Up till now, I have only heard that commands, of whatever kind, are made to be carried out."

The entire company broke out in a loud laughter, and I was told that I made a face that showed too much interest.

"Goldmann, you are a leader of sorts among these priestlings, and I will not command you to express your innermost thoughts—I will *request* it, with my assurance that you are free to speak your mind without fear of reprisal."

"Thank you, *Herr Major*. It saddens me that such a command should come at all, but especially that it should be made at Christmastime. During this holy season, our thoughts are directed toward higher things!" And I went on to quote Tacitus—in Latin, of course, which always makes a good impression—and what he said about the German maidens and their purity in Germania two thousand years ago. Next I quoted Caesar and what he said about the virtuous conduct of the northern people; then came the Middle Ages with appropriate examples; and I finally concluded:

"Now we come to those who consider themselves as true Germans and who consider Christianity as a deterioration of the German race, while masquerading as a Christian nation. They command the begetting of children—not caring how or with whom—and offer a premium for performance. Are these the true Germans? In my judgment, in all the history of Germany, never until this day and by the order of the leader of the SS, has such an outrage been proposed to the young women of Germany!" I must have spoken for about ten minutes. It was my first sermon.

The men sprang up and shouted, "Bravo!" A few muttered, "Let Himmler take care of the eager maidens himself."

A near riot broke out among the men. The meeting dispersed before midnight, and whole groups of SS men went with us six kilometers through the snow and bitter cold to the nearest Catholic church in Jordan.

The lovable old pastor, though he was accustomed to having us seminarians show up frequently, was shocked at this invasion by the SS, most of whom were non-Catholics. After Mass we were rewarded with delicious Christmas cake from the good parishioners, whom the pastor had roused out to join in the celebration.

The next morning, of course, the men returned to their accustomed brutal ways, some of them even grumbling at the opportunity passed by the night before; but they had had a lasting experience of righteousness and the peace of doing the right thing in the face of opposition. They would never forget it, even during the times when they might regret their participation.

The married men were given a Christmas furlough the following day, and I was given a special furlough by the base commander, who congratulated me upon my speech and my courage the night before. I was much surprised but hastened to take advantage of it before someone had a change of heart and decided I should remain in the camp. I spent a wonderful holiday with my family and returned to finish off my three-month training period, the last three days of which were being conducted by Reichsführer Himmler himself.

The day of demonstration maneuvers was a bitter one; snow blew from the mountaintop, and one of our units became lost there. At last, a command was given to them that saved them all, and during review of the unit at the close of the maneuvers, Himmler commanded that the officer leading it step forward.

No one moved.

"Come, come, no modesty. I wish to speak with the officer who gave the command and made the decision that saved that unit from sure death in this storm. Step forward!"

Finally, a soldier whom I knew well stepped forth. He was our Franciscan brother Roger Ricker. We were all amazed, and Himmler asked him, "Did you give the order?"

"Yes, *Herr Reichsführer.*"

"But who gave you, a mere soldier, permission to take over the command?"

"Sir, our leader was incapacitated. In our instructions, we have been told repeatedly that, in case of necessity, anyone has the duty to give a saving command."

Himmler exclaimed, "Bravo. Here is a soldier who knows his duty. You are worthy to be an officer in the SS. I will send you at once to a school for officers."

Roger's clear reply rang out in the stillness, "Sir, that is no longer possible; I have already been at officers' school."

No one understood his answer, and, when he was asked what he meant, he said loudly and firmly, "I attended the officers' school of the greatest and best-known army in the world—the army of Jesus Christ in the Order of St. Francis. I am in training to be a priest!" All became very quiet. Himmler whispered to the astonished officers around him, and Roger was ordered to step back.

In the evening, I was summoned with three other seminarians for a private chat with Himmler. He was very friendly, and he asked us, "Are you really students for the priesthood?"

"Yes, sir."

"How do you happen to be here—and do you wish to continue to serve in the SS?"

"We are ready to serve here, sir, since we have been promised that we will be perfectly free to fulfill our religious obligations."

Himmler talked briefly to those close to him and then said, "You are free to serve your God. There is no religious coercion here. But you must have observed already that whoever is among us undergoes . . . a change, and that without force."

I laughed.

He looked at me and said, "Why do you laugh?"

I blurted out, "We shall see who changes whom."

The others stared at Himmler: What would he say now? But he merely looked at us and said, with satisfaction, to his companions, "These fellows are all right; we need them." To us, he said, "You are free to go."

And go we did, with this assurance from him who frightened everyone that we were free to fulfill our religious obligations.

There was a sequel to this incident. The next morning, one of the higher officers received a communication from headquarters that had been passed on from the highest source. In it, we learned that the final goal of the war was to free not only Germany and Europe but the whole world from two adversaries—the Communists and the Christians. The more dangerous, they said, was the Church, which for two thousand years had enslaved mankind with its religion of hypocrisy and false love. "Until the last priest hangs on the gallows, the final victory has not been won!" the communiqué said.

"Yesterday, we were assured religious freedom from one of the highest sources; what we now hear is just the opposite!" I cried.

The officer sneeringly replied, "Yes, indeed. Religious

freedom, by all means—as long as the war lasts. Nothing has been said, though, about what happens after the war is ended!"

I have an unfortunate tendency to put my foot into it, so I could not refrain from asking, "Sir, what will happen when we are again in our monasteries?"

"If one of my men should dare to enter again into those nests of stupidity, I would personally tie him to the nearest tree for flogging!"

Now we knew where we stood. But it would be a long time before that happened, and I merely suggested that we should wait quietly and, in the meantime, continue to fulfill our religious duties.

When the officer sharply inquired if I doubted the final outcome, I answered, "I know only this, sir: that whatever transpires, the will of God will prevail. Only that which is right before him, and in keeping with his Divine plan, will conquer. This has been proved a thousand thousand times in the history of the Church and surely will not now be changed."

He said nothing further to me, but he reported my words to my superior, who called for me and said privately, "Be careful; it is dangerous to say such things."

"But do you not believe in the final victory of what is right?" I asked.

He shook his head. "There is nothing more one can say to you." Years later, at the war tribunal in Kassel, all these events were reported in the accusation.

At the end of January, in 1940, we set out on a march with our horses, going across Germany from the cold east to the warmth of spring in the southwest, in the beautiful region of Baden. We were quartered in the small town of Herbolzheim in very attractive private homes. It was a welcome change

*After a period of maneuvers in early 1940, Heinrich
Himmler visited the men at Camp Earthworm. Struck by
the courage of the seminarians, who refused to compromise
their ideals of faith, Himmler gave them permission to
carry out their religious duties without interference from the
hostile anti-Christian officers of the SS.*

*In the spring of 1940, Goldmann's
unit was sent to the village of
Herbolzheim, near the Rhine.*

*Frieda, the lovely dark-haired daughter of
the house where Goldmann was quartered.
A wily SS non-com had plans for her,
which Goldmann frustrated.*

from the maneuvers and drillfields we had left. I was particularly fortunate, for I was assigned to a new, small, neat home with a family of four, who took me to their hearts with a loving kindness that surprised me. Of course, I was put to the test by one of the good ladies of the neighborhood before I was accepted by the family.

An old aunt, a most formidable person indeed, questioned me before all the people present. "Are you a respectable person?" she asked, quite frankly.

I couldn't believe my ears, and simply stood there like a clod. She repeated her question, and went on, "There is a young lady of marriageable age in the house, and we want no wild ones here."

I couldn't help laughing, and the young ladies who stood about blushed deeply.

"*Gnädiges Fräulein*, have no fear. I am a seminarian, a Franciscan; I am not yet ordained a priest, but I am the same as one, despite this SS uniform. I have no interest in women, except as souls in need of salvation."

They all laughed, and I was escorted into the house quite cheerfully. The young lady, whose name was Frieda, was indeed beautiful and neat and friendly, and I could see why the aunt was so concerned.

Everything went along quite smoothly. Every morning before going on duty at seven, we seminarians attended Mass. The good pastor was surprised to see us there every morning in our SS uniforms, kneeling at the Communion rail with every evidence of deep piety and sincerity. The good Christian citizens of the town deemed it an honor to meet us and to extend many kindnesses to us during our stay. Since our officers were more taken up with pretty women than with their duties, we had a great deal of freedom, which we turned to good account with Mass in the morning and meditation each night; and in between we spent many precious hours in study.

One morning, I had to clean the office; it was a beautiful, clear spring day, and I was alone. I opened the window to let in the air and overheard the staff officer and our sergeant talking beneath the window. I wouldn't have missed that conversation for anything in the world!

The officer said, "What are the priestlings doing? Have they fallen yet?"

The sergeant made a disgusted negative sound.

"What?" exclaimed the officer. "Surely things must have progressed somewhat in that direction. We did not deliberately place them with the prettiest young women's families just to have them remain unchanged!"

Again, the sergeant made a disgusted noise. "That's just the trouble—they refuse! We placed them on purpose with the most beautiful women, and the tall one"—meaning me—"I gave the one that all the non-coms are wild about. And what happens? He runs off every morning at six to the church. I had him followed, and as long as he gets something to eat"— he meant Holy Communion—"from the pastor, there is no hope."

"Then begin the call of duty earlier", the officer suggested.

"That doesn't work either, for then he and all the rest would only run off to the church at five in the morning or go in the evening. The pastor loves them so much, I believe he'd say Mass at midnight to accommodate them! I have tried everything I can think of to change them. Nothing works."

When I passed on this interesting tidbit to my Franciscan comrades, we had a good laugh over it. The officers and non-coms had outsmarted themselves, for in placing us where they themselves would have desired to be, with the prettiest and purest of the young women, they had put the girls under our protection. It was not we who were in danger of "changing", as they archly put it, but they themselves who had been put out of commission. The families would not think of giving us up, for they knew that their daughters were safe with us— and we were ourselves safe among these good Christians from temptations that might otherwise have proved too much for our untried discipline.

Some time later, the sergeant asked me if I ever looked at a beautiful girl.

I replied, quite loudly, amid the laughter of the crowd, "Of course, I look at beautiful girls! God has not blinded me, just because I aspire to the priesthood. In fact, I see one every day, one of the best looking in town. I understand that many of the non-commissioned officers regret that I am lodging with her family. They feel I am passing up an opportunity they would not overlook!"

They all laughed louder as, red-faced, he sputtered, "You are the reason for Frieda's standoffishness. She won't even go to the movies. She says she never goes to the movies with strange soldiers. I think you are feeding her some of your religious claptrap!"

"Perhaps so. Perhaps she would prefer to go to the movies with one she can trust, one who goes to church every morning, even if it means going at five o'clock." That hit the mark.

He laughed out loud. "Did you hear that—the pastor and his girl friend going to the movies! That, I must see." And he strode off, still laughing.

When I arrived at the small house that night, I asked, "Frieda, would you like to go to the movies with me? I am sure some entertainment would not be amiss." Happily, her parents, who had heard my question, assented, as did she, and we started off. I timed our arrival for just after the show had started, so that all of the non-coms would already be there. At the first pause in the picture, we two marched in, and the corporals were wide-eyed and openmouthed with astonishment. I later heard that the sergeant was most profane in his comments.

If I have given the impression that our residence in Herbolzheim was a picnic, I must correct that. There was much unrest and disorder, and we seminarians in the SS were often called upon to quiet things down, the officers having decided for some reason that we exercised a little more tact and authority than the other elite guard men. As time passed, more and more wayside crosses were damaged or defiled outright, and more and more heartsick parents came to report abuses and outrages committed against their daughters. Relations between the soldiers and the residents grew worse and worse.

Suddenly, we were called to the Siegfried line, by the Rhine River; and for two months our unit lay there, in the flower-laden springtime, doing nothing. My duty was to attend to the communications network of the battalion, and throughout the weeks we were there, I lay in the woods from early morning until late at night with very little else to do but study and sun myself. I was almost like a child again, enjoying the wild animals and the clean, undefiled air of the woods and meadows. I knew it could not last much longer.

Chapter 4

CHALLENGING THE SS

We moved on to Kippenheim, and still no shell was fired. Then we went to Württemberg and were just settling down into pleasant billets when we marched out hurriedly one night; the movement was forward, and the war was on for us. Above Luxembourg, we invaded Belgium and France, and now things really became serious and, for me, quite interesting.

I knew French, which was a rarity, and therefore was pressed into service as an interpreter. I was placed in charge of all lodgings and other necessary requirements and arrangements, and I could therefore do much good and lighten many burdens. For instance, I would tell the French citizens, "Bury all the gasoline; I will take it all presently." And then later, in their presence, I would take only a small portion, leaving them the rest of it hidden from other soldiers, so that they could run their farm machines and other necessary equipment.

Later, in Paris, where so many were hungry while we had everything in abundance, I saw to it that many hungry French children were fed from the stores of the hated German army.

Being in communications, as well as an interpreter, I knew when SS raids were to take place on churches and other such places. One of the officers' pet means of degrading priests was to seize the Mass wine. When I had advance notice of this, I saw to it that the priest was warned in advance, so that when the SS arrived to carry out their dirty work, no wine was to be found—and often no priest, either, for to remain would have meant death. I was also able to warn priests who had been scheduled for execution. When I went along the next day, as interpreter, the nest would be empty, the sacraments safe, and the holy vessels hidden away among the parishioners. I found myself daily thanking God for the SS uniform I wore and growing in my faith and belief that my presence in that hated company was a blessing to those I encountered, as well as to myself.

The war progressed now with great rapidity. Several severe thrusts were made at the river Aisne and at the Channel, with heavy losses. Our enemy knew the SS would take no prisoners and fought accordingly; we had to dig many a grave.

In the Argonne, especially, we suffered heavy losses. And yet, such is the nature of man at war that, even while the dying were still lying alive on the ground, the plunder began. Our noble Germans of gentle birth, the highest of our officers, were among the leaders in the unbelievable looting, which took place in the midst of the screams of the injured and dying. They piled trucks high with booty and sent them on to Germany to be delivered to their homes. The soldiers, following this example, became like madmen in their ghoulish efforts. Nothing was too trivial, nothing too ridiculous, for stealing. Soon the streets of the villages were littered with all the possessions of the people, stolen and dropped when the soldiers spotted something else that captured their attention. The men were like animals; no girl dared to show herself.

The seminarians, of course, took no part in this miserable spectacle. We were cursed by our comrades as "sanctimonious

Nothing much stirred along the Siegfried Line in March 1940. The troops—including Goldmann—had time to construct this comical effigy of Neville Chamberlain and send it floating down the river on a "tour of inspection".

Seen here practicing in the Rhine forest, these young gunners soon had a chance to show their prowess in the invasion of France.

In May 1940, the unit marched north to invade France via Luxembourg.

By June, the German troops had
penetrated France and received their
baptism of fire. Knowing that the SS
took no prisoners, the defenders fought
stubbornly and inflicted heavy losses
on the invading Germans.

German losses were
especially heavy in the
Argonne. This captured tank
did its work well until the
ammunition was exhausted.

Not a shot was fired at the invaders by these captured guns. Capitulation was near.

At Les Islettes, the Germans came upon the graves of their predecessors killed during World War I. In the background, the bombarded town is in flames.

Les Islettes burned for three days before the Germans entered in safety. All throughout this battle, as in others to come, Goldmann never fired a shot, nor deliberately caused the death of an enemy soldier.

fools", but we held our ground. Later, a number of us were decorated and were praised for our position at this time. We stuck to our broadcasting post and killed no one.

I was promoted to *Obersturmmann*, and the commander told me he was sorry he could not give me the Iron Cross. But, of course, that would never do!

We pursued the enemy, who fled so quickly that only forced marches enabled us to keep close to him. We traveled many kilometers through abandoned and plundered villages. We ate off the countryside, occasionally coming so close to the enemy that we feasted on fresh-killed chickens they had stuck on pikes along the road, never dreaming that we would be so close we could steal their dinner. Finally, the guns quieted, and the long wait began.

It was a pleasant time for me, in a melancholy way, since this interim allowed me time to be with the people, to improve my French, and, if I could find a priest, to attend Mass. Many times during this march, I received Holy Communion at times from pastors whom I had first to find and then to convince; for who in possession of all his senses would believe that one of the hated SS would reverently desire the sustenance that came only from partaking of the sacraments and participating in prayers and Mass? After I had gone to confession to them, however, they would at last believe that I was really a seminarian and not just an arrogant Nazi come to entrap them. Often they were so bitter because of the war, but so devoted as pastors, that I was bewildered and full of pity for them. I smuggled out many articles of food for their own use and for distribution among their people.

On July 14 in Vaux sur Blaise, the French celebrated their national holiday—which we did not know at the time. We went to Mass as usual, and three or four choirgirls began to whine away at singing the High Mass. We could not long endure that, and some six Franciscan seminarians opened up and sang a true choral Mass. The French were speechless— and so were we the next morning. The entire staff was in an uproar. Word quickly got around that we sang, in SS uniform, in a French church on Bastille Day. As we entered the headquarters building, we were called down and denounced as traitors and enemies of the German people for singing for the enemy on their national holiday.

"This is an outrage, a disgrace to the entire SS. You are confined to camp!" shouted the sergeant. "How could you attend a celebration held by our enemies?" He was purple with rage.

That did it! "Sir," I replied, "the Catholic Church is supranational! Before God, there is no Frenchman, no German, no Aryan, no Jew!"

The sergeant roared again. "What are you saying? You are traitors!"

"We shall lodge a complaint concerning this matter." And we refused to say anything further.

We wrote at once to the general, stating our case, and he replied that he was familiar with our group; that we had permission from Reichsführer Himmler himself to attend Mass. He enclosed a note for each of us to carry stating that we could go anywhere; we used these notes often.

While the others had to drill on Saturdays until late in the evening, my group and I would don our dress uniforms and give notice at 1400 hours. Strutting past the apoplectic sergeant, I would shout for all to hear, "SS Obersturmmann Goldmann gives notice that he is leaving the camp to go to confession!" And my companions, with straight faces, would shout equally loudly their names and rank and their destination. The sergeant almost died from rage, but what could he do? I went to confession until midnight!

Priests, treated as ordinary civilians by the Nazi regime, were inducted into the army as common soldiers. Here a man of God lies in an anonymous grave.

Here his memorial catafalque stands before the empty altar he served.

In the fall of 1940, we received orders that soldiers who qualified could obtain a leave of absence for the winter in order to continue their studies. As I met all the requirements, I put in for five months to pursue my theological studies. At first my comrades who were not seminarians laughed; but when the leave was granted—all five months of it—the rage of the Nazis knew no bounds. I left for Freiburg, studying less of theology, it is true, than of art and literature. I tried to return to Fulda, naturally, to be with my family, but I found that this was impossible. The monastery had been disbanded on December 13, 1939, by the Gestapo; the Franciscans were literally driven out of Hessen, and the monastery used first by a group of SS police and later as a hospital.

At Freiburg, I had five wonderful months of study and relaxation. I had to laugh at my fellow students who complained about the rigors of their studies. To me, they amounted to a rich and rewarding rest from the horrors of war. I had the pleasure of causing a terrific stir by attending my first few lectures in full-dress SS uniform—and then coming into the halls in the brown Franciscan habit that was so much more familiar and comfortable to me.

When I returned to camp, I was temporarily refreshed in body and in spirit but was distressed to see how badly morale had deteriorated, along with any progress I might have made in the religious uplifting of my fellows. I had taken up the private mission of bringing some ray of truth and light into their bare and unfulfilled spiritual lives, and I thought, before my leave, that I was making a little progress with some of them. Now it seemed I was right back where I started, and my fellow seminarians with me.

The young officers, most of them former university students, began a campaign to show us how stupid and useless the Church was. It included harassment such as showing us filthy books captured in Paris in full assembly and asking our opinion of them as works of art. One of our number put a stop to that, however, by one day calmly and deliberately tearing the book to shreds before the astonished officers could stop him. They flew into a rage and threatened all sorts of punishment; but he replied with a threat of his own, which he carried out, to report the whole shabby business to Berlin. He had friends in high places there, and the result was that the officer involved in that little charade disappeared the next day, no one knew where, and an abrupt end was put to that nonsense.

Somewhat later, a unique opportunity for "underground" apostolic activity presented itself, and we eagerly took advantage of it. Upon our return home for our study furlough, we had learned that one could purchase absolutely no religious articles, such as rosaries and crucifixes, in Germany. Bibles and prayer books were also *verboten*, since the paper needed in the printing was scarce. Of course, there was plenty of paper for the anti-religious propaganda, but that was another story, quite beside the point.

It happened that, when I was on leave in Paris, I was strolling casually among the bookstalls one day, and, glancing down, I chanced to see the emblem of my old monastery in Fulda on the cover of one of the volumes. I had been told that the monastery had been closed and looted of all its beautiful old books, but this came as a terrific shock to me. I learned later that the Germans had sold them, but I never found out how they came to the bookstalls of Paris.

Meantime, looking around, I discovered that there were many other volumes here from our monastery, together with some that bore the seal of other monasteries. I contacted my religious superiors and told them of this, and they asked me to deal with matters as well as I could. I had plenty of money, and so I went about buying up all the books I could find, eventually ending up with a room in which I could hardly move for the books stacked to the ceiling.

Somewhere along the line, I received an inspiration to buy up all the rosaries and crucifixes I could get my hands on. I was blessed in having thousands of marks placed into my hands by friends and relatives for this purpose. Next, I spent considerable time pondering how to get these valuable things back into Germany. Friends who were returning home helped some, carrying them as personal baggage and taking them to the place I told them of. Soldiers going home on leave were willing to help for a small fee. But it wasn't enough; it was too slow to do much good.

At last, I found a good Christian in the office of our regiment, a man who was a decided enemy of the Nazis, like so many of us. We risked falsifying papers to cover the books, putting them into many boxes and crates stamped TOP SECRET: SS MAIL. Every day, truckloads of goods being taken out of France for transport to Germany contained more than half books in the carefully marked crates. The drivers knew their contents and consented, for money, to watch over them and deliver them to our Monastery of Gorheim-Sigmaringen, to Dr. Heinrich Hofler, the leader of the German Catholic group who ministered to the spiritual needs of the army.

It was very difficult and dangerous, of course, but so rewarding. Sometimes we went so far as to send them by plane!

The men helping were soldiers of the SS; I was in the SS. The drivers we bribed were Nazis, soldiers of the Reich. And yet, no one ever betrayed us. No traitor ever rose up from the ranks to reveal our activities, and the many blessings that accrued in doing this particular work strengthened all of us in our hearts.

Reports came back to us about how our religious superiors had succeeded in receiving the material and distributing it to the spiritually hungry Christians. We rejoiced, and we continued to think of it as an interesting adventure. The Nazis, who had robbed us of our monasteries, who had snuffed out the lives of countless thousands of innocents, whose every act was depraved and evil, never caught on to our campaign. We knew by this that the angels were truly on our side; and though it went somewhat against the grain to conspire against our own country, we felt that the sooner these despised men were defeated, the sooner we could return our Fatherland to her rightful rulers—the people—and her rightful King—Christ.

A certain Sergeant Stummel, whose hatred for me was to become a byword in the camp, caught on to all these machinations; but, since I was being helped by some of the higher officers, he could take no punitive action. Not all of the men in SS uniform were animals, even though not Christian. The worst the sergeant could contrive to get away with in the form of punishment was to transfer me to another company, but even that turned out to be a blessing. The commanding officer was a man who truly lived in the heart of Christ and gave me liberty such as I had never been able to enjoy in the service. He gave me leave to travel to Paris—we were camping in Rueil, Malmaison, and Bougival—where I could follow my religious bent. Not long after I joined the company, we were transferred to Paris, where we were billeted near the Arc de Triomphe, which made it even better, from my point of view. I roamed far and freely among the cathedrals and chapels—and after the noise and bustle of the barracks, the contention, the devastation and degradation of man fighting man, these hours spent before the altars became oases to my soul.

My friends and I were like hungry children, devouring the many cultural and artistic riches Paris had to offer us. We had plenty of money and as much leisure time as we could reasonably hope for; we seldom saw our beds before midnight. While our non-Christian comrades partook of the eternal soldier's fare of wine, women, and song, we became acquainted with Abbé Stock, the spiritual director of the Germans in Paris. He underwent great trials of soul and danger to life, being constantly under surveillance by the Gestapo and more than once in danger of death. He trusted the French brethren too much, they said, and they maintained their watchfulness and their suspicion of him without letup. We would gather in his house in the evenings for instruction and devotions, learning many things that would help us to learn to live as Christians in the un-Christian world in which we found ourselves.

We saw little of war. I was transferred to another communications group with quarters in the best section of Paris, near many large parks; I was given quarters containing a bedroom, living room, and bath, with a maid to care for it. I lived like a prince, although I had a premonition it would all end soon.

We were given an opportunity for officers' training, and I gladly signed up. I felt that, having been able to do much good already while not an officer, if I had higher status and more power, I would be able to do even more. With my scholastic training, I easily came out first in the group and faced only one final test before the promotion would come through. We had to go on a forced march in stifling June heat with heavy packs. Each day's march was some eighty-four kilometers.

We seminarians were amused to watch what transpired on this march, for we had long been the butt of barracks jokes for our refusal to go along when the trucks would come by

One of Goldmann's tasks was the requisitioning of gasoline from the civilian population. He instructed the people to bury some of the fuel secretly.

Goldmann did his best to commandeer food from German supply dumps in order to feed the starving French children.

In October 1940, Goldmann's unit reached Paris, where he stayed until the following May.

once each week to carry the men off to houses of prostitution. The officers felt that, since we were men, we must be in bad condition if we were deprived of such sport. We, of course, refused steadfastly to go, and they jeered about our manhood, or lack of it, and laughed at us as weaklings. But on that forced march, it was they who dropped like flies and had to be loaded onto trucks and carted on to our destination. Even the officers ultimately collapsed. What a pleasure it was to us to see the proud Junkers lugged off like sacks of grain! The only two survivors in our division were myself and another seminarian. The commander commended us; the whole experience was a lark to us, accustomed as we were, from our rigorous days in the Catholic Youth Camps, to long treks and strenuous exercise.

Ironically, my endurance during the march was to prove the turning point of my life in the armed forces. One evening the other seminarians and I were called to report to the commander.

"Gentlemen, you have conducted yourselves quite creditably—far more so than I would have expected. I always imagined that preparation for the priesthood was a sedentary occupation, producing nothing but weaklings. Well, I congratulate you! You are to be promoted in the SS, to become officers in the finest military group the world has ever seen."

We looked at one another, wondering what the catch was. There had to be one.

"My dear sirs, there is but one barrier to your service in this elite corps, which has no equal in the history of the army. Would you kindly sign this piece of paper?"

With that he distributed forms to us. We read their contents in stunned silence: *I hereby declare that I am leaving the Catholic Church and make the firm resolve never again to enter the Franciscan Order or the Church.*

This, then, was the freedom of belief that was promised us! Now they thought they had found a sure bait, to draw us out of the Church, dangling the carrot of an SS officer's commission in front of us. We stood at attention, motionless.

The commander asked, "Are you ready?" The man he addressed was from Berlin, and, with a face white with anger, he replied, "Commander, I am not accustomed to change my religion as I do my dirty shirt on Saturday." He spoke in a Berlin dialect, which made the answer seem comical, though the situation was grave.

The next man merely said, "Commander, before I came to the SS, I was a soldier in the army, and there I found a motto: *God with us*. Here we have known the motto of the SS: *My honor is loyalty*. I have nothing to add to that. Do you really wish to make an officer out of a man who is disloyal and traitorous to his God? For if a man will betray God, he will surely betray man!"

Nobody else said anything. I thought instinctively of the words of sacred Scripture where Christ told the disciples that they need not be concerned how they should answer their judges and persecutors, for the Holy Spirit would suggest the right answers. The commander asked only, "Do the rest of you think the same?"

"Yes", came the firm, unhesitating answer.

He turned to his assistant. "Let the men remain in the office", he said and left. Now what?

He returned shortly in full uniform, complete with steel helmet, and we expected some punishment to come without delay. He ordered all of us to remain where we were, took a firm stand, saluted with his left hand—his right arm had been shot off—and said, in a voice charged with emotion: "Gentlemen, I thank you. I expected nothing else from you."

We were again speechless, for a different and far better reason. Such recognition came as a surprise; we were not a little proud of ourselves as we left.

However, there must be consequences to such rashness. Our officer in the information division was raging mad that we refused to be commissioned. At night he came to our lodging and started up a conversation on religion and the army. Before all the soldiers, he said, venomously, "Whoever is a Christian is by that very fact a second-class soldier—and a poor German!"

That was, of course, more than we could take lying down. We protested at once, but he continued.

"And whoever has the capability to become an officer, and does not do so, is a traitor to the German cause."

That hit hard. I sat down at once and wrote a sharp protest, stating that although the commander praised us publicly after the maneuvers, although he had said he wished he had a whole battalion of such seminarians, one of our officers dared to insult us publicly, saying such things that the honor of the SS was deeply offended. We were forced by this to make a complaint.

The officer to whom we had to give the report for referral to higher authority was furious. The commander himself called us in to tell us to withdraw the complaint, lest it be sent on to the division headquarters. But that was just what we wanted.

"The officer must be removed, sir. Surely you see that."

The affair rapidly grew all out of proportion. A few days after submitting the protest, I was ordered to report to the division HQ on the matter. I remained firm in my complaint and emphasized the fact that, not too long before, Himmler himself had promised us religious freedom with no evil consequences and without prejudice.

The matter was taken to a higher authority, and, after three weeks, the final decision came back from Berlin. Himmler had read the report, since his name had been brought into the matter, and he had written his decision in red pencil on the margin of my complaint: "A declaration of these men's personal philosophy *(Weltanschauung)* is to be demanded."

I was ordered to comply. This was dangerous, but I was determined to have an end to it. I typed out eight pages, beginning, "I declare that I reject the *Weltanschauung* of the SS and the National Socialist Party."

I argued, as logically as I possibly could, that my rejection was based on three things: history, philosophy, and religion, using every ounce of preparation I had received in my training. The writing was incisive and decisive—but I was to make my declaration alone. When I asked my brother seminarians to sign with me, they refused. The writing was too strong, they thought. I was, after all, a German and should not write in that style.

"But can't you see, it is just because I am a German— perhaps more so than these so-called high-minded Nazi leaders of ours—that I am compelled to write this way!"

I pleaded and argued with them, but something I never thought could happen did: not one of the others signed.

What followed came as absolutely no surprise. I was confined to camp until the reply came from Berlin. When that arrived, four days later, it was short and to the point: I was to be expelled from the SS as unworthy and be sent back to the *Wehrmacht*.

That suited me well enough. I was summarily packed off to Holland. My former SS division was sent to Russia a few weeks later. I subsequently learned that all the seminarians had been killed. They were put in the front line. If they had only signed with me!

After completing officer's training, Goldmann was called upon to renounce his Faith. He refused and was expelled from the SS. This photo, taken in May 1941, is his last in the SS uniform.

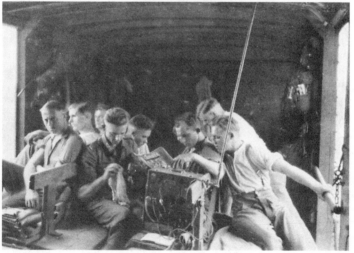

Back in the Wehrmacht, Goldmann was sent to the eastern front along with members of a communications unit.

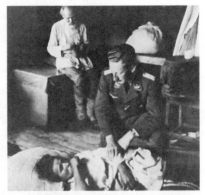

ABOVE: *Scorning the cross of Christianity, these Germans rest in death beneath the "rune of the dead", a pagan symbol adopted by fervent Nazis.*

RIGHT: *Receiving medical training at the Russian front, Goldmann cared for the wounded through the winter of 1942. Then, perhaps fortunately, he contracted dysentery and was invalided to southern Germany.*

Goldmann's habit of reading the Bible made him the butt of sarcasm and insult—until he taught one Nazi a well-remembered Sunday School lesson.

Goldmann recovered quickly and regained his strength by sightseeing in the Bavarian Alps.

Watched by the SS all during the Russian tour of duty, Goldmann was confronted with a list of twenty-eight charges against him—virtually a sentence of death. His trial took place in Kassel, site of this lovely palace.

After the trial, he was permitted to study at Freiburg in September 1942.

Chapter 5

A MATTER OF LIFE OR DEATH

I went to Roermond, in the Lowlands, where some troops were encamped, and there I was dismissed from the SS and sent back to Fulda. It was 1941. I had been in the army at this time for some three years. The return trip to Fulda, thanks to an oversight on the part of one of the officers, who forgot to date my pass, was leisurely and pleasurable. I spent a few days at our monastery on the Rhine and came finally to the city itself, where I was surprised to find the same officers and sergeants who had been there when I entered the SS.

They tried once more to amuse themselves at the expense of the theologian, but now I was no raw recruit but an experienced soldier. Since I had no more desire now than I had ever had of bearing arms against the enemy, I requested, and was granted, a transfer to the medical corps at Kassel, and from there was sent on to Meiningen.

My tour of duty at Meiningen became one of the more unforgettable experiences of my life. There I became acquainted with a Protestant comrade, a member of the Evangelical Church, and through him I came to know a group of Protestant Christians. This acquaintance was one of the decisive experiences of my life, for it reaffirmed my faith in humanity. While my faith in God had never faltered, my recent experiences with my fellow man had left almost everything to be desired. These good people did much to restore it. I spent many blessed hours, almost every day, in a house in Hessen where belief and trust in God's word as found in Sacred Scripture were strong and where an inexpressible stream of blessing flowed. This house near Bebra became for me a spiritual home as no other place on earth, not even my monastery. The conversations I had there and the love I was shown by my "dissenting" brothers were truly remarkable, and I count those days among the most treasured of my years as a soldier. When at last I had to leave them, I took with me a deeper knowledge of their creed, their ideals, their goals; things that in a later time, and a far country, were to stand me in good stead in understanding non-Catholics who were nonetheless stalwart and upstanding Christians.

We moved on to Erfurt, then on to Russia. While traveling through Poland, I was moved by the extreme misery and the deep piety of the people. It was there that I first learned of the terrible things that the Germans—that is, the police and SS troops—had done to the Jews and to many priests—and, if the notion took them, to mere ordinary people who stood in their way. Here I saw what my soul had instinctively known— that this was what the victorious Nazis had in mind for the whole world. We drove through Russia, passing endless columns of prisoners sunk in utter misery.

The front line came closer. Though I was not an officer, I had been trained as one and had leadership abilities; and so I was given a hundred men to lead to the front. We marched south from Smolensk through endless plains. On the way, I read daily from my little Bible, as I had done when I was with the SS.

This elicited from one of the soldiers such vile remarks as I had seldom heard even in the SS. He really was talented, but his talent was being misused on me.

"I'm warning you, friend, it would be better if you would shut up."

He became more brazen still, and he finally reached a peak of profanity that I simply couldn't let pass.

"Look, soldier, I've asked you to stop. If you don't close your mouth, I'll close it for you."

"What makes you think you could make me shut up?" he jeered. And with that rhetorical question, thinking he had a pushover, since I was obviously a pious weakling, he attacked me. Seizing my arm, he tried to break it by bending it around behind my back. Muttering a prayer for forgiveness under my breath, I returned the little Bible to safety in my deep pocket and proceeded to teach him his Sunday School lesson.

After a short struggle, he lay bleeding on the ground. How he was wounded, I don't really know, unless it was from a terrible blow on the head from a large fist swung in great anger. Nevertheless, however he came by it, he had a deep gash on his forehead, which bled profusely.

He lay unconscious for minutes. That could be serious, for I was the leader of the group, and the use of force against enlisted men by a superior was punished severely. I did not regret the incident, but neither did I want to lose my command. I treated his wound and sent him back from the front to recuperate, not knowing how it would turn out.

He returned after three weeks, not having opened his mouth. He was very quiet after that when he was around me, and, surprisingly, so were the others. They knew—having had undeniable proof—that no nonsense about religion would be tolerated in this company.

When we finally came to our headquarters, I learned that the papers about my SS affair had arrived. Things became very interesting once again. By now I was quite accustomed to being in hot water most of the time, so I didn't worry too much when I discovered I was being followed everywhere I went. They were gathering evidence.

They even went so far as to draw me out in conversations to try and determine what I thought about the war, the Jews, the Church, and the concentration camps. They wrote down everything, sometimes three or four of them at once, and I gave them everything they asked for, pretending to be innocent of their intentions.

My letters were opened. A friendly soldier surprised me by warning me about what was going on, not knowing that I knew fully what they were up to. His action heartened me, even though he had to come at midnight, in the dark, to do it, for it meant that even here the spark of human decency had not been extinguished.

I really didn't care what they did. I wrote homilies for the soldiers like the sermons of Cardinal Galen. Thousands of copies came off a little printing press, which we set up here and there along the line of march. A group of Catholic and Protestant teachers had organized the underground religious newspaper, to which I was an enthusiastic contributor.

In the autumn, heavy fighting took place and we were in that unfortunate encircling of Moscow by the Panzer thrust which ended in the flight and destruction of whole armies. Winter suddenly came upon us with such severity that nothing could withstand it. At Christmastime, what remained of the German invasion force was on its way back, retreating, as we had started to do weeks before. Morale was at its lowest ebb; many thought the war was lost, and, indeed, this first winter brought losses from which the German army could not recover.

In January of 1942 I was ordered, at last, to take the course in nursing that I had requested and that had been so long deferred by the fighting. I had still not fired a single shot, having been kept for one reason or another in non-combatant positions, such as in radio, communications, and so forth. I really don't know to this day what I would have done had I been ordered to shoot someone. The nursing course was given directly behind the front lines, frozen in the winter's snow. I came out so well that I was made a non-commissioned officer. For a while, life was as pleasant as life can be under such difficult circumstances, for a non-com in the nursing corps has very little to do during the winter. Fortunately for me, I contracted a case of dysentery that they could not cure at the front and was taken by ambulance to the south of Germany, to Rosenheim.

The good people there were very religious, and they came each morning to escort the limping soldiers to the nearby church of the Capuchins. They showed me so much attention upon learning I was a former seminarian that I could hardly bear up under it. There followed six peaceful months to recovery, broken only by two incidents.

The first was my attempt to get to Dachau, where my superior of the Franciscan Order was imprisoned. I had heard so much of that infamous place that I wanted to see it for myself; nothing but the testimony of my own eyes could convince me that anything so foul and corrupt could exist in Germany. When I arrived, I found an old SS acquaintance at the entrance, one of whom I was especially fond. He was surprised and pleased to see me and gladly showed me around. That was far more than I had expected. And conditions were far worse than I had expected. I had heard of how they mistreated the prisoners; but I had not heard that they killed them too, mercilessly, laughing at their defenselessness. The particular targets of their baseness were the priests, whom they forced to drill in formation for hours at a time, shooting those who fell down from exhaustion or malnutrition or some other dreadful prison hardship. Just as I was about to inquire for my superior an alarm rang out, and we had to leave so as not to get caught inside by the inspectors. My hatred of the Nazi regime became more intense, and I resolved to return as soon as I could to see if I might ease somewhat the burdens of these suffering souls.

But when I returned to the hospital, things began happening. The medical superintendent of the sick wards, a sincere Protestant, warned me that something was in the wind; the Gestapo from Munich were here to get reports from the students about me. I was examined, and, after being released from the hospital, I was taken under guard to Kassel and put under house arrest in the barracks. With the aid of the commander of the barracks, who was, in his heart, anti-Nazi, I was able to get out every day for Mass or Holy Communion and go somewhere to take in a decent evening meal, for the food situation in the armed services was becoming steadily worse. I still didn't know what the Gestapo was planning for me until suddenly in August I learned that I was to go on trial. The charge was "weakening the armed forces of the German people in the face of the enemy". I was also accused of violation of the law of secrecy—one of the most important laws of Hitler's day.

There were twenty-eight points in all against me. The judge made it clear that I had been closely watched since my SS days and that many hundreds of men had spoken against me. He himself was unsympathetic to the Nazis; but the pages and pages of witnesses left him no alternative but to press the case. I was truly amazed that a lowly would-be priest, ex-SS officer candidate, and nurse should come in for so much attention from higher authority. The judge convinced me of what I had merely suspected before—that my situation was now a matter of life or death. Such offenses as mine always resulted in the execution of the accused.

I tried to keep my thoughts from dwelling on it too much, and I took advantage of the time to visit Fulda and to commune with my Protestant friends near Bebra. I was finally summoned to the court in August. One of the high officials, who was very sympathetic to my case, took me to his room and behind locked doors told me there was no hope. The deliberation and decision were set for mid-September.

"I trust you, Goldmann, and will see to it that you are given furlough to go and visit your family one last time, if you will give me your word of honor that you will be back here on September fifteenth."

This was an unprecedented privilege, and I quickly agreed. I went to Cologne, finally beginning to realize what a spot I was in. Strangely enough, I was not even remotely tempted to try to escape. While I was worried, I had also a persistent feeling that everything would some how turn out all right. I was not lighthearted, by any means, but I was not afraid either.

I said nothing to my parents and enjoyed a really joyous reunion. On September 14 I was back in Kassel, and on the fifteenth, in the afternoon, I was called before the assembly of judges.

"Goldmann," said the chief judge, not looking at all as I had pictured one who was handing out a death sentence, "you are free!" With that he smiled, as did the other members of the court. I was astounded. I could not believe my ears, but he gave me proof for my eyes. He handed me a copy of the proceedings, and I read there the amazing fact that my right to freedom of speech was confirmed. The verdict was worded in a way that left no doubt as to the court's opinion of the Nazis, and in this I found further fuel for astonishment; this was a group of really brave men. That they were determined to do something positive in opposition to the Nazis was clear to me, but I learned nothing further at that moment. I was so happy over regaining my freedom and my very life that I had very little thought then for the reasons. These were to be revealed to me later.

When I went immediately afterward to bring my commander the news of my acquittal, he was so glad he gave me a five-month leave of absence to pursue my studies—to recover from the shock, as he said. Thus I spent a second winter on furlough in Freiburg, studying. In the meantime, my comrades were shedding their blood in Stalingrad, and I would have been there also, had this trial not kept me at home.

My entire division remained in Stalingrad, buried deep beneath the snow.

Chapter 6

SISTER SOLANA MAY'S FAITH

After spending the winter of 1942–1943 devoting my time to studies, I returned in April to the camp. Prior to being sent again to Russia, I was given a day's leave of absence to go to Fulda to visit my mother's grave.

I arrived on the morning of May 17, 1943, visited the grave and some relatives, and still found myself with some spare time, the delay being caused by an air raid. I was on Lindenstrasse and suddenly realized I was in front of the convent of Sisters in whose chapel I had served my first Mass, nineteen years ago. I quickly made a visit in the chapel, and, as I knelt praying before the altar, a small, aging Sister came up to me. It was Sister Solana May, the sacristan who had taught me to serve. My little "foster mother" had recognized me at once, and she asked me to come to the sacristy to talk. It turned out to be one of the more memorable conversations of my life.

She asked me sharply, "Do you pray devoutly?"

Though it was, on the face of it, a rather strange question to ask a soldier, I replied, "You saw how I prayed in the chapel, Sister."

"And do you pray that you will be ordained a priest next year?" I was stunned.

"Sister, me? A priest? And next year? That is impossible!"

Gently, she asked, "Why impossible, my son?"

"I have not yet studied theology! I had just finished philosophy when I was drafted, and what I have since studied on my leaves of absence is far from theology. I still have at least four more years in the seminary, after the war, before I can be ordained—if I come out of this alive."

She looked at me with a soft, confident smile. "Do not worry—you will be ordained a priest next year."

My mind told me she was talking nonsense, and I asked her how she came to have such a notion.

To my astonishment, she said, "But you are an exceptional case!" She took a book from a drawer and gave it to me to examine. There I found written that, on the day of my mother's death, she began to pray for me, that I should become a priest at the end of twenty years. She reckoned exactly that my years in school, from start to finish, would take twenty years. She had prayed to our Lord and made sacrifices for nineteen years to the end that I should be ordained a priest in the Franciscan Order. She had offered up all her prayers during the day, the night—in fact, every single act of devotion during that entire time had been offered for the single purpose of making me a priest! And, since she considered her own prayers alone too weak, she had asked the other Sisters—280 of them—to join in, and they promised to add their prayers to hers. Many of the Sisters who had died were begged to remember the altar boy now that they were in heaven.

Still smiling, she took the amazing document from me and said, "You see, you *are* an exceptional case. And since Holy Scripture assures us that our prayers are heard, there is no doubt that you will be a priest next year."

I answered, somewhat sadly, "But Sister, when you began

to pray, you could not know that this unholy war would break out and all your plans would be changed!"

Shaking her head, she replied with great assurance, "War? The Bible says nothing of war. It does not say, 'All these things are true, except in case of war, in which event the Bible has no validity.' It says our prayers are heard and will be answered. The answer to our prayers does not hinge on a foolish thing like war."

I had to laugh. Such childlike faith—almost childish faith! She saw me laughing and asked, "Do you not believe that God is mightier than the war?"

I could only say: "Yes, indeed; but the war is on, and I am a soldier and have not completed my courses in the seminary. There is still the law of the Church that says no one can be ordained a priest who has not studied—and the most fervent prayers, dear Sister, can not change that."

She looked at me, surprised at my weak faith, and asked, "These laws, who made them?"

"Why, the pope", I replied.

Then she laughed joyfully. "The matter is very simple. The pope, who made the laws, can also dispense from them."

"That he could do, if he has a good reason; but it is out of the question that he would ordain someone a priest who has not studied. And I am not in Rome."

Again, that sweet, childlike laugh of confidence: "You will get to Rome. Today I will begin to pray that you will see the pope in Rome. Then you must ask him boldly for this ordination."

I was rendered speechless by her mad confidence and drew from my pocket an order that I was to march on the next day to Russia. I said, "I must be on my way to Russia tomorrow morning, early. The pope does not live there, Sister."

She merely said, "You will see. You will not have to go to Russia. You will see the pope." Such ideas!

I said, "Thank you for your hopes and your prayers, Sister. I must leave now for the station. *Auf Wiedersehen!*"

Asking me to wait a minute, she quickly returned with her mantle and permission from the Superior to accompany me to the station. We made a strange sight, the tall soldier in uniform and the little Sister, and I had to laugh thinking of it. Fortunately, the station was not too far. All the way, she kept reminding me to trust firmly in her prayers and to remember when I got to Rome that I must be confident and ask the pope to ordain me. I said nothing; I was beginning to be annoyed. She went to the platform with me, so I had to buy her a platform ticket. I boarded the train, and she gestured that I must open the window. I leaned out and heard her say, "I've thought it over; you need the help of the Mother of God, the Mother of all priests. And so you will first have to make a pilgrimage to the Mother of God and ask her help. Then all will succeed."

I had recovered my humor, but I lost it quickly when she said this, and, waving my orders angrily under her nose, I shouted, "Here it says Russia and nothing about a pilgrimage, or Rome, or the pope—and certainly nothing about the Mother of God!"

She simply said with the same confident, smiling face, "When you are in Lourdes, pray fervently!" Fuming, I slammed the window, for the train was starting. I tried to put her nonsense out of my mind, but during the entire two-hour ride to Kassel, I could not simmer down and kept pacing the crowded aisle. Arriving at my barracks, I began preparing for the trip to Russia the next day.

Morning came, and it was like being in an ant hill, with two hundred soldiers getting ready for the march. I was to

lead the company to Russia. At eight o'clock, we went to the
railroad station and boarded the train, which was to leave at
9:10. Five minutes before that time, I left the coach to see if
everything was in order. Suddenly an auto drove up with an
officer, a soldier with a gun, and a sergeant in uniform. "*Ach*,
he wants to go along too", I thought. I approached the officer
and informed him about the departing troops. He looked at
me, asked my name, and said to me coldly, "You are under
arrest." To the sergeant, he said, "You take over." I handed
over the papers and was put into the auto, with the soldier
and his gun at my back. They took me to the barracks.

I was put into the stockade at once, and the commander,
who had gotten me out of trouble before, came to see me
immediately. He told me that an army official had called from
Berlin to say I was to be detained, and my commander had
not been told why. "If you will tell me what you have done,
perhaps I can help."

But I simply did not know. He left, shaking his head. Then,
as I sat thinking, I began to wonder if my association with
the group who wished to assassinate the Führer had been
discovered.

In November of the preceding year, I was among my Evangelical friends in Imshausen, where I went from Kassel in
order to gather new strength and courage. I became acquainted with Adam von Trott zu Solz, a man of noble birth
who impressed me greatly. In the early morning I was walking back and forth in the garden, saying my prayers. The
nobleman came up to me and asked me to take a short walk
with him. I could not refuse, and so we walked along the road
leading to the castle on the hill, which belonged to him. On
the way he asked me what I thought of those who were rul-
ing Germany. Since he was the brother of the lady of the

Sister Solana's improbable prediction came true: Goldmann visited Lourdes in May 1943.

This picture shows Goldmann in late 1943 during the Italian campaign, twenty-seven years old, a hardened veteran non-com often finding himself bolstering the courage of faint-hearted officers even younger than himself.

In November 1943, while visiting friends at Imhausen, Goldmann became involved in the plot to assassinate Hitler.

house where I was staying, I had no intention of telling him how intensely I hated the Nazis. He told me suddenly that he was a member of the secret group opposing Hitler's Third Reich. He said, "You can help us free Germany from its disgrace."

"How is that possible?" I asked.

He said merely, "*He* must go. All things are prepared. But we still need a messenger for important dispatches that cannot be written." I did not understand. He said, somewhat impatiently, "You must know what I mean. You have been in contact with us before, since you were given your freedom in Kassel in so unique a way."

Now I understood that the judges of the war court were part of the anti-Nazi conspiracy. Gasping for breath, I asked: "Is Hitler to be killed?"

He looked at me with fixed gaze and said: "*Jawohl*, that is the only way."

I said at once that I was a soldier and had taken the soldier's oath, and as a Christian I could not break that oath. He said that he was also a Christian, as were also those who were with him; they had prayed before the crucifix and had agreed that "since we are Christians, we cannot violate the allegiance we owe God. We must therefore break our word given to him who has broken so many agreements and still is doing it. If you only knew what I know, Goldmann! There is no other way! Since we are Germans and Christians we must act, and, if not soon, it will be too late. Think it over till tonight." And he went up to his castle.

When evening came, I had thought the matter through and was able to give my consent. I received some messages intended for certain gentlemen in Paris and Rome, but I did not know if I ever could deliver them. They could only be transmitted verbally. The messages did not seem to me to be particularly vital, but he stressed their great importance. I must not try to evaluate the contents. But I had to keep the secret, come what may.

For three days I sat in the stockade and wondered if the entire plot had been exposed. On the third day, a message came from Berlin. The commander opened it in front of me. Now I would know my fate.

But, amazingly, I was to be transferred at once to southern France to a new division with special duties! I asked, "Where?"

"Pau", he replied. "Do you know Lourdes? It is close by."

How fantastic, I thought. Sister Solana's faith had been vindicated! Evidently my high-placed coconspirators had heard of my orders to Russia and had taken this means to see that I was not sent where I could be of no use to them.

Once I arrived at Pau, I went immediately to the shrine at Lourdes. I was extremely agitated. Two of Sister Solana's predictions had come true: I did not go to Russia, and I *did* go to Lourdes. I prayed with all my heart, as much that the little Sister's faith might be justified as that I might be made a priest within the improbable time of one year.

I wrote Sister Solana what had happened, and she wrote back on a card, "Be brave and continue to pray." I tried to do both, and I went to the grotto as often as possible. Every afternoon I went to the chapel of the Sisters of Perpetual Adoration in Pau, where I felt at home as seldom before. I was shocked and dismayed to have had the doors of the Franciscan friary in Pau closed to me, simply because I was a German soldier. But the good Sisters fed me and cared for me in such a way that I gained some compensation for this coldness on the part of my brothers.

One evening, while carrying out one of my special duties monitoring radio broadcasts, I heard a message that preparations for invading Africa were concluded. I wrote it up and showed it to the officer in charge. He merely laughed. No American or Englishman would set foot in Europe, he said, since Germany held it securely. I was not so sure, but I thought that, if they did come, it would be to Italy. I purchased an Italian grammar and, for six weeks, studied Italian furiously. My comrades laughed, for they were convinced that we would all go to Russia—where I would have no need to know Italian. But I smiled and continued to study, trusting my intuition.

I had a bad moment when orders came through for us to go to Russia through southern France. But suddenly, en route, we were ordered to turn south, going along the Riviera to Genoa, where we were sidetracked. Our equipment for Russia was turned in, and we were given lightweight uniforms and sent south into Italy, where the enemy had landed in Sicily.

We passed Rome—the Holy Father was near! The prayer of the good Sister Solana May and her "foolish" faith seemed to be not so foolish after all. I remembered her statement in Fulda that God was more powerful than the war, and that Scripture says nothing about prayers not being heard in wartime!

Chapter 7

ITALY AFTER ALL

Toward the end of July 1943, our troops were ordered into Sicily to protect the retreat of the badly beaten remnant of the German army. The greater part of the island was in the hands of the Allies, and the outlook was very bad for us. Though we were fresh troops, fewer than 10 percent were experienced soldiers who had felt the hardships of the campaigns in France, Russia, and Poland. The remaining 90 percent were, for the most part, young students who had been taken straight from school and drafted. The greater number of them were under twenty years of age; some were only sixteen or seventeen. The younger ones even boasted of how they had falsified their ages in order to be drafted. These were the Hitler Youth who, in all good faith, were fired with enthusiasm for the German cause. All had one thing in common: they were badly trained.

Many of their officers were no better, being young lieutenants with no experience whatsoever. They were eager, pathetically so, to show the veterans what they could do.

We were dispatched immediately to the northern part of Sicily to hold back as long as possible the terrible offensive push of the enemy, who was advancing from Palermo, so that the soldiers from the southern flank of Sicily could reach continental Italy.

We set up our defense line not far from the city of Patti, some forty kilometers west of Messina. We took up a position behind a promontory that projected into the sea. Tunnels were constructed under the steep sloping cliffs, the only street in the city running through the tunnels. A deep valley and steep sloping cliffs, combined with only one small bridge, offered us a good place to build our defenses.

We set up our machine guns in the cliffs; we had no heavy weapons, not even mortars, and no extra ammunition for the weapons we dragged with us. We had no cannons. There were a few tanks but not much ammunition for them. Below, in the deep valley, a poor little village hugged the cliffs; the residents fled when they saw we were building a line of defense right above their heads. The Ninth Company was ordered to take up positions on the opposite side of the valley in order to prevent, if possible, the enemy's approach to the bridge.

The invasion was not long in coming. First, many reconnaissance planes put in an appearance. We had no anti-aircraft guns, so we were forced simply to sit and watch them do their work. Then six heavily armed warships appeared on the sea and extended to us their greetings. We hid in the cliffs.

Next, swarms of soldiers appeared along the mountain ridge on the opposite side. Undisturbed by our silent presence, they dug in. We had orders to save our precious ammunition for the attack. We watched as they set up mortars. The terrain began to look like an Allied maneuvering ground, and we were helpless to convince them this was not simply a demonstration of Allied firepower. On the top of the mountain they set up heavy artillery, and, alongside the heavy cannon, mounds of ammunition began to take form. They realized, obviously, that we could not reach them with the weapons we had.

After two days, the enemy began their bombardment. Day and night they showered us with shells. From the sea, from the mountain, and from the air, they rained death on us. None of our soldiers even dared raise his head without becoming a target for many weapons. Although we had protection, our losses were still great because the entire terrain was systematically bombarded.

After three days of this, we had more than four hundred dead and wounded. How was this to end? The enemy made two attacks but retreated when we met them with our machine guns, inflicting many casualties. Then they began the bombardment again.

On August 5, 1943, we arranged a place behind a projecting cliff to care for the wounded. It was located under the street in a huge sewer that served to carry off the rain water. The wounded were being brought in from the front when a friend of mine, a man from Baden, approached and asked me if there was no way of helping the dying.

"What do you mean? Can't you see I'm doing every thing I can?" My exhaustion made my voice more harsh than I had intended, but I had not slept or even rested for quite some time.

"I'm not thinking about their bodies, Goldmann, but about their souls. They are dying like dogs, without confession or Holy Communion. You speak Italian, don't you?"

I nodded, so numbed by all of this that I was not even surprised to realize that, of them all, I should have been the one to think of what he proposed.

"Drive back to Patti and get a priest; ask him to bring Holy Communion. You'll manage."

The thought aroused me and gave me new strength. I asked

and received permission to take an ambulance truck back to the city. My driver and I arrived in Patti about five in the afternoon with the double assignment of finding a priest and, if possible, finding some surgical supplies. We were perilously low on everything. The place was nearly deserted, since the sound of the cannon had reached the inhabitants.

I found a little church at the edge of the town, and, to my joy, there was also a Capuchin friary. I met the two aged Capuchin Fathers and asked one of them to get the Blessed Sacrament and come with me.

The old priest said, "I am sorry, I cannot do that. You must ask my bishop." He pointed out the cathedral on the top of the mountain.

We drove up the winding, narrow trail all the way to the top and parked the ambulance in the square in front of the cathedral. At the farthest side of the square three men sat at a table, on which a map was spread out before them. With the help of field glasses, they could see the positions of the Germans beside the sea. Some of the Allied positions were also visible.

Behind the table was a priest, a small, rotund, kindly-looking man. He was a little the worse for wear, his soutane not having been washed for quite some time and his black jowls proving that he'd either lost his razor, or his interest in using it, or both. However, in wartime one overlooks many things. Leaving the driver at the wheel, I approached the group, and they looked up in surprise. They had been so engrossed in what they were doing that they had not heard the approach of the ambulance up that steep road.

"Would one of you kindly direct me to the bishop?" I asked politely.

The gentleman at the right of the priest rose, made a deep bow, and presented himself as the mayor of the town.

"I am Karl Goldmann", I said, with as deep a bow. "Forgive my abruptness, Herr Mayor, but I do not wish to speak to you. I wish to see the bishop on a matter of great urgency. Would one of you kindly direct me to him?"

Then the gentleman to the left of the priest stood up and asked if possibly he could help me; he was the town magistrate.

This was really too much! "Sir, I appreciate your kindness, but you cannot help me either. It is the bishop I need."

Now the priest stood up, looked up at me (for he was much smaller than I), and asked what I wanted with the bishop.

"I do not want to speak with you, but with the bishop; I will ask you as I have asked these other gentlemen—will you please lead me to him?" I did not like the impatience of my own tone, but I was tired and more than a little put out by this game they seemed to be playing with me.

The priest replied in a sharp voice, "You can safely tell me your business. I am the bishop of Patti."

I looked down at him, the unspeakably soiled soutane, the unshaven face—and laughed. I blurted out, "You, the bishop? Never!"

He looked at me indignantly. Then he took a ring from his pocket, put it on his finger, and held it out before me. "Am I the bishop or not?"

He was! Blushing, I bent down to kiss the ring. But he, perhaps to teach me a lesson in humility, bent down low and held the ring so close to the ground that I had to kneel in the dust and bow very low to kiss it. We both straightened up, he with a satisfied and absolutely forgiving smile. He returned to his place at the table and kindly asked what I wanted with him. I pointed to the battlefield below.

"I am a seminarian, serving in the medical corps. Many soldiers are dying there, Catholic soldiers who have not seen a priest or been to confession for months. The wounded are in agony, and their souls are in mortal danger. The dying are without the sacraments."

"Do you not have a chaplain with the army?" he asked.

"No, we do not. The newly formed divisions have no chaplain, and the one who was with us before is on a leave of absence."

"In that case, there is nothing we can do for you", he replied.

"But there is. That is why I came here."

"What is it? What do you have in mind?"

"I ask that you give me a priest to bring Holy Communion to the wounded and comfort to the dying."

He looked at me as though he doubted my sanity. "What? A priest to go down there into the thick of the battle?"

"Yes, down there. And I will try at every cost to bring him back safe."

"Can you guarantee that?" he asked.

"Of course I cannot. Who can guarantee that anyone will return from the battlefield alive?

"I will not send a priest, nor will I order or command one to go to the front in a war that does not concern him."

I replied, "The Italians and the Germans are allies! They fight together in the same war, against the same enemy!" The three smiled at me, which did nothing to lift my spirits. Not long after, I learned why they smiled.

Right now, however, my only interest was in getting a priest, and in a very clear voice I said, "It is not a question of Italians or Germans, but of Catholics; we are Catholics, and we are in the diocese of the local bishop through no will of our own, so it seems to me the bishop is in some way responsible for us."

At this the three laughed out loud, and the mayor said,

The famous letter from the Italian Bishop of Patti, obtained under extraordinary circumstances, which authorized Goldmann to bring Holy Communion to German troops.

"There is no responsibility between the citizens of this country and the enemy."

I replied, "I am not an enemy, but a German!"

"To us, there is no difference; the Germans are not liked here."

With that, I lost all patience. I shouted, "It is not a question of whether the Germans are liked or not! It is a question of whether Catholics in danger of death are going to receive spiritual help—of whether I am going to get a priest or not! The philosophy can wait until after the guns stop firing!"

Still the answer was a determined "No."

I pleaded with the Italian bishop. "If you only knew what it's like down there! The screams and moans of the wounded— the dying. I beg you to reconsider!"

The answer was still, icily, "No."

What was I to do now? "For the last time, Your Excellency, I beg of you: Will you give me a priest?" I put it in the form of a very cold, formal request.

"Never", was the answer.

That finished it; there was only one thing for me to do. Mustering all my resolve and inwardly promising all kinds of acts of penance, I pulled out my Lügcr and held it under the bishop's nose.

"You have three minutes' time; then I will either have a priest to go with me and bring the Blessed Sacrament to the troops—or you will accompany me to the battlefield yourself."

He turned deadly pale and trembled.

"You have thirty seconds left!"

The bishop stammered something about extortion, but I countered with: "Don't you know there's a war on?" The time was up. I ordered the ambulance driver to guard the two gentlemen with the submachine gun and not let them move from their places.

"The bishop will accompany me to the church to get the Blessed Sacrament."

In obvious mental agony, he stammered, "Will you first do me the kindness of accompanying me into the house?" I could not refuse.

The bishop sat down, wiped away the perspiration, and asked whether, in my clerical training, I had yet received any Holy Orders. I told him, "I am a professed Franciscan, but not, as yet, even a subdeacon."

"I cannot give you a priest," the bishop said, "but I have something here—" he fumbled in his desk, searching for something that I devoutly hoped was not a gun! "—Ah! It is a document from Rome that will permit me to entrust the Blessed Sacrament to your care, keeping, and distribution."

I was shocked. I said, "But that is such a holy matter, I will first have to go to confession! Please excuse me, Your Excellency!" And I was off and running, after placing him under the care of the armed driver on the terrace. I literally ran down the mountain to the Capuchins, never thinking of saving time by taking the ambulance.

I made my confession and asked for a certificate that I had received the sacrament of penance. I hastened back up the mountain and found the three still sitting at the table under the watchful eye of my driver. I presented my certificate to the bishop, whereupon he wrote this note:

The Bishop's Residence
Patti 4.8.43

In view of the extraordinary conditions and the special faculties granted by the Holy See, we grant the Catholic cleric of the 29th German Panzer Division to bring with due reverence Holy Communion to his comrades, especially the wounded.

(signed) + Angelo Vescovo

That was more than I could have expected, and I sincerely thanked the bishop and asked his forgiveness. He gave it graciously, and, when I left, I saw tears in his eyes. I could not help wondering if they were tears of relief and joy that the dangerous German was leaving without having used his pistol.

Chapter 8

BAPTISM OF FIRE

Back once more at the Capuchin friary at the foot of this much-climbed mountain, I obtained a small pyx and ten consecrated Hosts. Full of joy, and having obtained also some medical supplies, we drove back to the soldiers.

The first soldier to receive Holy Communion was my friend from Baden who had urged me to get a priest for the wounded and dying soldiers. I myself was to be the next to receive the Blessed Sacrament, but at that moment a messenger on a motorcycle rushed up; a bomb had exploded in the midst of a battalion on the field—there were many wounded and dead. The Ninth Company, on the other side, also reported that more than half their number were wounded or dead. They were without surgical help. Medical corpsmen were needed immediately to care for them.

This was very serious indeed. The village, with its shattered houses, was about a mile away. To reach it, we would have to cross a street in full view of the enemy and then, a little farther on, cross a bridge that was completely enfiladed by the Allies.

It was "a trip to heaven", as we called such assignments. My doctor was of the opinion that we had no corpsmen to spare for such a hopeless task; no one could possibly arrive at either place safely. I looked around the corner of the cliff and saw salvos of bombs explode on the street.

Down on the other side of the bridge, our wounded soldiers were bleeding to death, their screams audible this far away—and no one there to give aid. I stepped aside in a corner, took the pyx from my left breast pocket, and gave myself Holy Communion.

Then I turned to the doctor and said, "I am going down there." Staring at me, he said, "Do you realize you will not return?"

"Perhaps." My faithful driver, Private Faulborn, was willing to drive me down in the truck, for there was no other transport available. This same chauffeur had many times saved my life and the lives of others by his skillful driving. I seized the Red Cross flag and, sitting on top of the driver's cab, I shouted, "Let's go!"

At once, the motor roared. Swaying madly along the dangerous curves, we were on our way down the mountain to the village. Instantly, the enemy opened fire. But we raced on heedlessly. With my left hand I held onto a wooden framework attached to the rear of the cab; with my right, I waved the Red Cross flag, all the while praying fervently. Finally, the enemy recognized the flag and ceased firing. All was quiet, the roaring of our motor the loudest sound in the entire valley.

As we passed the commander of the totally demolished battle line, he saw me and shouted, "Are you crazy?" We rushed on behind the ruins of the houses and came to a stop behind a half-fallen wall. I ran under cover of the fallen wall to the bridge, which was guarded by a machine-gun emplacement. Less than a hundred yards away on the other side, I saw the English soldiers in their dugouts. Between them and me was the bridge and, beyond them, in a large farmyard, the rest of the Ninth Company. I had to get there! But how to get over the bridge?

I raised my head just a bit, and at once the machine gunners went into action. Not even a mouse could get through alive! Again I raised my Red Cross flag over my head so that only my arm and the flag could be seen. I used my left hand so that if a bullet should find a target, I would be spared my right hand. But not a shot was fired. All was quiet, and I heard someone call out, "Cease fire! Red Cross!" I stood up and, constantly waving the flag, crossed the bridge. From both sides the soldiers looked on at this little scene. Unmolested and undisturbed, I reached the other side and entered the wine cellar of the farmer's house where the rest of the Ninth Company, some thirty men, were holed up. There were many wounded among them. I was able to lift some onto my shoulder and, with the help of other soldiers and under protection of the flag, bring them out to the truck on the other side.

The whole sector remained quiet, watching. I was again on the bridge, when suddenly I heard a dangerous sounding roar overhead. I looked up and saw a pursuit plane, whose pilot was obviously unaware of what I was doing, diving down on the bridge. Just as I threw myself against the parapet for protection, he let loose with half a dozen bombs, which all struck near me but mercifully left me unharmed. Presently, I managed to reach a narrow room in the cellar, where there were large round wine casks. One of our men rushed in with the news that the English had begun to attack.

Our machine guns fired wildly against them, but half of our gunners were dead. I ran through the dark corridor to reach the wounded at the machine guns in front of the house. I pressed my left hand, holding the Red Cross flag, over my left breast pocket, where the Blessed Sacrament was. When I reached the light coming in from the open door, I saw, not twenty yards away, a number of German soldiers lying dead over the machine guns and six Englishmen in two groups setting up two guns on the wall that formerly had been in our possession. The guns were pointed at the open door of the wine cellar in which I was standing. Suddenly, a terrific fusillade whipped by me from the two guns not twenty yards from me. All the bullets passed my left arm, tearing open my coat repeatedly, but not even bruising the skin. Instead, they landed in the cellar and wounded or killed some of those in back of me. I dived down and crawled back unharmed.

It was now too late to give further aid; everyone ran out of the rear door and tried to cross the bridge, which lay in the path of the machine guns. How many reached the other side I do not know. I found myself in a demolished farmhouse on the other side of the bridge, under the ruins of a sitting room.

I had to recover my breath; my chest threatened to burst. How long I lay there listening to my heart beating in my throat, I do not know. At last I became calmer, but the tension of the last few hours and the strain of many nights with no sleep and no rest was too much. I was too weak to move. Suddenly, I heard a noise in the same room. Someone was moaning in the corner. An Englishman?

Carefully, I crawled among the ruins in the direction of the moaning. I found a very old Italian lying in a collapsed bed, no doubt the patriarch of the house. He was sick and bleeding from the wounds received during the bombardment. Moreover, a beam lay over the bed. When I came near him, wearing my helmet and covered with blood from the wounded I had carried, the old man looked up at me in terror and cried out, "Do not kill me! Do not kill me!"

I quieted him and assured him that I came not to kill but to help him.

I soon realized he was dying. In addition to whatever illness had made him bedridden, he had several wounds in his abdomen and more broken bones than I could count. Each touch of mine as I tried to examine him brought fresh groans from the poor old man.

I asked him if he was Catholic—a rather unnecessary question, seeing he was Italian and clutched a rosary in one hand—and asked if he wished to receive Holy Communion.

He looked at me incredulously, so surprised he seemed to forget his pain for a moment, and asked, "Are you a priest?"

I could not answer his question with a simple "Yes" and felt there was little time for explanations, so I said instead, "I have the Blessed Sacrament with me."

He looked at me doubtfully, yet joyfully. When I held the Host before him, he attempted to kneel, notwithstanding his pains. I prayed an act of contrition with him—of course I could not hear his confession—and gave him the Holy Viaticum. He wept tears of joy and happiness and lay back on his bed breathing shallowly. I felt the end to be very near.

During this time, I had been totally unaware of the battle outside. Now I heard many footsteps and wondered who it might be—friend or foe?

Carefully, I peered through the smashed window. To my consternation, I saw Englishmen in long columns marching over the bridge in front of the house, loaded with weapons and supplies. An immense file of enemy troops crawled past the window. I was cut off! Between me and our newly formed position was the enemy's line. There was no possibility of escape. There was nothing for me to do but to wait and marvel at all the wealth of soldiers and supplies. There seemed to be no end to them! For two hours and more there was a continuous flow across the bridge. At last, toward sunset, it became quiet. I wondered what to do. The old man had breathed his last some time during the period when I kept my vigil at the window. I carefully crawled out, only to scramble a quick retreat. Not ten yards from me, two guards stood on the bridge. It was impossible for me to get out; the soldiers would either see me or hear me. Yet, there was no other way of escape available to me. It was growing dark.

The two guards stood at the bridge approach, just where I had to pass if I wanted to get back to my own troops. Not really believing it would work, I nevertheless tried one of the oldest tricks known to fighters for getting away from their enemies. I picked up a stone and threw it over the heads of the guards to the other side of the approach to the bridge. They heard the noise and at once took cover. Immediately I threw another stone, which landed a little farther away. One soldier quietly stood guard while the other crept in the direction of the noise. I threw a third stone even farther than the previous one. Then I stood erect, for their attention was drawn to the other side of the bridge. The one who had gone to investigate called out to his companion. He, too, went to the other side.

I hastened to the parapet of the bridge where they had stood guard. Carefully holding onto the projecting stones, I let myself down the precipitous side to the bed of the dried-up mountain stream. The soldiers went up the incline on the opposite side, and I went down to the bottom of the gulley, boots in hand. Soon I could no longer hear them, so I hurried along as fast as possible. To the right and left were groves of olive trees, whose silver leaves shone in the soft light of the moon. Somehow, though not surprisingly in the midst of this mortal peril, the sight of those softly shining leaves made me think of our Savior and his vigil in the olive groves at Gethsemane. I prayed softly while I hurried through the olive groves in the direction I thought would lead me to my own comrades.

Suddenly I saw figures before me. The British soldiers had not yet noticed me, since they expected no one from the rear. It was impossible for me to get through.

The only remaining way to reach the German lines was by wading through the water, for I had come out of the olive grove right on the edge of the sea. This was quite dangerous for me, since I am not a good swimmer, and there is the always-present danger of stepping off into the deeps. But, since no other choice presented itself, I carefully stepped into the water, which fortunately was not very cold. I held the Blessed Sacrament aloft in my left hand and carefully waded forward, meanwhile keeping a watchful eye on the opposite shore. But no one thought to look for a possible German wading through water up to his chin, holding his left hand high, as if in supplication. Out to sea lay the big warships that guarded the coastal emplacements. I was walking in a sort of unwatched no-man's-land between two sets of enemy forces.

I had just gained a position opposite the enemy's sentry when I heard a plane overhead. Immediately the searchlights from the ships illuminated the sky, first fingering the heavens and then the water. It became daylight, so there was nothing left for me to do but put my head under, holding the hand with the Blessed Sacrament just above the water level and praying with all my might.

This danger finally passed, and I raised my head from my unpleasant immersion, my mouth filled with salty ocean and my heart with fervent thanks. There were yet a few reefs to crawl over in order not to expose myself above water. Finally, I thought I was far enough away so that I could risk climbing out of the water onto the shore. I was successful and began to run forward, still with great caution. It was biting cold in my dripping uniform. I didn't even take time to empty out my boots, which were sloshing with water. An hour later, I was challenged. It was the German sentry.

My reception was so heartwarming that it surprised and touched me. I had not known that I was in any way a symbol to these men, but when they thought I would never return, they felt the loss strongly. Now that I stood dripping before them, they could hardly believe their eyes. When the commander saw me, he said, "Goldmann, you astound me! You must have had the devil in you to make such an escape. Of the entire Ninth Company, you are one of the few still alive. Everything went to the devil out there, and we certainly never expected to see you again!" He pressed hot coffee on me and sent someone to take a uniform off one of the dead so I could get dry.

I thought how strange it was that our commander should mention the devil, when I knew much better to whom I was personally indebted for my unusual survival.

The uniform was too small, but after a few days I was given one that fit; it, too, came from a fallen soldier. Our losses were to be very heavy in the next few days.

Chapter 9

"GET UP AND WORK"

For the next two or three weeks, we waged an ingenious fight against an enemy who far surpassed us in men and materiel. It became a cat-and-mouse contest in which, at times, we almost forgot we were fighting for our lives, so engrossed did we become in the numerous ruses and stratagems we employed to get our handful of men out of that valley death-trap alive. During the day it was impossible to make a move, so we relied on darkness as an ally. We found protection in the railroad tunnels from the ships' guns. Since they hardly had reason to fear us, they sailed up boldly, as close to the shore as possible. Then we found some anti-aircraft guns in the mountains and scored a few direct hits on the ships before they withdrew out of range. After that, we had a rest. Oh, we sent up occasional salvos of shells whenever we could, in order to hold the enemy off, but mainly we tried to rest and regain our strength. Since this was a coastal highway and our position was still fairly good, we were able to retain our new position for quite a long time.

We had adventures in plenty during this time. We began to run low on supplies and provisions of all kinds, but since we were essentially cut off from the main body of the armies, we

were directed to "take care of ourselves". For a while, we
lived by gathering grapes and many other delicious fruits that
were ripening in the untended, partially destroyed orchards.
However, this vegetarian diet would not long do for the German stomach, and by the end of August we had had quite
enough. One day, while out reconnoitering, we happened to
spot some wrecked Italian ships partially submerged in the
harbor of Milazzo. We decided it was worth taking a chance
to see if we could get out to the ships and perhaps obtain
some provisions there.

Emptying an ambulance truck, I set out with a few soldiers, whom I had ordered to arm themselves with automatic
pistols and ammunition. We arrived in the city of Milazzo,
which fronted on the harbor, and found it almost deserted
after the many bombings by the Allies. The harbor mole was
almost completely destroyed; we marveled at the power of
bombs that could crumple such walls. Several heavily damaged, half-sunken ships lay temptingly in the roadstead, only
a little way out from the pier. There were no sailors in sight—
all seemed to have fled. Four of us put a little boat in order
and rowed to the derelict we judged to be the most promising. Our judgment was good. We found fabulous treasures
in the ship, things we had only dreamed of even in time of
peace. We filled the boat, making three or four trips, loading
the truck as high as we could. Our comrades would feast for
a while!

No human being was in sight. No sooner had we stowed
away the last case of food and lashed down the tarpaulin on
the truck than a group of Italian sailors emerged suddenly
from a side street. They had been in hiding and had evidently
been drinking heavily. When they saw that we had taken provisions from their ship, they became very angry, as one can
easily understand, especially when they saw we had not over-

looked the bottles of excellent wine. About fifty of them blocked the road in a threatening mood and demanded that we unload the truck.

I didn't even need to give the order; my hungry soldiers at once drew their machine pistols and fired a few shots over the sailors' heads; the Italians fled into the ruined houses lining the street. At that moment, we ourselves had to move quickly. Unperceived, three bombers had appeared. They had noticed the gathering in the street, and at once bombs fell like rain. A few of them landed in the houses. We lay flat in the corridors of a house built of thick square stones, in the midst of some of the Italians, who cried out with fright, kissed their medals and rosaries, and continuously cried out, *"Mama mia!"* and *"Madonna!"*

They lay clutching each other, seeking protection, while the walls of the building shook under the force of the bombing.

My only concern, beyond staying alive, was what was going to happen to our truckful of food. While the planes could still be heard and our Italian companions still lay in the house, we hastened to where we had left our vehicle. But there was no truck to be seen, not even any wreckage!

We stood there perplexed, when suddenly we heard the sound of an engine. Turning, we saw good old Faulborn coming out of a covered driveway with the unharmed truck. He had had the presence of mind to drive it to safety, even while the bombs were falling. We jumped on board and off we went. In the meantime, the Italians appeared on the scene again, shouting curses. Though we had just been companions in peril, we drove off laughing, thinking only of the feasting we would have for a while.

Not too long after this, we got into another scrape over food that might also have cost us dearly. But then, in war, who counts things like that? Your life is forfeit from the time you go onto the first battlefield, and it is only by realizing this that you are able to maintain some semblance of sanity.

We had gone around destroying all viaducts, bridges, and so forth, and we supposed our enemies to be still quite far away. I was on the truck with the last group when we noticed a farmhouse not far away, with wonderful grapes hanging ripe for the plucking. No one was in sight, so we turned off a little from the road to enjoy some of the fruit.

Meanwhile, the rest of our trucks drove by on the street. We let them go, since we could easily catch up with them, and set our hands to the more important matter of the grapes. We also managed to collect a basket of eggs and some potatoes; a handy cow supplied us with milk, and we found lard in the kitchen. We had every thing we needed to make good potato pancakes, a delicacy we had missed for a long time. The estimable Faulborn was not only a good truck driver but also a very good cook, so he began at once to prepare the meal. I started the fire and collected fuel. Strolling around a bit in anticipation of the pancakes, I climbed up on a railroad embankment behind the house. For a moment I stood there stiff with astonishment—the British were approaching! First two armored cars, then long lines of happy soldiers, marching as if in peacetime. They were thirty meters away from the railroad tunnel and would soon appear on the other side of the embankment and cut off our escape. I ran quickly back to the house and told Faulborn of the danger. He started the motor immediately, and I jumped onto the running board; but, before we drove off, he ran into the house carrying my helmet and his own. I thought, "Poor fellow, he's lost his mind", and was about to run after him when he emerged with the two helmets, which he thrust into my arms. As we roared off, I saw that one helmet was filled with grapes and the other with potato pancakes!

We reached the street just as the British came over the top of the embankment, not five meters from us. We turned east and raced ahead. They seemed astonished to see the helmets hanging on my arm, and we took them so much by surprise that before they thought of following us or shooting at us we had disappeared between the houses of the city. We drove through the olive groves up the slope, and from the top we saw that the enemy column had halted and fanned out to search the terrain—perhaps to see if there were other German pancake-eaters around. We sat down on the hill high above and enjoyed our meal; nothing had ever tasted so good.

Not long after that occurred the strangest incident in my altogether improbable military career. After fourteen days of constant strain and the loss of 80 percent of our soldiers, we were relieved and lay perhaps three kilometers behind the front in a little town at the foot of a mountain. About eight o'clock one night, after a terrific bombardment began at the front, more than thirty wounded arrived at our aid station. There was no doctor present, and I was the only trained medic, so I was kept busy until midnight dressing the wounds, giving injections, and doing what I could for them. At last it was finished; the men lay under the olive trees of the small valley, some sleeping, some moaning, others, I knew, dying. I wrapped myself in my blanket and soon fell asleep from exhaustion.

Suddenly, I woke up; it was about 2:00 A.M. I thought I had heard a loud voice. I jumped up and went to the wounded, thinking one of them had called me. But they were quiet. Two were already dead. I went to the two sentries and asked if they had heard anything; they assured me I must have been mistaken, since all was quiet. It *was* quiet—very quiet. A strange uneasiness took hold of me, but since there was nothing wrong I lay down again, but I could not sleep.

Half awake, half dozing, I tossed about from side to side, and suddenly I heard a loud, almost threatening voice, "Get up and work! *Schnell*—there is no time to waste!" The voice was so loud that my ears tingled. Moreover, the sound seemed to fill the whole valley. I jumped up and looked around excitedly in the dark, but I could see no one. I ran to the sentries and asked if they had heard anything, but they said I had been dreaming and burst out laughing. It was indeed very peculiar.

I became alarmed. Who had called me?

Completely unnerved, I sat down under a tree. A strange fear took hold of me; I could not sleep and did not know what I should do. Looking up into the clear sky, I again heard the mysterious voice, this time really threatening me.

"Get up and work! It is past time!"

Completely unnerved, I lost control of myself altogether and cried out, "What is the matter?"

But there was no answer. The sentries rushed up and asked, "What are you yelling about?"

They assured me they had heard nothing, at the same time remarking to one another: "With some, it begins in the head!"

I did something I had not done for months; I took my pick and shovel and began to dig a foxhole. It was the first time during the entire Italian campaign that I had dug one, having little inclination for that type of work. But now I hacked at the earth as though I were being paid for it. After a short time I had blisters on both hands. About six o'clock in the morning the other soldiers awoke. They formed a circle around me and jokingly admired the half-finished hole I had dug in the rocky ground.

They asked, "What happened?" One soldier joked, "Now that we have won the war, even the non-commissioned officers work!"

I did not mind their jeering. They sat around, enjoying the spectacle. About seven o'clock, Faulborn brought my breakfast, well prepared. He could not understand when I told him to set down the food and dig a hole for himself. He knew me for a calm man and looked at me in surprise, as if wondering whether something had happened to my mind.

"I have no time to explain it all to you, but for the sake of your wife and children, dig, and dig fast!" He was manifestly impressed by what I said and the way in which I said it. That, coupled with the evidence of my half-dug hole, impelled him to begin with his experienced hands to dig a hole for himself. The other soldiers laughed, and said, "A contagious digging disease has broken out!"

We continued to dig while the others looked on. About nine o'clock, my foxhole was large enough for me to lie down in. Exhausted, I crawled out, put on my shirt, and stretched myself out on the ground to rest my weary bones. Looking up into the sky, I was suddenly struck with horror. High up in the heavens, ten bombers were circling like vultures. At once the alarm was sounded. The soldiers stood as if paralyzed, so as not to reveal our presence to the planes by any movement. But it was too late; we had already been seen.

They swooped down and dropped at least twenty bombs. Faulborn and I jumped into our foxholes while the others hastily sought safety behind trees or by lying down on the ground. I turned on my stomach so that I could protect the Blessed Sacrament, which I had with me.

All hell was loosed down upon us as the bombing continued. With my last strength I was able to pull myself up higher, lest I be suffocated by the shower of dust and dirt and pieces of rock and metal. Then I fell unconscious.

After the attack was over and the valley turned into a smoking wilderness, other soldiers came to search for survivors. Faulborn and I were the only ones. It took ten minutes of artificial respiration to revive me, after I had lain thirty minutes covered by debris.

Who had called to me in the night? Who had saved me?

Three weeks after this incident, I received a letter from Fulda. It was from Sister Solana May. On the very night when I had heard the voice commanding me to get to work, she had experienced such fear about me that she hastened to the chapel and prayed until morning, "Guardian angel, save him!" She asked that I write her at once and tell her if anything had happened to me. She also said that it was about two o'clock in the morning when she awoke with such fear, the exact hour when I first heard the voice.

Thus was my faith bolstered still further during these terrible times.

Chapter 10

WAR'S INFERNO, HEAVEN'S GATE

Not long afterward, just before entering a little town near the seaside, we made preparations to blow up a bridge to stop the advance of the enemy. We set up our machine guns in the homes of the town to give the enemy a proper reception. The citizens immediately fled when they saw that a battle was going to be fought there. Only a few old and sick persons remained. They assembled in the center of the town near the church, which had been severely damaged by aerial attacks. One side of it lay in ruins. I saw the pastor standing near the church, reading his breviary as if he were not in the least concerned.

I approached him—an old man with snow-white hair—and told him to hurry and get out because in less than half a day a battle would be fought there. He said nothing, only shook his head and continued his prayers. I repeated my request with even greater urgency, but he paid no attention. I suggested that surely he would want to keep alive for his parishioners' sakes; it was his duty to flee into the mountains so that after the war he would be able to serve his parish.

He looked at me as if he were angry for a moment, took me by the arm, and led me through the rectory and up into his bedroom. Near his bed, I saw the fifth station of the cross, which he had saved out of the damaged church. Pointing to it, he said, "Simon was not allowed to flee but was forced to go along up to Calvary to the place of the crucifixion. Today I am the Simon."

Then he let go of my arm, and I was so confounded that I could say nothing. I remembered the words of the Lord: "The good shepherd lays down his life for his sheep. But the hireling, who is not a shepherd, whose own the sheep are not, sees the wolf coming and leaves the sheep and flees." I knelt down and asked for his blessing.

He laid his priestly hands on my helmet and spoke the blessing: "The Lord bless thee and keep thee. May he show his face to thee and have mercy on thee. May he turn his countenance to thee and give thee peace. The Lord bless thee." I received his blessing with profound joy. When I heard he was a member of the Third Order of St. Francis, I showed him my certificate showing that I was a cleric of the First Order. The aged priest, with tears in his eyes, gave me the kiss of peace on both cheeks and rejoiced that two sons of the peace-loving St. Francis should be privileged to meet here in the unpeacefulness of war.

Shortly after this event, the fury of the war drove us on. Thanks be to God, we were ordered to evacuate the town and to withdraw farther toward the rear. So the town and the church were saved for the aged priest and his people.

In the middle of August, during heavy fighting at the coastal highway near Messina, we were shot at for the first time by our Italian allies, who had suddenly disappeared during the night and, in preparation for Badoglio's betrayal, had become our opponents. The battle became desperate when the British and American forces formed a solid unit at our backs, with the coastal highway the only retreat left open. Our entire battalion, with only four armor-piercing guns to check the advances of tanks, was surrounded. On a mountain to our rear, the enemy lay entrenched. The highway was so strongly guarded that there was no way of getting through; nearly a thousand soldiers were cut off.

We waited in one of the many railroad tunnels, having dynamited the other tunnels, bridges, and viaducts while we were bombarded from six large warships during the entire day. When darkness set in, a young commander of the *Luftwaffe* hauled out our only remaining artillery pieces from the tunnel and set them up on the highway within range of the British cannons on the mountain; we had carefully decided on this move the day before. The Sixth Company was ordered to make an attempt to get across the highway with covering fire from the artillery, but the result was disastrous. The fire from the enemy mowed them down. We had only one desperate gamble left if we were to escape. We fired the guns like madmen at the enemy, using the fire as cover for four captured Italian tanks that we rushed through the darkness, packed with soldiers. They hung like grapes from the sides.

The tanks, followed by ten trucks, went full speed down the highway, which was littered with dead and wounded soldiers—friend and enemy alike. It was a terrible ride. I was on the second tank, and I could only pray to our Lord in the Blessed Sacrament while the cries of crushed soldiers drowned out the clattering of the chains of the tanks. I will never forget the sound as long as I live—anonymous men who, having survived enemy fire, were now crushed by their own comrades whose plight was so desperate that escape was the only thing left in their minds.

We came through. The commander was given the cross of

knighthood for his brilliant plan—but there was much blood on it.

The next day, we lay hidden on the shore in the sand. Six English cruisers lay close by, just offshore. If one of us raised his head, he was shot at with a salvo. Although we were fired on throughout the day, we had relatively few losses. Toward noon, a motorcyclist roared in from the rear, in full view of the enemy.

I shouted at him: "You idiot, couldn't you wait until dark? You're betraying our location to the enemy!"

Breathless, he jumped from his motorcycle and handed me the message; it was an unimportant matter that could just as well have waited until nightfall. I forbade him to move from the spot. All of us were afraid that the British gunners would find us, with the motorcycle on the highway and us not a thousand meters away. But all was quiet. We uttered a heartfelt sigh of relief. I told the boy, not yet eighteen years old, that he must wait until night set in before returning, no matter what the commander might say about it. He promised.

Like all the others, I was tired, and I lay in my sandy foxhole and dozed off. Suddenly, the air was split with the familiar roar of a motorcycle—the boy had taken advantage of my dozing to race back. The enemy was waiting for just that. At once a vicious salvo was aimed at the cyclist. He raced as if possessed; the bullets fell in front, behind, above, and below him, and still he raced on. We held our breath; some of the shots were even reaching us. He traveled one hundred meters, two hundred meters; then he bent over the bike, turned, and drove slowly, slowly back to us. And, oh, wonder! The enemy remained quiet. We saw in our telescopes how they, too, were observing us through their glasses. The youngster came on slowly, at a crawling pace. I stood up and swung the Red Cross flag. Everything remained quiet.

The young men around me watched, awed, as the still younger soldier stumbled toward me. I caught him.

"Herr Unteroffizier," he said, haltingly, "I am so hot, so hot here in my breast." I put him down on the white sand and opened his coat. From his breast, the bright red blood spurted like a fountain from his lungs, a fountain of death. My face and my uniform were covered with it. I pressed my hand on the big hole in his chest to stop the flow, and still it oozed through my fingers.

"Must I die?" the young man asked, with a faltering and trembling voice.

"Yes, there is no hope." I was about to ask him if he was a Catholic, for I had Holy Communion with me. But then a smile brightened his face, a truly radiant, good, and joyful smile, and he said with a weak voice, "Please write to my mother and tell her I am waiting for her at the gate of heaven. She must not cry. I am waiting for her." With the happy credulous smile of a child, he passed into eternity. Rarely have I been so affected by a death, and I have seen so very many.

There were others, other deaths, I cannot easily forget. Once a bomb fell in the midst of a battalion. The sight was terrible. My faithful driver, Faulborn, brought me to the place. Many times he saved my life and the lives of other soldiers. We found that all but two of the men were dead. The two living we quickly put on stretchers and loaded on the truck. I told Faulborn to drive as fast as he could, for it would be only a matter of minutes for these two men. He raced on, unheedful of the fire from the ships. I sat with the wounded men and watched them. But it was too late to do anything to save them, and I finally told him to stop, to ease them at least from the jostling pain of the driving. One of the soldiers looked at me quietly. I took his paybook from his breast pocket; he was the son of a farmer in Westphalia, and a Catholic. I told him his condition was serious and asked if he wished to receive Holy Communion.

"Are you a priest?" he asked.

"No, but I have Holy Communion."

He smiled with joy, and whispered, "Hurry, hurry, sir."

I prayed an act of contrition with him and gave him Holy Viaticum. He whispered something I could hear only by putting my ear to his mouth. His last thoughts were about his mother. "Please write her and tell her, 'I die with the Savior in my heart.' "

What a death, I thought.

I looked after the other soldier. He, too, was a Catholic, a laborer from the Ruhr district.

"You should receive Holy Communion, also", I said. With effort, he replied scornfully: "Such a piece of bread will not save me. Rather, put a cigarette in my mouth." I took one from my pocket, lit it, and gave it to him. He took three puffs, dropped the cigarette from his lips, and died. He was with the other soldier now, before the judgment seat of God. This incident remained with me for a long time, and called to mind the words of our Lord, "He who eats my Flesh and drinks my Blood has life everlasting, and I will raise him up on the last day. But he who does not eat my Flesh and does not drink my Blood has not life in him."

We finally reached Messina after constant attacks, both during the day and the night, from our former allies, the Italians, who were keenly intent on ambushing us. There were possibly one thousand German soldiers left on Sicily, the northern part of the island being occupied by the enemy, who were setting up their guns on the pier without hindrance. The last boat, a speedboat, landed. We threw, more than carried, the wounded onto the boat. It was filled nearly to the sinking point. Three medics jumped into the boat; the wounded soldiers held on, many of them in vain. The motors roared and we were off, landing safely on the other side of the Strait of Messina, in spite of the constant firing from the artillery on the pier and from the aircraft. Our anti-aircraft guns from the other side shot down three planes; the rest no longer molested us.

The first night, we camped in a church building, and the next night we traveled north. We were running now, no doubt about it. We had to travel at night because the enemy's superior air power made daylight travel hazardous. Our next stop was Palmi. Then we came to a little mountain town, where the people received us most kindly.

Chapter 11

VIATICUM

The rest of the division escaped into Italy, but too many remained as dead or captives in Sicily. We delayed a few days to rest in Palmi, down in the toe of the Italian "boot". During this time, fresh troops came from Germany. They were mostly young men under twenty or older men over forty-five. They were the last whom the Fatherland could throw into the jaws of the hungry beast of war.

Our task was to delay the oncoming enemy and to leave nothing usable to fall into his hands. So it became a war on a small scale, mostly small groups against small groups, so that the enemy was forced to fight in the narrow streets of towns from the Aspromonte to Cassino and could not bring to bear the full might of his power, as he could do in the open field.

What we could destroy was destroyed: bridges and viaducts, electrical machinery and hospitals—even the small ambulance stations in little towns. The big supply centers of the Italian army went up in smoke. It was a pity to see such destruction, but, in most cases, no mercy was shown. The Italian prisoners we took were stripped to the waist and sent to the north barefoot. The forests and the hills were full of partisans; they showed little mercy to these men because of their bitter feeling over Italy's defection.

Soon the enemy took over the Strait of Messina, and then for week after week the small war raged in the mountains, with toil and courage on both sides. Again and again the enemy were at our backs, and this meant an adventurous and often unpredictable encircling movement was necessary if we were to cross the bridges and passages in the mountains. But here it was not as it had been in Sicily, a matter of superior equipment, but rather a matter of strategy and courage, and so the casualties were fewer; here there were no ships or planes.

I was surprised at the lack of precaution and the almost childish trust with which the Allies followed us. We mined all the bridges and viaducts and, more than once, when we dug into the mountainside to watch, the fully equipped columns of enemy soldiers came through as though they were on a friendly visit; first came light tanks, then the artillery, and the rest followed in close formation. We let them pass over the bridge and then blew it up; they were helpless in our line of fire. Here we saw many chivalrous deeds in deference to the Red Cross flag. Four bombers who saw me on the top of a truck, waving the flag, dropped chocolate bars for the wounded instead of bombs.

It was already September. On the way northward I had found a truly brotherly reception in the Italian rectories and monasteries, and the pastors renewed my consecrated Hosts with joy and astonishment. On September 5, we had been surprised by an English attack in the mountains, and some of our men were wounded. At night I drove them to a hospital. I knew that two battalions and three heavily armed companies were behind us. At about five o'clock in the morning, the whole mountain was shrouded in fog and quietness. The road led over sharp curves, down the mountainside toward the sea, where there were two towns on the coastal plain.

Here we stopped, and I asked for water for the wounded. A strong wind scattered the fog, and to my surprise I saw dozens of troop transports, small boats and cruisers, and a few large ships of war lying off shore. Thousands of soldiers were already landing, with tremendous quantities of supplies.

Our way was cut off, so I turned back and thirty minutes later came upon our rear guard. The field major and our commander hurried to a place where they could watch the landing. They set up their guns. The enemy never knew we were up there in the foggy heights, until at 6:30 all hell broke loose. Ships exploded as we found their ammunition lockers. We fired for ten minutes before a return shot was heard. Things must have been terrible down there at sea. At last, the big warships began to return our fire, but 99 percent of their shots either went over our heads or fell too short. For an hour, we suffered no damage, but with the enemy below, things looked very bad. Now we were ready to try a breakthrough. At the command "Stop", all was quiet while the trucks were loaded.

My truck was first, and down the mountain we went. No shots came from the shore, but the ships, though badly damaged, managed to fire back weakly. We came to the first town and formed new lines. We were commanded to drive the enemy back into the sea.

I thought this unwise, for it meant exposure to the ships' guns, which had now partially recovered. I set up a first aid station near a building in town. The doctor, a new one, was already wounded in the hand, so it was up to me to give the injections, write out the cards, and, more than once, sever limbs with only a knife. Now the wounded came fast, nearly a hundred; between bandages and injections, filling out cards, and performing crude surgery, I would ask, "Are you Catholic? Here is Holy Communion."

After hearing a short act of contrition, I placed the Body of Christ on quivering lips with my bloody fingers. But all too soon the Hosts were used up, and more had to be procured. The town was high above the battle, and many Italians had been watching the scene below. As they saw the Panzer Division and the Germans coming, they all fled into town. Before the old church stood three priests, two young and one very old.

I jumped off one tank with my helmet on and my face and hands and uniform covered with blood. I drew the note of the Bishop of Patti from my pocket, thanking God that it was in Italian. Though it gave me permission to carry the sacred Species, they claimed that they had no Hosts. I could well understand that they would not feel they could trust this blood-drenched enemy soldier with Holy Communion, so I spoke in Italian and gestured and produced a second piece of paper showing my membership in the Franciscan Order.

"Not for the price of blood", was their reply.

My patience was at an end. One of the soldiers came up with an automatic pistol and the three raised their trembling hands. A soldier in a tank covered the rest of the crowd of people, and we marched into church, I making sure that the priests came also to see what I did and how I did it.

"*Avanti!*" I commanded, as we reached the sanctuary; but they refused, and I had to force them. How strange that the few times thus far in this war when my gun was aimed anywhere, it was aimed not at the enemy but at priests and defenseless bishops!

We found the tabernacle key in the sacristy and I made a short act of adoration. The three priests with their arms still uplifted saw me open the tabernacle with obvious reverence and understanding of what I was daring to do. I took the Hosts I needed. The old pastor wept. I spoke to him.

"Father, the Hosts are for the dying. Will you give me, and them through me, your blessing?" At last he believed I was no thief or murderer, and he placed his shaking hands on my helmet.

Away we went with the tank. I heard from the crowd, "Ah, these German devils!" But devils with the most Blessed Sacrament!

This all took about an hour. Then I was back at my station, where I was caring for the wounded. The Hosts were almost all consumed when news came that the Eleventh Company had met the enemy and many wounded were lying on the battlefield. We had to go; the tank was our only means of transportation.

Soon we met the fleeing Germans, closely followed by the British. When they saw the Red Cross flag, the British came up to us and spoke friendly words and helped me load the wounded. Some Catholics among them understood what I was doing with the dying and knelt; others looked on in bewilderment. They gave the wounded tea and chocolate, and we rode back in safety. This was one of the most human experiences I encountered in the war.

We returned to our station, and soon the town was bombed by planes. We ran out of town on foot since our tank was also damaged; there I saw my ambulance truck standing next to the pastor, who merely said, "Finally. It is high time you got here." He saw the enemy coming, took in two wounded German soldiers we met so we would not be burdened, and we went away into the mountains.

During the next four weeks, life was a nightmare. How we ever managed to make headway, with the Italians and English all around us and planes dropping bombs, I'll never know. I was welcomed in many Franciscan monasteries and in rectories, in spite of the blood and my hated uniform.

It was a feast of Mary—I think the Holy Name of Mary on September 12. We had blown up the bridges and everything else that could be blown up and judged that the enemy was hours, perhaps days, behind. We spent the night in the mountains, under the high trees, soaking up some much-needed rest. The next morning at ten we were to continue our march. I thought it was time to hear Mass again and to go to confession. Since our chaplain was away, I decided to go down to the valley, about an hour's trip, to a Dominican monastery. At four in the morning, I started out. A big dog ran next to me, but he was not unwelcome for I was not afraid of him and he could protect me from sudden ambush. After thirty minutes I arrived at the monastery, but all was quiet. I thought 5:30 must be the hour for rising, but there was no sound of activity within. Finally, at 6:00 I knocked, and it took an eternity before a man's voice growled, "For heaven's sake, what do you want on a night like this?"

I said, "I want to go to confession."

He opened the door in surprise, and before me stood a Dominican Father not exactly dressed for choir. I was in uniform, and, once he recovered from his shock, he led me into the church and prepared for confession. Then I served Mass for an old Father, to the surprise of students and clerics alike. They began chanting in choir, but it was haltingly done, as they were watching me. When I received Holy Communion, they all left the choir stalls to take in this spectacle. I finally went in to the sacristy in order not to rob them of all devotion and attention at their conventual Mass. The old Father who had heard my confession led me into the refectory, where butter and cheese and wine were to be had.

I was hungry, and I showed the clerics who had come in how a German can eat! Naturally, they wanted to hear something about the war. I told them a few things and proudly showed them my rare papers. It was nearing nine o'clock, time for the High Mass, but the Novice Master postponed that in favor of their Franciscan guest. And so we talked and laughed, and they even began to sing. My spirit drank in this true brotherhood that was food for my soul.

Suddenly, the Brother Porter announced in all innocence that many of my comrades were outside—should he show them in?

I had my suspicions about who was there, and looking through the small window in the door, I saw British soldiers! The whole churchyard was full of them. What now?

The superior knew; he lent me a habit, and, with three brothers, I left by a side door. With beating heart, I walked slowly between them to hide my boots. The English greeted us with "Hello", and then we went through a passage near the monastery where I returned the habit and hurried back up the mountain. The others had all left; they had seen the British coming. Only Faulborn was in the village waiting. He thought my hour had come, but he was willing to risk his own life to share it with me! But we drove off instead and blew up all the bridges behind us. A word of thanks is due to the sons of St. Dominic!

Chapter 12

DEACON SERGEANT

We kept going north. The plains of Salerno greeted us, but we did not suspect that for many it meant an early grave. The enemy had collected their forces, and our old and very young men were not equal to them.

To the east of Salerno rose a hill known as 444, because it was 444 meters high. From here one could see the whole plain. The enemy took over and dug in. We were commanded to take the heights. It was a foolish, stupid order, considering our lack of troop strength and our sorry equipment. The evening before the assault, some companies were still without officers.

I was given Company 10. During the night, a young lieutenant came, fresh from school, with absolutely no experience on the front. We lay in the vineyard, waiting for morning. We explained the situation to him.

It was damp and chilly, and no one slept. The young soldiers, green troops, tried to imagine how things would work out, since they had no experience in such a drive. I got out my song book and hummed a few hymns. The lieutenant was the son of a pastor from Hamburgischen and active among the Protestant youth; he knew the songs and sang along softly, with a voice as clear as a bell. The others gathered around us; they were eating grapes as they listened to our singing. Finally, day broke, and the command came: "Get ready."

There were yet twenty minutes before the beginning of the attack. Through the fog one could see the mountain rising above us.

"Should we scale that mountain?" asked the young officer.

"Naturally."

"But the English are sitting on top, with their big guns."

"Yes. But we will overcome them."

"But that is suicide", said the officer. He was so young! "That should be done at night!"

But it was already daylight. Suddenly, he asked me if I had seen anyone die. My laugh was bitter.

"Yes, very many."

"How do they die?" And suddenly he was shaking with fear. "Is it true, one does not fall in the first attack?"

I was startled. This was not a good sign. Untrained though he was, the men needed a leader, and he was coming apart with fear. As I sought to quiet him, his whole body trembled. "No, no, I cannot fall!" he repeated again and again. "She is waiting for me."

"Who?"

He showed me a picture of a young lady. "She is the one. I promised her that one day she would be my wife there in the rectory." He wanted to become a pastor and hurriedly told me how good she was. And God could not want him to die now, not now! He was terribly afraid, and he was supposed to lead the company in the attack!

I told him that since he was a theologian, and the son of one, surely he must know something of trust in God. I told him to follow me and do exactly as I did. "Make no move unless I do," I said. He nodded.

We found new cover before the enemy could take aim. We prayed the Lord's Prayer together and lay in the last row of the vineyard; before us lay a sloping terrain about three hundred meters wide. At 5:40 the artillery let loose, our pitiful four guns firing away at the heights. We began to run. Not a shot fell from above.

Had the enemy moved on?

But suddenly shells burst all around us. We progressed like frogs, up, a leap, and down again. Surprisingly, things went well, until the machine guns started. Then only short leaps were possible. The lieutenant was close behind me. He did well, lying with me in the dirt. Now the dry stream was near. Only two or three more leaps, and the worst would be over; there was shelter on the other side. I saw him move, called out, "*Herr Leutnant*, wait!" but he thought he could make it in one leap.

He ran. And then he was hit in the chest and fell into the dry stream bed. I hurried to him. Blood was flowing from his shattered chest. He looked at me and said with his dying gasp, "My poor, poor sweetheart!" That was the end.

War is such madness—the young die before they begin to live!

Though we took the heights, our losses were heavy. After an hour the commander came up to me as I was about to dig a grave for the young lieutenant. He congratulated me and pinned a star on my shoulder because of "bravery in the face of the enemy". It wasn't often that a non-combatant soldier received such a field commission, and I should have been proud; but before me always was the face of the dying young officer. This was the third time I had heard "because of bravery in the face of the enemy". But I just ran as the rest did. I could not derive much satisfaction in receiving this star.

The following night we were ordered down from the heights because the mountain was under fire from the ships. We had so little artillery and ammunition that we could not return their fire. We joined the troops on the north side of the seacoast and were instructed to cut off the enemy from their ships the next morning, but we failed. We advanced toward evening, but the enemy retreated to within four hundred meters of the shore. There stood columns of tanks and cannons, row on row, one right next to the other. What could we do against them? The air was full of planes; we counted two hundred of them.

We lay hidden in the forest. Next to us in a large meadow lay a royal Italian horse stud farm. It was in the line of fire, and the cries of the dying horses pierced our hearts. The soldiers, in spite of the danger to themselves, went to kill the wounded animals.

That evening at eight o'clock, we moved quickly; only a third of the company remained. On the way we found a damaged enemy tank, from which we took a dead man. In his hand were an American prayer book and a medal. We buried him in a grave near the street. Again a brother was killed by hostile brothers. The folly of war filled us with sickness.

We lost the plains of Salerno. The enemy stood firm. We withdrew yet again into the mountains. The enemy came from the southeast, from Calabria. By now it was mid-November. In Murano-Lucanio, I visited the bishop; he reendorsed my note from the Sicilian bishop giving me the privilege of carrying the Sacred Hosts and so I could give Communion daily. If a pastor on the way refused, the drawing of a pistol brought what I needed, both for the dying and for myself. Many civilians received their last comfort from me; the old and the young alike fell like hunted animals in the line of fire from both sides.

On November 12, I received news that an air attack had damaged the home of my parents. This brought my long-promised, often-deferred leave of absence. How I longed to get out of this hell! Over the Brenner Pass and home!

The damage to our home turned out to be slight; so I left Cologne for Rottenburg, where a monastery with its peace and quiet and good food and rest awaited me. I had stopped in Rome for two days and succeeded in getting permission from the Congregation for Religious to take my solemn vows, despite the war and restricting Church regulations. Though I was bound irrevocably to God and to my goal of becoming a Franciscan priest, and no vow was necessary to keep me straight on that path, still I desired with all my being to speak those vows and to make the commitment irreversible. It was a rare permission, which caused some raised eyebrows.

My Superior was most pleased and made arrangements with Bishop Fischer to ordain me to the subdiaconate. After a retreat in Weggental, in a beautiful pilgrimage church before the picture of our Blessed Mother, I took the vows of poverty, obedience, and chastity on December 7, 1943.

Hardly anyone was in the church, but in the first pew knelt glowing little Sister Solana from Fulda, who had won this special grace for me by her prayers.

For her, it was a day of reward for her faith. The following day, when I received the subdiaconate at the chapel in Rottenburg, her joy knew no bounds. But I wanted more; subdeacon is but the first step toward deacon. However, the bishop declined; he needed permission from the Bishop of the Army before ordaining me a deacon. I hurried to Tübingen and phoned the bishop in Berlin. He remembered me, so it was not difficult to get his permission, which he sent by mail. It came on December 11, and the next day I became a deacon.

Suddenly, my desires burgeoned. Having already won the diaconate, I now wanted to serve as deacon at Midnight Mass on Christmas. But my leave was to expire on December 23. I wrote to my commanding officer requesting an extension until January 3, but, when no answer came, I took the train on December 22 for Munich. My train for Italy was waiting there. I took my luggage into the train carriage, but just before departure I heard my name called over the loudspeaker. I hurried to the stationmaster, and was told my permission for an extension had been granted. With the papers in my pocket, I celebrated Christmas in Rastatt, in Baden.

The "Reichsführer of the SS" inspects the camp near the Polish border.

*A common grave of thirty-seven SS soldiers. Here they repose,
not under the cross of Christ, but under the rune of death.*

In pursuit of the fleeing French, the German forces sometimes had to travel seventy-five to eighty kilometers a day.

Chapter 13

"TEDESCO FURIOSO"

On New Year's Day, en route back to the front, I found my-self in Rome. I wanted by all means to speak to the Holy Father. That, however, was so difficult as to be almost impossible, for the German troops had surrounded the Vatican and made the Pope a prisoner. I asked the General of the Franciscan Order one evening after supper in the monastery of St. Anthony if he could arrange an audience for me with the Pope. He asked me why, and I told him simply that I would like to ask for Holy Orders.

"Have you finished your theological studies?"

I had to answer truthfully, "No. I intend to begin in earnest after the war."

Father General laughed, as did those who were with him. "Oh, oh, this *Tedesco furioso!* This wild German! You would break into the Vatican?"

"No, but I—"

"I'm sorry, my son, that just will not do. Without finishing your studies, you simply cannot become a priest. And an audience with the Pope is quite out of the question."

So that request went with the wind, but I didn't give up. I was here, the time was now, I simply *had to* see the Holy

Father! Some of Sister Solana's faith had rubbed off on me, and the things that had come to pass in the past few months had engendered in me the abiding conviction of the rightness of what I wished to do.

The next morning, I went to the German Embassy and requested some advice from a certain Herr von Kessel on a private matter. He was one of those who were involved in the conspiracy to assassinate Hitler. He took me into his workshop, closed the doors carefully, and, as I gave him the password, he again looked around carefully. I informed him about the arrangements for "July 20" insofar as Baron Adam von Trott had informed me. I repeated the message several times, while he repeated after me, memorizing, for none of this could be entrusted to paper.

I heard some interesting things about the Allied powers that I was to bring to Baron von Trott at the first possible opportunity. After I had memorized the information, Herr von Kessel said, "You have done a good service to the cause. Is there anything I can do for you in return?"

I blurted out, "I would like to see the Holy Father."

"That is not easy, Goldmann. You know how things stand in Rome."

"But I must see him! Surely you know some way!"

"What is it you want?"

I told him.

He laughed and said, "You don't know the Vatican, or the Church. That is altogether impossible."

"But that is what I want to find out! You just get me into the Vatican, and I'll do the rest."

In the end, he called his secretary. "Try to get the Vatican for me, Fräulein Mueller. If possible, the office of the Holy Father."

She returned at once and said the connection was made.

Shortly after, Herr von Kessel said, "The Holy Father will see you. Your name has been sent in."

He summoned his auto, and I drove through the German blockade into the Vatican with a beating heart. Now doubts assailed me; how did I dare, I—a lowly, newly ordained deacon, rushing through things like a bull in a china shop, challenging the established order and proven right way of doing things within the Church—now to be bombarding the Holy Father with this request, at a time when his time, his heart, his spirit were burdened with the problems of millions of men and women? I trembled at my temerity, but the faith of Sister Solana rose up to chide me, and I tried to get a better grip on myself.

The Swiss Guard received me, and I wondered who had sent in a report about me. An official was waiting to escort me, and I was led up the steps. The prelate asked me on the way up what I wanted of the Holy Father. I hesitated and then was told I must be brief, for it had to be entered into the Audience Book, a red book he carried in his hand.

I told him I had two petitions concerning the care of souls from the Bishop of the Army and that I had greetings from a non-Catholic but Christian group who were praying for the Holy Father. He wrote that down, and then he asked: "Is there anything else?" I answered that there was a personal matter I could tell only to the Holy Father.

"But that will not do! You will have to tell me at least a little bit about it."

Finally, I said, "I want to ask for the priesthood."

The prelate beamed and said, "Fine! For whom?"

"For me." Even to myself, it sounded weak and uncertain.

"Oh, so you are a seminarian?"

I could answer that with good conscience in the affirmative. "And you have finished your studies satisfactorily?"

I kept silent. I was not versed in diplomacy, and so I came out with it bluntly and said, "I intend to finish my studies after the war."

He looked at me as if questioning my sanity; he took two steps up (he was much smaller than I was) and said, with the face of a Caesar, "Impossible, absolutely impossible!" Had the situation not been so desperately serious to me, I think I would have chuckled, he looked so perturbed at this notion of mine!

That was the end of it. We went up the steps through a large room with two Swiss Guards on each side. The prelate stopped again and said sharply and distinctly: "In regard to the last point, you will say nothing. The Holy Father has no time to listen to such absurd requests."

I was getting angry. "Who decides what the Holy Father will hear from me? Only he himself—and I!" I spoke clearly and loudly, causing the Swiss Guards to look at me in surprise. "I shall speak, no matter what!"

The little prelate's friendly face turned cold again; he looked at his watch and said, "It is eleven o'clock. The time for an audience has passed. Come tomorrow."

That was just a little bit too much. I said sharply, "I am a soldier; I will be with the troops tomorrow. I must see the Holy Father today. It was promised me, and I stand on it. I insist."

"I am sorry, you must leave."

I said in a tone of voice I am sure the prelate never before heard addressed to himself, "I have no thought of leaving. If you insist, then so be it. I will see the Holy Father by force, if necessary." With that I put my hand into my pocket.

Of course I had no pistol with me, but he thought I did. He looked at me, then at the archaic arms of the Swiss Guard in consternation, probably thinking, "A gun against swords—that means blood."

His face turned friendly again.

"Please wait here. I will see."

He came back quickly.

"Yes, the Holy Father will give you some of his time. But he wants to hear nothing of your last request. Do you understand?"

I understood, and it was bad. I went into the room and found others also waiting. I stood at the end of the row and waited and prayed to St. Thérèse. I remembered her experience with Leo XIII, when she went to him seeking his permission to become a Carmelite at the early age of fifteen. She, too, was expressly forbidden to speak to the Holy Father of what lay deepest in her heart and topmost in her mind. I promised her that I would make a pilgrimage to Lisieux if all went well.

The Holy Father, Pius XII, entered, and we all knelt. He let some explanations of their reasons for calling on him be made and then went to each one. The mothers cried; he comforted them and blessed the children they carried. Truly he was a father! My prelate with the red book was always next to him, with a few short words for each.

Finally he came to me. I spoke to him of the requests of the Bishop of the Army, which were granted at once, being two very important things. Then I relayed to him, the common Father of Christendom, the words of greeting from the Evangelical brothers and sisters; this moved him visibly, and twice he said he blessed them all, his children, from a full heart.

Now I did not know what to do next.

He noticed that I wanted to say something else.

"Do you have something else you wish to say?"

Here was my chance. "Yes, certainly, but I am instructed not to mention it."

In an audience with Pope Pius XII on January 3, 1944, Goldmann was given a note permitting him to be ordained a priest— despite the fact that he had not completed his studies.

Most Holy Father,

    Fr. Gereon Goldmann, deacon of the Franciscan province of Thuringia, prostrate at the feet of Your Holiness, humbly begs:

    1) A dispensation of one year and six months lacking in theological studies, so that he can be ordained priest.

    2) That any bishop can ordain him priest, on any day, because of extraordinary reasons.

    And may God etc. . . .

    In audience with the Holy Father, 10 January, 1944.

    His Holiness Pope Pius XII, referring the matter to the below-mentioned Secretary of the Sacred Congregation in charge of matters pertaining to Religious Societies, graciously grants all the favors requested, together with the faculty of hearing the confessions of the Military alone, having placed the serious responsibility on the conscience of the Superiors.

    Notwithstanding anything.

    Given in Rome, day, month and year as above.

"Why not?"

"The prelate told me you do not want to hear anything about it."

The Pope looked at him and me with a laugh and said, "You can tell everything to your Father."

It was like a dam bursting, and I let it all loose. I had spoken carefully in Italian up to this point, but it all escaped me and I lapsed back to German.

"Holy Father, I am, as you know, a soldier, a medic, constantly with the troops on the battlefield. I do not kill but try to save, both body and soul. The soldiers are dying by the thousands without a priest to hear their confessions. Nine completely new German divisions are without a priest. I beg you most humbly to admit me to the priesthood so that these dying soldiers may also have confession."

"Do you have a certificate regarding your studies?"

"Yes, of my studies in philosophy."

"And theology?"

"I have said this so many times recently, and I am ashamed to repeat it to Your Holiness, but it is my intention to complete my studies in theology after the war."

He showed great surprise. "But you have not studied theology?"

"No, not really."

"But without studies you cannot become a priest."

In my predicament, I stumblingly told him that since my eighth year I had been a server at Mass and knew the Mass well.

The Pope laughed at that and asked, "And do you think that every server boy should at once become a priest?"

Then it struck me what nonsense I had spoken.

"And then, you do not know how to distribute Holy Communion and preserve it."

I could answer that I had done that for some time.

"How?" he asked in astonishment. "You are not a priest."

"Nonetheless, I have the Hosts in my pocket now."

He was speechless until I showed him the letter from the Bishop of Patti, with some explanation of how I came to have it, saying nothing, of course, of the episode with the pistol.

He laughed and gave it back to me, saying, "You seem to be an enigma, rather grandiose, like some southern bishops in the display of Roman authority."

Finally, I told him very briefly about Sister Solana and her twenty-year prayer vigil and how she had insisted that I must ask for this audience; how I told her how impossible it was, since I was going to Russia; and how it was that I escaped being slaughtered and ended up instead, by a circuitous route, in Rome. I told him of how Sister said that, if I came to Rome, I would in a short time have a note saying that I was to be ordained—and that without examination—but with the obligation to complete my studies immediately after the war.

That did it. With the precious note and a blessing—and a twinkle from the Pope's kindly eyes—I left, without glancing any more at the discomfited prelate, who eyed me without much warmth.

On the way to the Franciscan monastery—and no victor ever returned home more joyfully—I stopped at Herder's near the Piazza Colonna and bought a number of First Mass pictures.

As I entered the monastery, supper was almost over. Father General saw me and, laughing, said something to those around him about the *"Tedesco furioso"*.

But when I showed him the note, he could hardly believe it, and he gave me the warmest kind of southern greeting. The food tasted very good that night.

Chapter 14

THE DREADFUL HARVEST OF WAR

Preparations were undertaken for my ordination on the morning of January 30 in the Church of the Catacombs of Domitilla. A Franciscan bishop would ordain me. I was delighted, almost delirious, and with this great feeling of exaltation I went to the front the next day, near Cassino. But my regiment was no longer there, so I had to return to Rome by the coastal road. I passed through ancient Ostia and thought of St. Monica, who died there. Not far away, where the road turned left, was a castle in the woods, with a small village and a church with a Capuchin friar.

I stayed there for two weeks, and every day the ancient priest explained to me the rubrics of the Mass. For fourteen days I was under the care of this good Capuchin friar, who went through the Mass untiringly with me and gave me much good advice for the priestly life. Suddenly, on January 24, an alert was issued early in the morning. I was ordered to march at once toward Cassino, where the British and Americans had started an unexpected winter offensive to divert us from their beachhead at Nettuno. Their plan succeeded; our troops around Nettuno were hurried to Cassino, and the shores were left unprotected. After a few days, the enemy landed with little opposition or difficulty and formed a beachhead there.

We hurried to Cassino. I had to send a message to Rome stating that there would be no ordination at the end of the month, that I would give more information later on. We engaged at once in the mountains south of Cassino, trying to stop an enemy who outnumbered us a hundred to one in men and a thousand times more in supplies. Somehow, we succeeded. We dug deep into the mountain, where they could not reach us, and our heavy guns were quite effective. The sky was filled with British planes day and night, but they too, because of our peculiar position, could do little damage to us. Now and then an enemy scouting patrol was sent out to find if we were still alive. They learned the hard way, and so the front remained fixed, although our equipment was meager. We lay in the mountains during the cold of January 1944.

I was fortunate, for I was encamped in a small place called, if I remember correctly, San Giorgio, and from there I went out every day with wine and other articles of comfort to care for the wounded. There were some dangerous paths, particularly at night, but the view was beautiful. January 29 came with an air attack the night before that left many wounded. I made for the place where they were, near the birthplace of St. Thomas Aquinas. I arrived safely and cared for the wounded, and then I took a walk through the bombed village. I was about to return by way of Cassino but found that was impossible. Bombs were falling everywhere. We decided to try it anyway, but driving was out of the question. The only human beings visible were dead, and they were mostly civilians. We went under the trees and traveled through the forest for protection. However, it was not possible for us to cower there under the trees all day. I found a path leading up the mountain, but a sign at the foot of it said:

ROAD TO ABBEY
FORBIDDEN TO ALL SOLDIERS.

I remembered the abbot was also a bishop; perhaps he could ordain me. How strange, that through all the grave danger we found ourselves in, with bombs falling and death threatening from every direction, the single thought I entertained, the abiding passion I felt, was the drive to achieve at long last the ordination that had seemed so impossible for so long!

I called Faulborn, and we began to drive up the steep, curving, rutted road. At the very first curve, we were stopped by four field police, lower in rank than myself, who blocked the way. As imperiously and commandingly as possible, I said, "You must let us through. We are on a special assignment—we must see the abbot." I showed them my papers; the one in Italian from the Bishop of Patti regarding Holy Communion and the Latin sanction from the Bishop of the Army. These made a big impression, but they did not dispel all their doubts, so I showed my certificate from Dolmetscher and, finally, the note from the Vatican with the papal seal. That did it.

The police showed great respect, and we were allowed to proceed. Higher, higher, we went, until we reached the top, and the world-renowned abbey. Behind the abbey were hundreds of people who had fled here for shelter—mostly old people, women and children, seeking safety in the shadow of the holy place. But how these poor people were to be deceived!

Two more military police stopped me at the main entrance. They were to make sure that the people did not force their way into the empty monastery. I was told that no soldiers at all were on the mountainside or top; the closest troops were eight hundred meters away, where the artillery was set up. General Field Marshal Kesselring had ordered the mountain to be kept free. A few hours later, the Americans bombed the mountain and completely destroyed the abbey—because they thought the Germans were occupying it!

We parked the vehicle outside, and I went through the gate. Before me were the wide courtyard and the many steps that lead to the church. There was no one to be seen. I entered the church; the doors were wide open. Except for the magnificent altars, the church was empty; it still showed all its beauty and majesty. The sacristy was open, but still no one was in sight. I walked through the wide corridors of the monastery, where the monks began their days of prayer and toil. From here they had spread culture throughout Europe, but now every room in the building was empty. The high arches echoed and reechoed the sound of my heavy boots. I went up to the second floor and looked down the long corridors from which one could see the beautiful view to the south.

At last, from the opposite side, the figure of a monk appeared, his arms folded, hands hidden, and the *capuche* drawn over his head—like a being from another world. He was absorbed in prayer and did not see me. I stepped forward, my heavy step startling him.

"Can you direct me, please, to Father Abbot?"

"This is really not an opportune time to see him, I am afraid; he is praying in the cave of St. Benedict." He was courteous, but obviously my uniform led him to believe I was up to no good.

I showed him the note from the Pope, and he responded as if struck by a lightning bolt. Face radiant, he hurried to call Father Abbot. Shortly afterwards, two monks brought me food, which they had to serve on a windowsill, as no table or furniture were to be had.

Finally, the abbot, bishop of the diocese of Cassino, came. He was a reverend old man whose mild appearance reflected a prayerful life. One could trust such a man, and I told him my story.

He chuckled at some points and said to his companion:

Months before, all
the art treasures
were brought to
safety. Abbot
Diamare is sitting
exhausted on one
of the many boxes.

In riconoscente memoria
al savatore dei tesori d'arte
dell' Abbazia di Montecassiono
Julius Schlegel

In dankbarem Gedenken
an den Retter der Kunstschätze
des Klosters Montecassino
Julius Schlegel

25. 5. 1969

This copy of a document sent by the Abbey, a bronze
engraving made by a German soldier, is kept in the mayor's
office in the city hall of Monte Cassino. Translation: In the
name of our Lord Jesus Christ. To the illustrious and beloved
commanding officer, Julius Schlegel, who saved the monks and
treasures of the Abbey of Monte Cassino. All the citizens of
Cassino express their sincere gratitude and beg God's blessing
upon him.
Monte Cassino, November 1943

> + Gregory Diamare, O.S.B.
> Bishop and Abbot, Montecassino

"Things happen in war that are not written in the history books of the Church."

"Reverend Father Abbot, will you ordain me a priest if it so be that I cannot get back to Rome in time?"

He looked at me for a long time; suddenly, he took me by the hand, as a mother does her child, and led me to the center window, where the view opened upon the long plain and the distant mountain. Tears flowed unheeded down his cheeks, and with a shaking voice he said, "Look closely at those towns and villages", and with a trembling hand he pointed them out to me, naming them in a voice that was full of sorrow.

"There I had a church, there a hospital, there a Sisters' convent, and there a school. There a new parish and a kindergarten; for ten long years we have labored here to make this small diocese a little garden of God. Almost overnight, the war has destroyed everything. The buildings are gone, the people dead or fled. Only the monastery remains, here on the mountaintop—and who knows but what God may ask this sacrifice also? 'The Lord has given, the Lord has taken away; blessed be the name of the Lord.'" Then he looked long at me and said, "Only Divine Providence knows what will happen to this monastery in the next few days. It may be that even the supreme sacrifice of my life and the lives of the holy monks under my care may be required before this is over. The entire place has been sacked by the German army. There are now only ten remaining here in the care of St. Benedict. My son, it would give me great joy to ordain you here, as one who can continue to offer the Sacrifice of the Mass—but it may prove impossible. Come at any hour of the day or night, and I will ordain you at the grave of St. Benedict."

"I will try to return tomorrow night, if my orders do not call me to Rome", I replied.

He embraced me with fatherly affection and gave me his

blessing. I drove back down the mountain filled with joy and anticipation.

Around noon there were fewer planes aloft, and we were able, after overcoming many difficulties, to rejoin our troops. They were getting ready to break camp. At night we moved backward over Portecorvo to San Giorgio and from there to the mountains and into the wilderness, where we relieved a company of paratroopers who had held back the enemy for days.

They, a picked, seasoned group, had had great difficulty in holding this place; and I shuddered to think what our green troops, our old men and young boys, would come to in this place. We were in camp about half a day when the enemy began the attack. We finally took a stand around five o'clock in the evening in an old farmhouse that had been hit often. About a third of our men were gone. We had no field officers. At six o'clock, a large number of enemy troops came pouring in, and we had to retreat, at a cost of many more men. For some reason, the enemy stopped; we would have been completely routed had they pursued us. After three hours we reached the mountaintop and found an old farm called Massa Constanza.

There was only one stone building left, two stories high. The small front faced the enemy, about a kilometer away, with all his heavy war machinery. The house had three cellars, all made of stone. The men began to throw themselves down in the first cellar and fall asleep at once. The second cellar contained the radio operators, and I set up my first aid station there. We had had no doctor for weeks, and I had to do my inadequate best to help the wounded. The last cellar held the lieutenant and some sergeants.

Looking out of the house, I saw sleeping soldiers on both sides; there were not three hundred left.

I went to a nearby stream for water, and, as I was returning to the house, I heard a radio operator giving our position openly to our company in the rear. I was furious.

"You idiot! Don't you think the enemy hears that?"

The youngster looked at me in surprise and said, "Why, who can listen in here in the mountains?"

But it was too late. Anyone could have tuned in on our position. I treated the wounded by candlelight, trying to keep worry out of my mind, for there was nothing I could do to change things now. I went to get water again and stumbled over the still sleeping soldiers; they were too exhausted to move. Hardly had I reached the house when two shells shook it and stones came raining down. Lights went out, and from the outside came a dreadful cry; a shell had made a direct hit among the sleeping men. Those who were still alive stumbled into the cellar. Soon another shell exploded, amid indescribable screams. Those who could, fled. I was lying amid the ruins and heard a cry for help from the other room.

With the ever-present Faulborn as my companion, I crawled inside in the darkness and found there nothing but blood and flesh; here a hand, there a head. It seemed to me there, in that black hole of horror, that I realized the full depths of human degradation for the first time. I wept and prayed with grief and frustration as I heard the cry for help growing weaker and weaker. I kept trying to find the source of it and could find nothing but the severed parts and warm blood of men who only moments before had been alive, warm, real! I felt my heart would burst; surely, nothing could ever again be as bad as that!

Finally I found not one but two men and dragged them to the door and then through a small opening, one under each arm. I had just reached the third cellar, which the officers had been using as a staff headquarters, when a direct hit finished destroying the building above. Only this small cellar remained intact. The officers were gone. About us was piled a mountain of stone, and we four were alone in that small place.

And now, hell let loose in truth. Every two minutes there was a double explosion; this continued until 5:30 in the morning. When we could, Faulborn and I searched outside for the wounded and pulled them into our cellar. When we reached twenty, the room would hold no more, and we had to end our trips out into the shell-lighted dark. This was the most miserable night I ever had to endure. Later on, when I was confronted at my trial with the thought of my own imminent death, I was somewhat afraid—though it seemed too unreal for me to believe it. But this! *This* was reality—severed limbs, men drowning in their own blood, the cries for help when none could be had! This was evil; this was Darkness incarnate, and I trembled with fear and anguish. My soul cried out for relief from the suffering of these men I could not help. I felt their pain, their tears, their deaths.

My driver and I stayed awake the whole night. When the water gave out, there was no thought of trying to make it to the stream for more, for then the men would have been completely without comfort. So we stayed on our feet, there being no room to sit or lie down, and the men around us crying out for water died for lack of it. True, I tried to go out twice—and twice was driven back by shots that shattered the flasks. Finally, the well itself was demolished, so that finished that.

Suddenly, at 5:30 A.M., all was quiet. It was a ghastly stillness; there were only four of us still living in that room. I went outside, and my eyes were met by a sight I shall never forget. Shell-hole after shell-hole stretched out before me, and there in the distance the British warships stood offshore. Now we knew who had shot at us so accurately. Just in front

of the door lay the young radio operator who had so innocently and stupidly sent that fatal message. There were very
few to be buried; little but pieces of human bodies, the dreadful harvest of war.

Chapter 15

HE HAS GIVEN HIS ANGELS . . .

We had to leave; to remain meant capture. The two soldiers, having serious arm wounds, did not want to go; they wished to wait for the British. Two others we found with leg wounds said they would try to escape, so we helped them along on the slow walk down to the valley. After about an hour of this snail's pace, we came upon the formerly self-confident young lieutenant and two aides hiding in a shell-hole. When he learned that we had come out of the house whose bombardment he had watched in frustrated fear all through the night, he took off his Iron Cross and tried to give it to me. But I had had enough of that.

"Later on," I said, "not now", and fell asleep. I awoke after two hours and found a note next to me saying that I should follow slowly with the wounded men; the others were going on to a new position.

We got started, following a zigzag course down the mountain. It was terribly tiring, helping the wounded men. Every step they took caused them great pain, and I had no drugs, no narcotics, to ease them a little. Suddenly there was a sound from the rear; perhaps some two hundred meters across the mountain, long columns of the enemy were marching! They shouted and gestured: "Hello, boys! Come on!" They wanted us to surrender. We went on, they leveled their guns, and the chase was on. We ran and fell, crawling up the mountain. The wounded men moved as if they were not wounded at all, and across the way the enemy kept up fire from three or four guns. It was like a peacetime hunt for a fox or a rabbit, only we were the animals the hue and cry was about! Shots fell all about us, but we ran like madmen, and at last we fell over the crest of the mountain.

There we lay nearly unconscious for an hour. I thought my heart would pound through my chest. No one said anything. We knew that if the enemy came after us, we were finished; we had no strength left for further flight. But they did not come. We looked, and saw them lighting a fire to warm their food. When night came, we started out again, somewhat rested, but hungry and thirsty; by nine o'clock we reached our lines. Scattered over about thirty meters, soldiers sat and lay on the ground—mostly children, sixteen years old.

To my amazement, I found the lieutenant was no longer in command. An insolent young fellow, a second lieutenant, was in charge. I was the oldest in service of all those present. As I reported to the officer, he said, "What, retreating? Is there such a thing? Did you never learn that a German soldier never yields a meter? And you want to be sergeant-major!"

That hurt, but with tired control I merely stated that, as a soldier, I was reporting on duty performed and said, "Not everyone has gone through what I have experienced." He was wearing a shiny new uniform, and he caught my meaning immediately. As the lieutenant, the former officer of this company, who was standing nearby, reminded me that I was to receive the Iron Cross in a few hours (for he intended to go through with it), the second lieutenant laughed "Yes, like the one your clean lieutenant is wearing! *He* is to be relieved of duty by the war court because of cowardice in the face of the enemy. And anyone else retreating one meter will be shot!"

That was too much. Faulborn took out his machine pistol and coolly aimed, saying, "Sergeant-major, should I quiet him?"

The second lieutenant turned white and speechless; he dared not move, only muttered something about mutiny. I couldn't restrain myself and said: "A Hitlerite!"

Our former lieutenant said, "Let him be, he'll get his nose full."

The young officer saw that things were not going too well, so he tried to become friendly and told us what our situation was. When he heard we had left two wounded behind (I did not tell him that they did not want to go on), he went at once to the telephone and asked for the commander. He returned shortly: "Here is a command from the general. You are to go back at once and bring the two here. We are not letting any wounded who are still able to fight fall into the hands of the enemy. The front needs every man who can still hold a gun."

I assured him that it was hopeless, for we saw the enemy with our own eyes on this side of the house. It would be impossible to get through; to return would mean death or capture. Meanwhile, eight men came up with litters to carry the wounded we were instructed to bring back; they were all over fifty years of age.

"Here is your company", the lieutenant said. "You have a Red Cross flag in your boot; use it, and you will come through safely."

What were we to do? He understood, of course, that it was not cowardice that made me unwilling to go back into that ruined mountain, and he said to me very quietly, "It is not my command, Goldmann; it is the general's."

I was furious, but helpless. I told the group, who were as bitter about it as I, to give their arms to their comrades, for, if all went well, we were going to be captured—and, if all did not go well, we would not need guns. They obeyed sullenly. I made sure of the safety of the papal note by putting it into my inside pocket, with the Hosts. We started out at 10:00 P.M. The mountainside was very steep; a single misstep meant death. The enemy was in front of us.

After about thirty minutes of this, the men gave up. "Sergeant, this is madness! We have wives and children. What are we doing, walking straight into the enemy like this? They will hear us coming! Let us stay here—tomorrow we can return and say no one was to be found at the house. No one can prove that we were not there!"

They were adamant; they wouldn't budge. I really couldn't blame them too much; who but a fool would walk right into the guns of the enemy for the sake of two men who, if they were not already captured, had said they wanted to surrender, and would do so at the earliest opportunity? I ordered them again to move on, but they would not.

"All right. Wait here. I'll go alone. If I am not back in a half hour, then it will be some time before I return. If there is danger, I'll shout—you can hear it easily, it is so still up here. If you hear gunfire, you can go back." They agreed, and I went into the dark night.

The clouds hid the moon; the visibility was poor. I took off my boots and walked the stony path in what was left of my socks. I was so afraid, I didn't even feel the pain of the stones under my feet. My heart seemed to beat in my throat; I expected to be discovered and shot at every turn. I was ashamed of myself, but every dark rock seemed to be the enemy, and the cold sweat came pouring out of my shaking body. It got so bad I couldn't walk. I sat down and called myself a coward.

But nothing, nothing relieved the anguish and the fear. I had simply had too much, seen too much, in the past forty-eight hours.

Suddenly, as if someone near had started to say it, I repeated the words of Psalm 91 (90), over and over again:

> You who dwell in the shelter of the Most High, who abide in the shadow of the Almighty, say to the Lord: "My refuge and my fortress, my God in whom I trust." For he will deliver you from the snares of the hunters, from the deadly plague. He will protect you with his wings, and you shall take refuge beneath his wings: his faithfulness is a shield and a buckler. You shall not fear the terror of the night nor the flying arrow in the day; the plague that wanders about in the night, nor the calamity that destroys at noon. Though a thousand fall at your side and ten thousand at your right hand, it shall not come near you. . . . For he has given his angels charge over you, to keep you in all your ways. In their hands shall they bear you up, lest you dash your foot against a stone.

These words of Sacred Scripture have been said thousands of times at Compline, the Church's night prayer, and souls have felt no stirring of devotion, but of a sudden they impressed me deeply, quieted me, and gave me trust and courage. I went on, repeating the words over and again. Fear vanished; the angels were with me!

Then I was on the ridge where we were shot at the day before. Carefully, I scanned the opposite side, but there was nothing—no enemy to be seen. To the right, a small hill arose from a hollow, with the bombed house, Massa Constanza, looking like a ghost in the night. Still I heard nothing, so I kept going over the ridge in my stocking feet, zigzagging toward the valley at the bottom. The way was full of curves, and all was deadly still except for the soft bells of the cows in the distance. It was pitch dark. The moon was hidden by heavy clouds.

I reached the bottom and walked through ice-cold water up to my knees. Suddenly I saw a helmet! I lay down in the water. Above me, I could see someone looking down into the valley, but he did not see me. Now I knew where they were. They must have heard something, for now many helmets of the enemy became visible. They were talking quietly and looking into the valley. I realized my litter bearers must be coming. The soldiers took their guns, and from the rear I heard the sound of boots and rolling stones. I knew they would let our men get through and then shoot them; that would not do!

What could I do? My hand, seemingly of its own volition, found the Red Cross flag in my boot. Just as I held it aloft, the moon broke through. To their surprise, the Englishmen saw the Red Cross flag waving frantically, down where they had thought no one was. They jumped up and looked down into the valley. I shouted, "German Red Cross! Don't shoot! Don't shoot!"

At first they were speechless; then one called out, "Come on." I rose and got up the hill, still waving the flag. They must have thought they were seeing some giant spectre, for they drew back and then formed a circle around me as I proceeded. Coming out of the deep that way, it must have been a truly amazing sight to them. Now they all stood about with rifles ready. Finally, an officer came, moving slowly, slowly, with the pistol in his right hand while he searched me with his left. His hand shook visibly. He had been scared as badly as I had been. I told him, "Sir, I have no gun." He believed me finally, and then I told him that the old men behind me also had no guns.

"Call them", he ordered.

I did, for otherwise they would have been shot. They arrived at last and looked at me fearfully; they relaxed only when we were given chocolate and hot tea. We were held captive. Around three o'clock some shots were fired from our artillery, which drove the English under cover. We possibly might have escaped, but, to be perfectly honest, I was so tired and exhausted that I was not able to dare anything.

Toward morning we joined a group of twenty-five men, who led us away. They searched us again, and all that could be taken, they took. We began our march into captivity. For us it was a march full of surprises. We saw countless numbers of soldiers, mountains of supplies and equipment. We saw Italian men and women being pushed into the mountains. We saw guns and cannons and tanks without number that were to bring death to our famished, ill-equipped, badly trained countrymen.

There was one pleasant episode at this time. As we came to headquarters, the guards ordered us to put our hands on our heads. The members of the staff came out to see us, a dirty, ragged, emaciated crew. I stood there, the tallest, as usual, and as sergeant I was the object of unusual attention from these fine soldiers whose uniforms looked as if they were ready for a parade. Suddenly I noticed a cross on the uniform of one of the officers. Could he be the chaplain?

I ventured to speak to him. "Father!"

He started at the address and looked at me in surprise. I took courage, and said, "I am a Franciscan."

He looked at me incredulously and said, in a cold, unfriendly voice, "You—you are a dirty German."

I thought, "Poor fellow, he does not fully understand the Gospel of love toward enemies." I said, "Yes, outside I am dirty, but inside I am a Franciscan."

He did not believe me and repeated, "Dirty German."

I said, "I have a letter for you."

Surprised, he laughed and said to the other officers: "Look, this dirty German has a letter for me. From whom, perhaps the Pope in Rome?" All laughed loudly at this good joke.

I said at once, "Yes, from the Pope. It is sewn in my inner pocket." Still laughing, he approached me; my hands were still over my head, and he felt around in my pocket, found something inside, cut it open and took the writing of the Holy Father in his hands.

He read it, looked at me, read it again, looked around as if to discover something and gave the letter to the general without saying a word. The general did not understand Latin, so the priest had to translate it for him. They stood around me, and the priest asked me in a surprised and conciliatory tone of voice, "Who are you?"

I could not keep it back. I said: "Just a dirty German."

They stood there, not knowing what to say. At last, someone asked, "Do you want anything?"

"Yes, I would like to lower my arms." It was a great relief, and the others followed my example. "Anything else?"

"Yes, I would like to have my watch returned, and the other things they took from me." The major turned in anger and shouted at the soldiers, "You robbers! Gangsters!" They not only brought out my watch but all the watches they had taken from the dead, the wounded, and the captured. I could have started a business in selling watches! I put a few of them in my pocket, and the other prisoners filled their own pockets. (But in the next place where all the captives were brought together, we lost them all once more!)

The priest became more friendly, though he was obviously a little leery; the big German might still be a dangerous animal! I seized the opportunity and told him frankly that such a letter from the Pope was a command for every Catholic priest. "You should take me to the nearest bishop."

"That is very difficult, but we will see. You will, of course, be taken to him eventually, but first the higher officials here would like to see you."

And so we were all loaded into autos and taken to the next headquarters. What a luxury, to ride! We were taken to the internment camp at Aversa, near Naples, a miserable lodging. I was instructed to wait for the highest ecclesiastic from Naples, who was in charge of all the Italians. Until he came, several days went by in which we were really in bad condition, miserable. Afterward, I was called up for examination together with a young soldier named Hans Petermann, whom I got to know quite well and who was to remain with me all through the following years.

Chapter 16

FATHER GEREON

So this is what it all came to. A military chaplain of the Allied forces, who acted as the chief chaplain for the Italians, came to visit me in my tent, and a few hours later I sat with Petermann in a Jeep; we went to Naples to see the Allied commander for all of Italy. A building resembling a castle housed the staff, and we stayed there for two days. Many high officers came to see the former SS man with a note from the Pope. It was too incredible, and there were many interviews concerning this, after which we were finally brought to the airport, where a plane awaited to take us to North Africa.

Hans, my young companion, had been a paratrooper, and so he was accustomed to flying; this was my first flight. The plane was not the latest model, and at times it swerved from side to side so badly that I became horribly airsick and was convinced that I was going to die. We had been undernourished for months in the field and were weak and exhausted, so I fell victim to the deathly sickness quite easily. The friendly English major who was accompanying us brought a haversack full of sandwiches; hungry though I was, I could not eat. Hans, however, suffered no such disabling malaise and fell to heartily. In the six hours of the flight, he managed to consume the entire sackful. Not a crumb was left for his weak copassenger. No onlookers could have imagined that one person could do away with so much food, but they simply had no idea how famished we were.

At last there came an end to this flight, which was one of the most awful experiences of my life, and I had to be dragged out of the plane half conscious. But as soon as I felt firm ground under my feet, I recovered. We were interrogated at a place called Birkadem, in Algeria. We remained under arrest, being ceaselessly questioned; and for two months we had to live in a very small room that had in it only two steel beds. The food was good but terribly meager. The guards were friendly, and the daily bath and the supply of soap they brought were appreciated, even though we had perpetually empty stomachs. We tried every way possible to get the amount of the food increased, but to no avail. Petitions of protests to the general were no use. He visited us occasionally and seemed to be greatly amused by our proposals in regard to food. Occasionally something extra would be added; that was the total result of all our protestations.

After week after week in a cell, without books and with no diversion, one can become quite miserable. Forgotten are the sounds of battle, the death, the stench of burning flesh, the dreadful cries of fallen comrades. Now there was only the terrible sameness of day following day with nothing to do. I had only a small Latin prayer book, and, at my request, an English Bible was given me. So Hans and I passed our time in reading Scripture, and I explained the word of God to him. I had hours to meditate, and it proved profitable for my spiritual life. But what was poor Hans to do, whom destiny had brought into prison with me? I decided to instruct him, since he had merely an elementary education.

On small scraps of paper, which we collected and begged everywhere, and with a small stub of a pencil, which I treasured, I wrote down what I had thought through in countless hours from my studies in the history of philosophy. It began with the Greek philosophers and ended up with Nietzsche. Because I had devoted two full years (plus numerous leaves of absence) of intensive study to philosophy, the knowledge I had gained came back to me gradually.

So we spent many hours in studying the apparently endless fund of learning I had managed to cram and retain in my head. Hans was quick, thirsty. I was surprised at his rapid grasp of things, his questions, and how easily he retained it all. I could not quench his thirst for knowledge; often we had heated discussions, as he, thank heaven, had ideas of his own, born of the times, and especially from the nihilist school of thought. At times, our clash of ideas nearly ended in a fist fight. We had little bodily exercise, and, although our daily schedule began at 5:00 A.M., we were seldom tired out.

I marveled at his control and strength; he was so trained that he could use his body as a plaything and accomplish the most difficult exercise with the greatest of ease. I was also an athlete, and my years in the Christian Youth and later in the SS gave me some physical ability; but what I saw in this young man was remarkable. His strength and agility were enough to bring me to the floor in every tussle, as if all my strength were but little.

So we lived in hunger, in a narrow room, and there were times when the atmosphere was not the most friendly, for he could not admit that his nihilistic ideas were nonsense, as I tried to prove to him with my years of education. The greatest thing about this running debate of ours and the lessons was that I could hold him and myself to a full day's schedule, so that little free time was available from early morning until late at night. To keep him busy, I convinced him that he was made for higher studies and said I was willing to prepare him for that if he would apply himself in earnest. He was a good student; he did not have to be told twice, and so began a course of teaching that was quite unique.

Oh, he was fast! It was a challenge to me simply to keep up with him. Gradually, I remembered all the Latin I had had to memorize, together with all its rules of use and syntax, and these he committed to memory. Within a few weeks, I had written out a sizeable dictionary in five languages: Latin, German, French, Italian, and also Greek and English, with a little Hebrew thrown in. I gave him almost two hundred words, and he fell to with a will. After only nine weeks, he knew them all. It was unbelievable, how this fellow could learn! Such intensive study, under these conditions, taxed our endurance to the utmost, and there were times when my explanations of the Scriptures, which usually took place at night, were interrupted by the none-too-gentle snores of my tired companion. Then I would go over the notes I had made during the day as my evening meditation and study.

We had been captured in January 1944. In May, a high official informed us that the investigations were ended, and that we could go to any prison camp we chose, in Canada, Australia, or here in North Africa. I asked where I might be ordained priest the quickest and with the greatest certainty and was told that not too far from here a place was under the care of the Franciscans. Many seminarians were interned there. I asked to be taken there.

At the beginning of May, we crowded into a Jeep and were driven over a mountain that rose high above the plains to a former brewery called Notre Dame du Mont, located near Rivet, not far from Algiers. At first I was pleasantly surprised. A prison camp without barbed wires! Only two soldiers and a sergeant kept guard. Up till now, our every step had been dogged by armed guards, and now we had freedom on the mountaintop in a section marked off for walking. In a massive stone building, forty soldiers with all kinds of weapons kept guard over the seminarians. The former Abbot of Beuron, Dr. Raphael Walzer, was Superior. After his flight from Germany, having helped Jews and anti-Nazi men and women flee to foreign countries, he had been permitted to gather here the German seminarians from the camps of the south. He gave his word of honor that none would attempt to escape. The cellar of the old building had been converted by the prisoners into a chapel where services were held that would have pleased the best liturgists. The Abbot gave us freely from his store of theological, philosophical, and patristic knowledge from morning till night. Though it was only a one-man faculty in the beginning, we learned much. What a man he was! His lectures were the best I have ever heard; every hour was a pleasure and full of profit.

It was here that I first heard things I did not want to believe about the starvation in the desert camps and the ill treatment that up till now I knew of only from the German concentration camps. What I heard now concerning the French Foreign Legion froze my blood, but I could not believe it until I experienced such things for myself. It is good that we do not know the future, or I could not have experienced so much pleasure on the mountaintop for thinking of what the future would hold for me.

We stayed there for three months. Of course we were always hungry, but the good Abbot did the best he could. With the English as our guardians, the amount of the food was very meager, but the quality was first class. I never tasted better food before. Surprisingly, with the French the quantity was still less, and its quality made it fit only for swine (which I suppose they considered us). Even so, it was better than what we got later on. If worms crawled out of the cabbage soup, made from old and half rotten cabbage, the prisoners who had been there longer would comfort me by saying that that was better than no food at all. If the bread was hard as a rock and smelled putrid, then the word went around that at least it wasn't full of sand or camel's dung. Nothing was said about straw!

At any rate, the Abbot tried to make things as pleasant as he could. He himself had brought the seminarians together from the camps in the south after endless tussles with the military and other authorities and tiring trips that made him ill. Here we were now, under his care on the top of the mountain, with a splendid view of the shore and sea. We could move about freely. That, indeed, was an almost unbelievable accomplishment. Every Thursday he drove the thirty kilometers to Algiers, where the Marian sanctuary stood some distance from the mountains. In the evening, he returned with a heavy load, almost breaking down under the weight, perspiring profusely as he made his way up. Often, as we watched him from the heights (for we could not leave our compound to help him), it seemed that he couldn't make it.

After all these hardships, which were far too great for his age, he stood in choir, even after his travels on Thursdays, and gave us each evening a masterly homily. Every morning at 4:30, he was the first one in choir, where we prayed the entire Benedictine Office from our new breviaries, which he had procured from Spain. Everything was done exactly according to Beuron practice, which he had directed for many years. Every day, after the conventual Mass and breakfast and an early study hour, came the solemn Tierce and High Mass. We "monks" stood in whitish-yellow sacks, strange habits indeed, around the altar. Even though we were from various dioceses and orders, our choir was fairly good in the Benedictine style, and our ragged clothes were the bond of true poverty that united us all closely.

Priests and students, seminarians, and others who were not seminarians but were glad to be here celebrated the Holy Sacrifice of the Mass under the devout leadership of the Abbot. I attended all the lectures the Abbot gave, for I was preparing actively for my ordination, which was scheduled to take place here. The Abbot had taken my papers to the Archbishop of Algiers, who after some doubt and investigation became convinced of the genuineness of the note and planned to administer Holy Orders here in the camp.

Therefore, I was zealous in following the rubrics of the Mass and in preparing my soul for the great day. More important than any other studies were my studies in the hearing of confessions and the care of souls; I had much to learn in a very short time. I started my day at 3:00 A.M. and finished late in the evening, lecturing young Hans, who accompanied me. And so with much hard work, feeling the pangs of hunger, in prayer and solitude, possible only under these cloistered circumstances, the day of my ordination drew closer and closer.

It was to take place on June 24, the Feast of St. John the Baptist, a Saturday. The days preceding were spent in a private retreat. The Mass of the Vigil of St. John, with the beautiful text of the election from all eternity, struck me, by God's grace, as never before. And then the morning of June 24 came at last. The event that a humble and believing Sister in Germany had prayed for trustingly through twenty years was now to take place, in spite of war and captivity, and in a way that could hardly be imagined: a French bishop was to ordain a German prisoner who was still technically attached to the SS and who had not taken the regular course in theology. This day would be the fulfillment of the promise that God answers the prayers of those who believe.

Shortly after 6:00 P.M., the archbishop of Algiers, Monsignor Leynaud, a venerable old man, arrived. He was somewhat surprised to see so many emaciated soldiers clothed in shabby prisoners' garb standing before him. It seemed that even my ordination, a most divine service, could not move forward without surprises.

The throne of the abbot, which served as the throne for the archbishop, was too high for him, and his feet dangled in the air when he finally managed to sit down. Getting off the throne again was a work of some endeavor. The prostrations, when I lay before the altar while the seminarians sang the Litany of the Saints, had a peculiar rubric all their own. The attending "seminarian", who was not a seminarian and who, for the first time in his life knelt beside a bishop and held the *bugia* in his hand, did not know how close he should hold the burning candle. Suddenly it happened—the flames came too close to the beautiful beard of the archbishop, and at once an odor arose that was quite different from the smell of incense.

The archbishop and the flustered candle-bearer put out the fire, but the smell remained.

The seminarians jokingly said afterward that, if the devil himself had come to attend the ceremony, he could not have invented a more disagreeable smell. They laughed when they said that the validity of my ordination was doubtful because the flame of the Holy Ghost did not appear visibly over the one being ordained, but instead a fire was visible in the beard of the bishop!

But finally the rites of ordination proceeded. The imposition of the hands of the bishop at last made me share in the eternal priesthood of Jesus Christ.

My first Holy Mass concelebrated with the bishop had its own difficulties. The Latin of the French prelate did not harmonize perfectly with my German accent, as the

Captured by the Allies and sent to a prison camp in Africa, Goldmann was placed in a group of other captured seminarians who had been gathered at a monastery above Algiers. After studying briefly in this "seminary", he was scheduled to be ordained by the bishop of Algiers.

The chapel in which Gereon Karl Goldmann was ordained to the priesthood on June 24, 1944.

seminarians were quick to notice. It was evident that the ordination was taking place during wartime, with the conse-
crating bishop and the ordained priest belonging to opposite
camps. But even in war there is a love that transcends fighting
armies, for here a French general was present in person and
knelt before me to receive my blessing; he kissed the hands,
just anointed with holy oils, of a German soldier, a newly
ordained priest.

The festive meal was better than usual, but even so it was
no doubt the poorest First Mass fare in the history of the
Church. The wealthy French landowner who lived nearby
came the next day with his family to my Mass and asked for
my blessing; but he conducted himself otherwise toward us
as if we were less than human. In his orchard and vineyards
much fruit was going to waste, for there was no one to pick
it; but it never entered his mind to invite the hungry prisoners or the poor people of Algiers to help themselves. As it
was beginning to spoil, we thought ourselves justified in
helping ourselves in the darkness of the night, and so spent
many hours filling our empty stomachs with grapes and other
fruit.

The abbot preached the sermon of my first Mass in French.
The theme was: think deeply, as did St. Augustine, in whose
country we were; live profoundly, as did St. Francis, to whose
order I belonged; and forget one's self, as did St. John the
Baptist, on whose feast day I was ordained. The seminarians
sang with all their might, and in the evening I received a gift,
a bowl of fruit, that Hans Petermann had prepared. I ate the
fruit with great delight and gave no thought to its probable
source.

For two months more I remained in this haven, absorbed
in the mystery of the Mass and lost in daily study. Never before in my life had I studied so intensely. No newly ordained

priest in the world could be happier than I was, in spite of poverty and want.

But in September 1944, my days were numbered. I had to leave "the seminary", where I received so many graces. It was a departure I made with mixed emotions. I did not want to leave, and yet I had some willingness to do so. These past two months, which I had spent under the fatherly guidance and spiritual direction of the abbot, had been a source of spiritual joy and growth that I never felt before or after. The whole atmosphere of the house, with its strict yet mild Benedictine routine, was too good for me not to miss it. Where else could a prisoner-of-war find such an ideal prison? What I had heard of other camps increased my sadness in leaving this place.

But, on the other hand, I left with a feeling of relief, for, unfortunately, during the months in our seminary, certain discords arose among the war prisoners. The outcome of the war was now no longer doubtful: Germany had lost. Two factions among the captives became increasingly well-defined and in sharp opposition; one side sympathized with the Nazis and were disturbed and shaken by the way things were going. These soldiers were, for the most part, in good faith in the ideology of the Nazi Party, for they could argue that the Pope had entered into a concordat with them and that our bishops had never come out openly against this criminal system.

The others, who for the most part secretly opposed the Nazis and hated them like the devil, dared not openly show their attitude for fear of reprisals—either against them at the close of the war or against their families if word ever got back to Germany. The attempt on Hitler's life that took place on July 20 failed, but it brought all the differences out into the open. The break was public, and words like "traitor" and "perjurer" were frequently heard. Despite my own basically peaceful nature, I still agreed with those involved in the attempt that his death was the only solution. I prayed for forgiveness for my part in it while still holding to my belief that it was the only way.

The arguments raged back and forth through the house, and our good abbot even became involved, though, as a leader of these men and a man of peace himself, he should at least technically have remained above political matters. We who were not Nazis said often that we wanted to be good Germans for a true and better Germany. In this, the Nazis themselves could not shake us, even though our best advocates stood now in a criminal court in Berlin. Things became quite unpleasant, and I was therefore relieved when I left the place. I felt, too, an impatience to be on with "my Father's work", which I could not really do in an active sense as long as I stayed where I was. If I had known what was waiting for me, I would gladly have stayed and put up with the unpleasantness on the mountain.

I took Hans with me, of course; we were to pass through still more experiences together later.

Chapter 17

JOURNEY TOWARD IMPRISONMENT

The journey from Algeria to Morocco took almost three weeks. On the first day, we realized fully that the pleasant days of peace and relative freedom on the mountain were gone as if they had never been. Nights, we lodged in dirty, stinking local jails, swarming with vermin, among men who were criminals. It was a world of corruption; we saw strife and thievery and unnatural depravity among the prisoners, especially among the Moslems. I said Mass once during a night's stay in Blida; then the long journey to Morocco continued, always under the guard of a sergeant who, though he made no effort to conceal his hatred for Germans, still sought to protect us from harm. Once, though, in spite of his protection and vigilance, we nearly lost our lives.

We arrived at the border and came to the first town in Morocco, Oujda. It had a station and railroad junction where we were to change trains, but the next train was not due to leave for several hours. I saw how the Moslems were controlled only by the threat of weapons, and how the inhabitants were treated by the French—not like slaves, even, but like animals. Most of the Frenchmen, with few exceptions, treated the Arabs with brutality, reducing themselves to a semblance of the lowest form of cruel overlords. We had nothing to declare at customs, for in our sacks were only a few clothes; so the guard wanted to take the two of us to a place where we could wait until the train left.

We had to pass a group of workmen, and, to my surprise, I heard them speak in German. When they saw our uniforms, they suddenly became wild men, surrounding the three of us and coming at me as a representative of the evil men who had driven them from their homes in the Alsace to live their lives here as beggars. I was, to them, one of those who had burned their children alive and had disgraced their wives and daughters—all this I heard for the first, but not the last, time. Our sergeant tried to quiet them, but there were over a hundred men, and suddenly the sergeant was separated from us. We were dragged to a lamp post, and one man climbed up while another got a strong rope. We were surrounded; we could not move.

All of a sudden I saw, thanks to my height, a priest in a snow-white soutane passing by on a bicycle. In great fear, I shouted, "Father, they are trying to hang a priest!"

He stopped at once, and, to my surprise, I saw a row of medals on his chest, for he was a military chaplain. He came up to the mob, took in the situation at a glance, and commanded the men to make room. Using his pistol, he forced an opening and came up boldly to rescue us. The would-be hangmen recovered their wits and started to attack us again.

At that, the chaplain blew his whistle, and at once twelve or more black soldiers came from the railroad station, with a sergeant who had a gun; at the chaplain's command, they pulled us along with them into the station, while the brave chaplain stood his ground before the angry crowd, holding them back with his pistol. The black sergeant asked me what this was all about, and when he found out that I was a priest, he knelt down and kissed my hand, and most of his men, who were Christians also, did likewise. When they learned that I was newly ordained, they all wanted my blessing. So close were hate and reverence in so short a time!

The sergeant made a telephone call, and soon an auto full of soldiers arrived and surrounded us. Hundreds of angry civilians had gathered outside by this time, threatening us, but, with the guns pointed at them and the priest in charge, they dared no further violence. We got into the car and went to a barracks. As soon as the priest–officer and his men left, the new guards treated us like animals, thrusting us into a prison that nearly belies description.

It was a narrow building, lined with dungeons. There were no doors, for the openings were but holes through which the men crawled in the day. Or were they still men? They had not seen bathing facilities for a long time, and the rags they wore scarcely covered their bodies. There was no sign of a haircut or shave. They sat in the sun and sought to free themselves from vermin, or else crawled ominously toward us, who, though emaciated, were better clothed. A big, strong, wild-looking fellow came up, looked at us for a moment, and before we knew it he had seized one of our sacks, which contained the few things a prisoner is permitted to have, and began to open it. As we tried to retrieve it, the others all became angry, and a fight broke out. We learned right then that, in prison, might makes right.

I did not know what to do, for I did not feel equal to this fellow; but young Hans did not hesitate a moment. With his incredible strength and agility he seized the wild man and placed him firmly in a corner. The big fellow hardly knew what hit him. The bag was once more in our possession. The other men shouted at this surprising show of strength, and no one dared approach us. But I wondered what the night would bring.

The group of hostile prisoners sat together, with the big fellow in the middle, and there was no mistaking their intent. We simply had to get out of there, and that was my task. I went to the door and called for the general of the camp. No one answered. I shouted louder and louder, but no answer came. My patience was finally exhausted, and Hans and I sought to push through the door. Now some soldiers came, and luckily they were black soldiers. What did we want? I told them I wanted to see the general, but no one would make a move to disturb him.

When I drew out my cross, the emblem of a chaplain, they all ran away at once, and, within a few moments, an officer appeared.

"What do you want?"

I spoke sharply, and asked, "What kind of treatment is this, to imprison a priest with criminals? You must know from my papers who and what I am. Don't you know the claims of the International Red Cross, which France recognizes?"

With that, I pulled out the battered Red Cross flag, and once again it did me good service. I wanted to lodge a complaint over this mistreatment and the breaking of the international agreement on the part of France. I spoke loudly, sharply, in quick French (though I am sure, in my excitement, that it was far from perfect French). I made myself understood. The officer was struck dumb. I saw that courage and audacity had gained some ground; he took Hans and me to a guard room and there apologized. He did not know I was a priest; surely we should have every protection, as the Red Cross demanded.

I produced my copy of the stipulations of the Red Cross, but it was in English. The English major who had handed me over to the French gave me the copy, for he thought I could make good use of it in the French camps. At the time, I wondered what possible need I might have for such reinforcements; now I knew. Though the French officer knew no English, and I had not as yet studied the copy, still the impression had been made.

He asked me what rights I had as a priest. I answered at once, "The right to say Mass." I added that France was a Catholic country, the first daughter of the Church, and at this he assured me he was also a Catholic.

"Wait awhile, Father."

In the next room, he used the telephone, and ten minutes later a car drove up, and we were invited into it. I thought I heard the word monastery, but surely that could not be. And yet, that was the very word, for after some time we came to a church and entered a side door, where the Father Guardian of the Franciscan monastery was waiting for us.

What a joy to be once again with my brethren in a Franciscan monastery! They were all very friendly, and soon the white-clad Father who had saved us from the furious mob of Alsacers showed up. I was able to say Mass at once, as I had not eaten anything, and then a good meal was served, "a delayed First Mass celebration", as the Superior expressed it. He went to the telephone and soon brought the welcome news that we could remain here, if we would give our word not to leave the house under any circumstances. That we did, gladly. We enjoyed our relative liberty in fraternal surroundings, took a bath and put on clean clothes, and slept in a real bed. It was wonderful, though it lasted only a day.

The next day at noon, a sergeant took us to the railroad station where the train was waiting for us. And again the men from Alsace had some "friendly" words for us. The guards were prepared this time, however, and we left the city without hindrance. We journeyed in the direction of Meknès. Our new guard, though a man of one syllable, was a good person and gave us good things to eat. Our trip through North Africa was very interesting.

In Meknès, we were imprisoned immediately in one of the barracks of the compound. It was a high cement building, cold and uninviting, with water standing in the cells and rats running around in broad daylight. Dirty coverings, thin and torn, were lying on the hard cement. This was our lodging. The food was Arabian millet-pap, and only hunger forced us to eat it. Again, I tried my Red Cross appeal, and a guard who knew some English respected it and told his officer, who laughed a bit, but left to see what could be done. Soon I heard a truly frightening loud voice, using words of endless obscenity such as soldiers are wont to do, and my name was called. I became fearful; I heard steps nearing our dungeon, and suddenly there in the doorway stood a soldier. He was a big, stout man with a friendly face and a loud, cursing voice—a Franciscan. He was the military chaplain of this post. His many years among rough soldiers made him express himself like a soldier, but he had the heart of a child, and as he saw our plight he cursed the soldiers and the army for putting us in such lodging. He upbraided the innocent soldiers and wanted to take us with him immediately. He did not succeed in that, as we were due to leave the next morning, but he got better covers and better food and much fruit, which he brought for us. Good Father Bonaventure Hermentier was later to save my life.

Next morning, we were put in an auto and taken out of the city, but we did not go very far. We stopped shortly at a place where many men had gathered. They seemed to be waiting for something. The Frenchmen naturally had separated themselves from the natives, who sat on the ground. Finally, a large omnibus arrived. It looked like a tottering Noah's Ark. The Frenchmen took the first section, which was partitioned off from the rest.

The natives ran like crazy to the rear section, and a struggle began among the men and women. At last some of the men found a place on the top of the vehicle, and the women and children and animals of all kinds were behind the windows. I wondered how many men and animals could find a place, and at the end the sergeant showed us into the section with the women and children. How we managed to get in, I don't know, but there we were, among the grubby children and the young and old women who had not seen water for washing in many months. There were chickens and a dog, two goats, and a cat. The women wore some stinking perfume, and mingled with that were the rank fetid odors given off by both the men and the beasts. The journey went over the hills, around the curves, up and down; those inside began to eat—and soon threw up what they ate. The vehicle became a mess as it grew hotter and hotter. Clothes were stripped off until most of the passengers were nearly naked. The air very rapidly became heavy and putrid. Those who felt an urge of nature eased themselves then and there, and so the bus also became a rolling toilet. I could stand it no longer; I saw black and fell over, as far as I could fall. When I opened my eyes, I was resting on the bosom of a woman who was very kindly trying to revive me. When I saw how she did it, I again saw black and again fainted. For lack of water, she kept spitting on the back of my neck and tried to revive me with the breath of her mouth.

It was a journey beyond description, almost as bad for me as the airplane flight from Naples to Africa. We finally stopped in a village in the mountains for an hour's rest. I crawled out of the car, and to my joy I saw fresh water. I took off my shirt and washed myself. The women looked shocked by my lack of modesty and turned away, forgetting that they had sat before me in the bus nearly naked.

I felt better after the wash, and, as we started out again, I tried to get on the top of the bus; but our guard was afraid that we would run away. I assured him that here in this wilderness I would never try to escape—obviously, there was no place to go. I also assured him that under no circumstances would I go back inside. Finally he climbed up to the top with us, and we squeezed in among the men, who didn't look too friendly. We knew how intensely these natives hated the French, and from the treatment they received, I could understand their hatred. As soon as these brown inhabitants of the wilderness heard that we were Germans, all enmity disappeared; they showed their respect for Germany and gave us all kinds of food which, of course, was not very appetizing, but we had to eat in order not to appear unfriendly. Besides, it *was* food.

After many hours of travel through this grandiose yet frightening land of the Moyen Atlas, we came to a village called Midelt. Here we paused briefly, grateful for a chance to stretch our legs.

Toward afternoon, we started the journey through the narrow passes of the Grand Atlas range. What we saw from the top of the bus surpassed all the beauty we had seen so far; a fantastic road, winding in endless turns from the mountains to the Sahara, and, in the depths of a valley, hundreds of meters down, there was a foaming mountain stream and whole forests of date palms. I remembered reading descriptions of these places in the books of Karl May.

The two of us held on tight; we had all we could do to escape being thrown into the depths below, for the driver maintained a furious speed; we came only a centimeter from the edge. It was quite dark when we finally came to a place south of the last Atlas chain, the entrance to the Sahara, where the famous—or infamous, depending on which side of the fence you occupied—camp of Ksar-es-Souk was situated. There were a thousand or so Arabian families and a rather large garrison of Frenchmen of the Foreign Legion. Then came the camp for the prisoners, who were mostly non-commissioned officers. Among the camps in North Africa, this one had the reputation of being the most fanatical Nazi stronghold. It seemed that there was always to be this challenge to my faith; it seemed my destiny always to be surrounded by the most bitter kind of political enemies. I prayed that I would have the strength to meet it head-on.

Midelt in the Moyen Atlas.

The memorable bus that carried Father Gereon to the infamous prison camp at Ksar-es-Souk, French Morocco. Women and animals rode inside. Men clung to the roof.

Meknès, on the way to Ksar-es-Souk.

Chapter 18

THE PRIEST OF KSAR-ES-SOUK

The camp was in a former barracks compound of the Foreign Legion. The small huts were built of bricks of sand, camel-dung, and water, dried in the sun. The water came down from the mountains. We were watched day and night. Walls of barbed wire and high towers with machine guns obstructed every view into the surrounding countryside. There were fifteen hundred prisoners inside the camp, crowded some thirty to a room. All lay on the cement, covered with thin sacks; all felt the pangs of hunger, for the food was absolutely insufficient; and vermin abounded. For months there was no news from home, and the new prisoners who came in from time to time did not dare tell the truth to these Nazis.

Worse than the privation and the annoyance from the French was the spirit that pervaded the camp, the unquestioned and unquestionable loyalty to Adolph Hitler and the sureness that in the end victory would be ours; no one dared to believe otherwise, and woe to him who thought to express his misgivings in any way.

There was a company called *Rollkommando* among the prisoners, a detachment of some fifteen or twenty young men who were strong and able to do their duty. This "duty" was to beat half dead anyone who dared to disagree with the discipline and the leader of the camp. In regard to the discipline, I could understand the necessity for it; for in such conditions the animal in man comes quickly to the fore. When one is hungry and almost mad from years of imprisonment, living in narrow quarters in the scorching heat of the Sahara, everything that pertains to civilization is not only lacking, it is forgotten. One is ready to sell anything, even one's integrity, to acquire a morsel of bread or to betray a friend who rescued him at the risk of his own life. When each man threatens to become an enemy to his neighbor, and when he can win a bit to eat by committing murder, then an iron form of discipline is the only means of maintaining some kind of order. I must admit that drastic measures had to be used. I saw Knights of the Iron Cross whipped at the post because of theft.

However, it is one thing to maintain necessary discipline when men are like beasts, but it is quite another to insist on the maintenance of a faulty system of thought in the midst of such hardship. Here the system was Nazism. It was so strong that even the Frenchmen, our captors and guardians, dared not mix in it.

Every morning after counting the inmates, the camp leader, a Marine named "Dönitz", greeted all the men with a loud "Heil Hitler!", and we had to answer, "We greet the homeland and the Führer. *Sieg heil!*" Three times we shouted this nonsense. We could not even talk privately—the leader had a spy system throughout the camp. No one knew who belonged to it, and through this system he brought everything out into the open, even things that should never have become public. Later I was made to experience this on many occasions. Those who opposed the Nazi spirit in any way were beaten so badly—how often we heard the cries of the ones so abused—that they spent weeks in the sick ward. The result was that eventually no one dared to express himself. An air of mistrust, a kind of paralysis, pervaded the whole place. After some months, through the grace of God, this was to be changed—and I had something to do with the improvement.

At first, though, things went very badly. I was locked up with the others in a room and felt their mistrust like a tangible thing. A number of men entered into conversation, but I felt at once that it was really some kind of clever trial. They asked all kinds of apparently unrelated questions. The tapping foot of some unknown comrade gave me a warning, finally, but already I had said too much. The next morning I was called into the leader's room. There I was confronted by a group I had known in my SS days. There were seven, some non-coms, one a leader of the so-called school of the Nazi worldview of things (*Weltanschauung*). The atmosphere was just too inviting. In pretended good fellowship, they discussed the spirit of the camp and spoke of how they had to take care, on this "German soil", as they called the camp, to maintain an exclusively German spirit. I was a German soldier, and it was their great pleasure to welcome a sergeant-major who had distinguished himself in battle. I was to tell the leader how I thought I could cooperate with him in promoting good spirits.

I asked, "What are the possibilities of working with you?" I was told that they had a distinguished group of actors, an outstanding orchestra with instruments supplied by the Red Cross, and a school of higher learning where the men could, if they chose, prepare to take their examination after the war. When I discovered that teachers of philosophy were needed, I thought I could qualify. I was told that naturally there was only one kind of philosophy to be taught—German philosophy based on Nazism.

On asking them who were the National Socialistic philosophers, I heard the names of Kolbenheyer and Nietzsche, Rosenberg and Baldur von Schirach. I could not repress a smile and said that in my school of philosophy these names were not included among the leaders.

"Where do they belong?" I was asked.

I was suddenly fed up with all this duplicity and said so. Bluntly, I replied, "Among the visionaries and the spiritually sick."

That was, of course, too much for them. The leader lost his patience and asked me why I had come here and what I wanted.

I said, "I came here of my own free will to work for the Catholics and for those who may wish to become Catholics."

He said, "There are no Catholics here, nor Protestants—only Germans—and there is no need of a religion here that is a stranger to art and was founded by a Jew!"

To that I replied: "Germany was a complexity of different races before religion came, and what Germany has been in history since 1200 has been due to Christianity; would you dare to characterize the German Christian culture of the Middle Ages as a stranger to art and as Jewish?"

Silence followed, and as they really didn't know what to say, they changed the subject. They asked, "What do you intend to do here in the camp?"

I answered, "I intend to offer up the Sacrifice of the Mass and to announce the Christian message and to administer the sacraments to all who ask these things of me."

"From whom do you have this commission?"

"From the archbishop who sent me here."

"Who is he?"

"The Archbishop of Algiers."

"A Frenchman?"

"Yes, a Frenchman."

*View of the prison compound.
Father Gereon remained here
from October 1944 until
February 1946.*

Roll call in the POW camp.

"An enemy of the German nation—and you take orders from an enemy with whom we are engaged in battle?"

I answered that, for a Catholic and a Christian, these standards do not exist; the Church is supra-national.

He replied furiously, "This international group is well known; they are all criminals!"

I said then with some satisfaction that the Führer had entered upon a solemn agreement with these "criminals", a concordat had been made, and one could hardly accuse the Führer of treating with criminals, could one?

"*Ach*, that was but a clever strategy on the part of the Führer."

"Such a strategy, I repeat, would be criminal, and one must not say that of the Führer", was my reply for the second time.

Again they were at their wits' end; the Führer's tactics had more than once helped me out of a similar spot. I simply took for granted quite literally and innocently that he meant all the things he said and did. I was reminded of Shakespeare's *Julius Caesar*, the speech where Mark Antony said often, "But Brutus is an honorable man", with moving irony. These men were too smart to fall for what I myself said, but they were beaten down by the very acts of their beloved Führer.

Now the leader really let loose: "Be careful," he said, "you are on German soil. And you know, perhaps, how we deal with the enemies of our country."

I asked him with icy coldness if he had ever heard of Dachau. He had heard the name but knew nothing more. I said I was there and could tell him exactly how things fared with those who were marked as enemies of the German people. I told them, holding back nothing, of my trip into that hellhole; they turned pale and became speechless at such audacity. No one knew what to say next, so once again the leader changed the subject. He said, "Whatever is said and done and spoken in this camp is under my command. If you want to preach, you will have to submit your sermons to me first."

Slowly growing angry, I said, "You go too far! These things are not even done in Germany—there a priest does not have to submit his sermons to a censor. Are things to be more German here than they are in the Fatherland? I will preach what I think is right, and if you want to know what I am preaching, come and listen!"

The whole group laughed at that, but there were two in particular who seemed deeply pleased. I learned later that they were upright men, real Christians, who were admitted to this group only because of heroic service to the Fatherland. They stayed with this distasteful task because their presence made the lot of the prisoners who came before this leader somewhat better.

Next came the question of whether I intended to hear confessions.

"Surely, for there are people here who certainly need it." Demoniacal laughter greeted this remark; to the question of whether I thought sinners were in the camp, I said I did not think that, I knew it.

Dönitz came at me furiously, "We are Germans. We have no sins that we need have absolved by a human being. For us, there is only one sin—the disgrace of our race. For that there is no pardon, only death. And anyone who preaches a strange religion is an enemy of the people and is a disgrace to his race."

That did it. I told him that his prohibition could not hold, that it had absolutely no meaning for me. In Germany pastors could hear confessions, and they would do so even if they were not allowed, for no nation or power on earth could prohibit what God commanded.

"You say yourself that this camp is German soil; do you have more authority than the leaders in Berlin?"

Again, he did not know what to say. One of the leaders of his gang advised him to cut short the discussion, and he did so, with the words. "I warn you."

I merely said, "Do you know that I spent years with the SS, and that I am still technically attached to their service?"

They all stood openmouthed in surprise, and I left before they had time to recover.

An hour later, a soldier came; he was the servant of Dönitz, as I learned later, and he told me to meet him at the rear of the camp as unobtrusively as possible. There he warned me to be careful, for they were going to get me.

"Father, you must not go out at night, at least not alone."

I followed his advice, and it saved my life. One of the commanders, who later identified himself to me, told me they were waiting to make me one of the "suicide" cases—their practice was to hang a dissenting individual and make it look like suicide. This happened in some of the other camps, too, with the full knowledge of the French, but they did nothing to stop or prevent it.

After a short while the leaders recovered from the shock of our conversation, and a good-sized crowd gathered at my door to see the bold new chaplain. As I stepped out, they all laughed and asked what I wanted and when would I be packing my luggage. I felt it was not necessary to start anything with this pack of hounds, so I went inside. The crowd increased, and the French camp interpreter, who roomed just opposite me, noticed it. Shortly, I was taken to his room, where the French general also came. He despised priests as liars and gluttons, but, since I was there in Ksar-es-Souk by command of the bureau of war prisoners, the general of the camp was responsible for my safety. If something should happen to me, it could also happen to him. I had been sent here because the prisoners had refused a French priest; now they had a German priest, and I was to be permitted to exercise my priestly powers.

He told me, "It was not my idea to bring you here, it was theirs, despite their behavior. You will present your sermons to the interpreter and talk them over with him freely. You may leave camp once a week to see a French priest to go to confession." He laughed as he said that, but I was delighted. I had what I wanted. He gave orders that I was to have one of the rooms in the corner, which was to be used both by myself and the Protestant pastor; I felt my victory was complete. It was really more than I had expected.

The leader of the prisoners was made directly responsible for my safety. It was his opinion that few of the men in the camp had any interest in Christianity, and he told me I had no authority over those who did not come directly to me.

But over those who needed me, I was to have supervision. I chose a corner room, from which in the next months many blessings would come.

KSAR-ES-SOUK

After the war was over, Father Gereon was given a scrapbook containing the following watercolors, cartoons, and other mementoes of camp life. The town of Souk was entered through this gate.

Ksar-es-Souk, seen from the south.

*Two views (this page and opposite) of the
palace of the Kaids, showing the aqueduct.*

Lager XXVII, prison camp for unregenerate Nazi non-commissioned officers. At first, the camp leaders refused to believe that Germany had lost the war. Nazi ideals prevailed under threat of death.

The chapel, an open-air shelter where Father Gereon tried to win over the men with his sermons.

Night falls over Ksar-es-Souk.

Lagerlied. des Kriegsgefangenenlagers in Ksar-es-Souk

Worte und Weise von Uffz. Ernst Kellermann

Wenn dann am Abend die Sterne erglimmen, sieht manches Auge zu ihnen auf.
Und viele Bitten und sehnsüchtige Wünsche ziehen ganz leise zum Himmel hinauf.
Im Lager von Ksar-es-Souk, da denk ich an meine Heimat und träum' der Heim-
kehr zu, die uns einmal glücklich macht. ✠

Und die weiße Wolke, die nach Norden zieht, nimmt einen Gruß nach Deutschland mit.
Du strahlende Sonne mit deinem Schein, sag meinen Lieben daheim, daheim:
Im Lager von Ksar-es-Souk, da wart ich auf meine Heimkehr, die einmal kommen
muß auch für's Lager von Ksar-es-Souk. ✠

CAMP SONG

When the palms sway easily in the wind
And we wake in the morning to reveille,
Our eyes look toward the south
But our thoughts go northward.

> *Refrain:*
>> *In the camp of Ksar-es-Souk*
>> *I think of my homeland and dream*
>> *Of the happy homecoming that will someday be mine.*
>> *The white cloud drifting northward*
>> *Carries a greeting for Germany.*
>> *Beaming sun, with your light*
>> *Speak to my loved ones at home.*
>> *In the camp at Ksar-es-Souk I await my return,*
>> *Which must come sometime—*
>> *Even for the camp at Ksar-es-Souk.*

When the stars begin to gleam in the evening,
Many eyes gaze up at them.
And many pleas and yearning wishes rise to heaven
From the camp at Ksar-es-Souk.

CAMP CHARACTERS

the eager earlybird

the rations distributor

the physical culture nut

bookworms

chess players

kitchen orderlies

night musicians

the bread-weigher

The prison canteen, where Red Cross parcels were given out—partially.

A street in Marrakech, where Father Gereon had an adventure.

Chapter 19

NAZI OPPOSITION

News spread fast in the camp, for in such a world, as in any prison, very little goes on that is not soon common knowledge. The battle went on. The men avoided me, having been ordered by Dönitz to boycott me and my work. When I walked through the camp, no one spoke to me. This lasted for some time, but finally, one night after hours, one man ventured timidly to ask if I was a Catholic priest. I was delighted that at least one had finally had the courage to speak to me, and soon he brought three more; one evening came when there were seven who dared to defy the order of the camp leader. At first, they remained quiet, but on the next night, a Saturday, a lecture was scheduled for all the camp, and the leader invited me personally and with suspicious courtesy to attend. The subject was to be the worldview of things. I could hardly refuse, for I belonged, whether I wanted to or not, to the camp. The speaker, in civil life a teacher and a National Socialist youth leader, began his talk, and I found out why they had placed me in the middle of the first row. He spoke directly and exclusively to me. I sat and listened to the usual line of the SS school about the "Jewish, oriental religion" and its immorality; about a harlot who was called the Mother of God and her illegitimate child; about a church whose popes were for the most part immoral, whose priests were chasing after women, and whose nuns, pretending to be unmarried, were really immoral women. This filth went on for an hour, with the others sitting quietly and waiting to hear what I would have to say.

I fooled them. I said nothing, for it would have served no purpose; they were merely looking for an opportunity to laugh me to scorn, and I refused to give them the satisfaction. When it was all over, I thanked the camp leader in a loud voice for "this learned exposition which I heard often in the years when I was a member of the SS. I could add many more details, but it is getting late, and I will postpone my remarks for another time."

This had accomplished the double purpose of thwarting their desire to bait me and letting all of those who did not already know it know that I was a member of the SS.

The next day was Saturday; I celebrated Mass in my room. In the afternoon, I took my first sermon to the interpreter, keeping it brief. Then I asked Dönitz for a room to say Mass, and he, as I expected, informed me that none was available. I insisted on having a room, and he persisted in his refusal, and so there we stood. He had to make the announcement about the sermon, for it was already in the hands of the interpreter, so that evening he said, in a tone of mockery and disdain, that on the morrow there would be church service for the pious. Some laughed, but on the whole things were quiet.

The next morning, I set up my shaky table in the camp courtyard and began, with my seven loyal followers, to get ready for Mass. The others were dumbfounded, for many had never seen anything like this. There were many Protestants and unbelievers in the camp. The French interpreter took it all in from his room and then came down to be a witness, making it impossible for my adversaries to start anything. Where before the prisoners had driven out a French military chaplain, now a French soldier came to take part in my Mass. Near the altar, there were scarcely ten men, but hundreds of others formed a wide circle to watch what was going on. Clearly, they expected something unusual.

Then something did happen. Now that I had the whole crowd around me, I began my first sermon. According to the paper I had given the interpreter, the sermon should have lasted about five minutes; but I could not pass up this chance to tell the truth to the whole crowd, and so I went on for more than thirty minutes. Since I had never had much difficulty in speaking, and my heart was throbbing to answer the lies told the night before, I did so with warmth and indignation. Having had plenty of experience with the line of lies through the SS, I had no trouble developing the theme *Christianity and the German People*. They stood breathless as I carefully developed the theme, first historically, then philosophically. I called the untruths of the night before by their proper name of lies, and mentioned the names of Rosenberg and Schirach and others. In the beginning, many laughed, and some picked up stones and rolled them toward the altar; that angered me so that I gave vent to my feelings in a voice that reached the far corners of the camp. For half an hour such a torrent of words poured forth that, even if they had wished to do so, they could not have gotten a word in. They stayed and listened to the very end. My formal education with the Jesuit Fathers, my courses in philosophy, but most especially my experience with the SS gave me the historical data that I needed to name years and events. I must confess I even added some Greek and Latin words for the mere sake of making a deeper impression and of proving to them that I knew more than the Nazis did. This first sermon of mine was not without results. I was fully aware that it was not so much the word of God as much as it was the speech of an angry chaplain, but many years later I received a letter from one of those present who eventually found his way back to the Church because of this sermon.

Most of the men remained quiet, but during the Mass some derogatory words were heard. The interpreter spoke to me later on; he was delighted with the sermon, but he warned me to be careful, for what I had said was nowhere to be found on his paper, and, if the prison commandant were to catch me, there would be trouble. This one time, since he knew what had gone on the night before, he sanctioned my departure from what I had planned.

My open challenge to the leadership of the camp and its Nazi policies had one tremendous result: I was given a corner room in a new building for saying Mass. There was only one subject for conversation for a while, and the camp leader wanted to let it die down and prevent a repetition of my having such an audience every Sunday.

The new room was without walls, so that everyone on the outside could see what was going on. While that was not good in one respect, from quite another angle it was fine. Right in front of the barracks was the camp's largest cesspool, where every morning a long line of men stood waiting. Because of this, it happened that not only my faithful ten heard Mass every morning but many others waiting outside to relieve themselves, so I began to preach a sermon every morning. Among those outside who heard me were secret agents of Dönitz, who wrote down and reported to him every word I said. He eventually had volumes of my sermons; but they had no effect on him, although slowly they began to affect many others.

I must admit that in my sermons, especially on Sundays,

when so many curious people were present, I often overshot the mark and said many things that, though true, were imprudent and later caused me many difficulties. Some of the men urged me to be more careful and restrained; but my first zeal in preaching could not be held down, and relations with the camp leadership grew worse. Some of the Christians were beaten up during the night; my room was smeared with dirt and filth, and attempts were made on my life. The French general sent for me and asked me if I did not want to live outside the camp, which I could elect to do, for things were getting dangerous.

"It would be better for you to leave the camp alive at night than be carried out dead in the morning."

I knew he was making sense, but I could not bring myself to accept his offer. If I left the camp at night, coming only in the daytime when it was safe, I would be called a friend of the French, an enemy of Germany. I took care to see to it that a few loyal men stayed with me at all times, my "bodyguards", they called themselves; and when a Protestant pastor joined me in my small room, the Nazis didn't dare to use force openly.

This good man brought a spirit of peace and brotherly compromise to the camp; he was a man of faith and zeal, and he built up a strong Evangelical community in camp. I believe we both profited from living so many months together in one room. I know that I profited greatly, especially from the moderation and prudence of this man—virtues I sorely lacked; he helped to prevent many incidents that my excessive zeal and rashness at times would have incited.

If the open warfare in the camp lessened, the secret maneuverings of the Nazis increased. Anything that could undermine the Christian way of life was attempted. One day in the washrooms, I found a number of Bibles torn apart.

Hundreds of the best Bibles, which had been sent to us from the United States, had been used as toilet paper. All books sent to the camp were examined, and those that were thought in any way to be Christian were destroyed. So-called black-lists were prepared and sent back to the men's home towns so that the people there would know that, according to the Nazis, these men were "traitors to Germany", having become a part of a religion inimical to Germany. This is why many did not have the courage to join our religious community, even though in their hearts they hated the Nazi leadership.

The battle was carried from the open air into the rooms, where in the hot, dry, uncomfortable desert night, the Nazis would tell the usual jokes and lies about Christians and make fun of all that was holy. They wanted to incite the men to anger and strife. Mature men came to me weeping and troubled, for they could not bear to put up with such dirt and mockery; yet still it came forth every evening, hour after hour, in the heat and vermin-infested night, from the mouths of the Nazis. When they asked me what they could do, I replied, "Keep still, absolutely silent; don't say a word. One cannot argue with a dunghill. Take up your rosary and say it firmly and quietly. If they ask you about it, say, 'We are saying the rosary so that you do not go to hell.' Beyond that, say nothing." They followed my instructions, and every morning they came to Mass to gain strength for the day and the night. This was a small group of loyal men who by their very loyalty helped us slowly to gain attention, so that many returned to the Church after many years' absence; they told me that the quiet example of these men gave them the courage to acknowledge their religion.

Our slow efforts to reach every man continued. Mass was celebrated as becomingly and as beautifully as we could. Many hands worked throughout the day in copying the text of songs and the words from prayer books. A teacher of music from Austria started a small choir that in a very short time distinguished itself.

Every morning the small group of worshippers stood around the altar in the room without walls, where it was bitter cold on the early winter days. The men were wrapped in rags against the piercing morning chill. Every morning I explained the Mass, and these talks opened up for them for the first time the treasures of the liturgy. They were happy and thankful. One man said, "Why did I have to wait sixty years to begin to understand the Mass?" Altogether, I preached more than two hundred sermons on the Mass, and rows of listeners stood outside. I had to break the Host into very small particles for the morning's Holy Communion, but it was sufficient to give us strength for the day.

Soon, however, the men wanted more than a twenty-minute sermon, so we began what turned out to be a small school of theology. We had plenty of time on our hands, so we kept busy studying. I received a number of the best works in theology from a French chaplain and read them day and night. We began with a group studying Scripture, and in the common reading and discussion the word of God became alive for these men. Every week we spent a total of four hours or more on intensive Scripture study. Then I gave instructions on faith, the liturgy, Church history, morals, and all departments of theology that were of interest to these laymen. At their urging, Latin and Greek were also included in the curriculum. All told, I spent about five hours of every day lecturing on one subject or another. I gradually gained confidence in preaching and spoke on subjects of interest to all. I startled the Nazis in the audience when I did not omit from the lecture on Church history the scandals that had taken place from time to time. Since they had so often and so eagerly pounced upon these and twisted them by their lies, I tried to speak truth, without attempting to justify many things, giving the incidents as they happened, in the context of their times.

The next series of twenty sermons was on marriage. In such confines, with no women available, much of the talk was about the two things they didn't have—food and women. I learned from some of my loyal men that one effect of my sermons on marriage was a general cleaning up of the private conversation; when the Nazis began to peddle dirt, many of the men would rise and speak out against them, and that put an end to most of the smutty talk.

The big breakthrough came at Christmas. The camp leaders had prepared some lectures on the pagan German Yule Feast. From wood (that was stolen) our group made a beautiful crib and prepared hundreds of small candles; the choir was at its best, with violins and other instruments; we decorated the entire barracks with palms and artificial fir trees and waited to see what would happen. At 8:00 the Nazis began their Yule Feast; attendance was obligatory. The men went and heard what was said, but they said nothing and gave no sign of approval. At 11:00, after all had retired to their rooms, we all ran hurriedly through camp and began what we called a pilgrimage to the crib. Everyone who could walk, except a hundred of the most fanatical Nazis, came to our chapel in the barracks. Soon it was full. We had partitioned off a small section with blankets to keep out the cold, but that had to go to make more room. Then the hundreds of candles, which had been placed everywhere, were lighted. The crib became visible in the warm candlelight, and the choir sang the true Christmas hymns while the men joined in. It seemed for a while that there was no longer any war, no Nazis or Germans or Frenchmen, for we were all one in Christ.

It was Christmas, a time of peace to all of good will. It was not difficult to reach the hearts of these men then with the glad tidings of Christmas. After Mass I heard confessions for hours. Tears of sorrow, together with the sacramental absolution, wiped away all wrongdoing. As penance I gave a week's compulsory attendance at Mass; many kept it up for months after their "sentence" had expired. To this day, I receive letters from some of the men who were there, telling me it was the best Christmas they ever had. It could not have been more real; we were in a barracks without windows or doors, in a cold wind that brought snow with it; the men were ragged, thin, and hungry; we did not have to visualize the poverty and want and barrenness of the first Christmas—we were living it every day. We had nothing of those things that had made Christmas such a joyous feast at home, but we felt in our hearts as never before that the Christ Child came into this world in want and poverty, and we felt this peace and joy in our hearts.

From this day on the community of believers increased slowly and steadily. The Nazis' attacks were increasingly ineffectual. And we labored long to insure that the effects of this night would not be lost; we increased our work in education, intensifying our attempts to keep the men occupied in fruitful study and work from morning Mass until evening's Compline. "The Devil finds work for idle hands", it is said, and I tried to keep their hands and their minds from falling prey to his temptations.

Of course, in time, all this brought the roof down over my head. The Nazi leaders were furious and sought in every way to make the care of souls impossible.

When I was brought to the camp, it was suggested to me by the French that I should, from time to time, inform them of the condition of the camp's internal affairs. The Nazis had learned of this from the French themselves. Though I did not actively do this, they learned much from my sermons, which were taken down by the Nazi leaders' spies. In the third week of Lent, they made a forward thrust; they forbade everyone, under heavy penalties, to speak to me. "The enemy of the people" became an object of isolation. Those who still dared to listen to my sermons were beaten till blood flowed. This was the spring of 1945, and the war was nearing its end. The Nazis knew that their hour was drawing to a close, and they sought to save face by increased terrorism. What was I to do?

I took counsel with some of my close followers, and they advised me to abide by the decision. The alternative was to side with the French by making known to them what was going on in the camp, but that would give the Nazi leaders grounds for accusing the Catholics as enemies of the people. So I waited and kept still. Things could not go on this way for much longer.

Chapter 20

A MIRACULOUS DRAUGHT

For two weeks, I was alone. This was the loneliest of my entire time in the camp. In their bitterness at the outcome of the war, the leaders were capable of any violence, and I was cautioned not to tempt them or give them any excuse. Finally, one of the men of the Foreign Legion left camp, and, before he left, he told the French of what the Nazis were doing.

That was the end of the boycott. The camp leader was removed, and everything became known to the French: how the Nazis encouraged corruption, how they lived well and took most of the things sent by the Red Cross, without which we would have starved long ago. First the French guards took a good share, then the Nazis and their henchmen in the camp, and we got the rest. The Red Cross boxes came once a month, and only about half of the original shipment reached us.

With the war lost and with the change of leadership in the camp, there came an era of relative peace in matters religious, though obstacles were never wanting. Now that the Nazis had officially lost, anti-Nazi and Communist groups arose, and in their own way they were no better than the Nazis.

We had begun to talk of building a chapel, and in January of 1945 we had started to work on it. It was really almost too much for the starving prisoners. We had to make our own bricks from desert sand mixed with camel dung, straw, and water, burned in the hot desert sun and then dragged into camp. The bricks were so large and heavy that every now and then the men would collapse under the weight; it was truly a work of sacrifice. Everything we needed we had to smuggle into camp. Nothing so filled these men with pride and peace and confidence as this laborious work of building a chapel in a Nazi camp where six months before none existed, not even in our dreams. In addition to the physical difficulties, we had to overcome the opposition of the French authorities, who feared that a church might cause disputes.

Procuring the glass for the windows and the wood for the furnishings was, I blush to confess, a masterpiece of thievery. The prisoners became artists; they made a censer and a monstrance of wood, a ciborium from aluminum taken from a plane and polished until it looked like silver. On Holy Saturday we were able to enter our "cathedral" with the *Lumen Christi*. This chapel meant more to us than all the great churches in the world. It was a beautiful, quiet room, away from the noise of the camp, dimly lighted by the golden windows, very conducive to prayer. Two hundred persons could worship there; we never thought that in a few months we would have to enlarge it to twice its present size, and that even then it would be too small. Our chapel became a true place of prayer; I never found it empty. We kept the Blessed Sacrament in a tabernacle in the wall without a key. The men kept guard over their Eucharistic King, with the two kneelers being signed up for days ahead.

Soon a hundred men were attending daily Mass, and on Sundays many more came. These poor, afflicted, starving, and half-despairing men, many squatting on the floor in broken health, received Holy Communion and found strength to go on. As the news of our chapel got out, we received from the good Sisters altar linens and vestments, lamps, and many, many candles; in the end we lacked nothing. From early morning until late at night, men were at prayer or study in the chapel. Our schedule for theological studies broadened out; we even had examinations, and I was surprised to find out what the men had learned.

And as we were allowed to build a church, so God built the invisible church of faith in the souls of these prisoners; they came back to the practice of their religion, and some became believers for the first time in their lives. Young men who had never heard the truth about the Church before came in crowds, learning for the first time what a blessing it is to believe in God and to be one of his children.

Even if this chapel built in and of the desert sands has crumbled away by now, the unseen church of faith that God built in the hearts of these men still stands, as the many letters that still come to me testify.

Perhaps our greatest experience was to find the strength and the secret of prayer. In the first years of intensive study in our chapel-school, the subject of greatest importance was the credibility of the Christian message; it was the theme of many of my sermons and the subject of discussion in many of our groups. That first year was a year of planting the faith and letting it become deeply rooted. The second year we stressed living a life of faith and found here the value of prayer. I asked, first of all, who can pray? And who *is* praying? An inquiry revealed that hardly five percent would admit that they prayed; those who prayed did so from force of habit, and their prayers were mostly the prayers of children. For most of the men, prayer was a burden or merely a habit; in any case, it was an unpleasant thing, and for a man and a soldier it was considered an embarrassing occupation. The life of prayer among the devout is something vital and strong. Prayer means talking with God as a child talks to his father; there is no need of set formulas or, if there are fixed forms, which the experts in liturgy formulate, they are a song-prayer of body and heart; the true source of prayer in any form is the heart that overflows in love and faith.

That this is not merely something for women and children, but that first and foremost it is for the man, the head of the family, was not known to the prisoners, nor that the asking part of prayer is the last and least in importance.

So I preached dozens of times on prayer; in the end, we had to have two sermons a day. (I worked every free moment on writing out my sermons; when I left, I had more than two thousand of them.) By God's grace, I succeeded in starting in the hearts of these men an unquenchable fire of prayer. With faith and zeal, with perseverance and joy, many succeeded in reaching great heights in prayer and a supreme depth of communication with God.

Or, as one prisoner put it, the years in camp were an unbroken retreat, which no one found too long or burdensome. "Prayer is our secret weapon", was our slogan.

Groups of what they called "torpedo men" were formed with no help on my part; their function was to help those who had fallen away from God. Whenever one of these "torpedoes" met a comrade who had fallen away, he immediately said a prayer for his conversion, told his comrades, and they joined him in attack, an attack of prayer. It was a joy to all of us when one so "attacked" returned to his faith or when a sinner came and asked to go to confession.

From a life with the Lord in prayer, it was but a small step to life with him in Holy Communion. Before their imprisonment, these men would have scoffed at the idea of frequent or even daily Communion. Now they learned how sweet the Lord is in the Blessed Sacrament. The supply of Hosts gave out, and the French chaplain of the garrison did not want to give me more because he thought they were being used as bread to satisfy our hunger. He was right, we used them to satisfy our hunger, but it was the hunger of the soul, especially visible in this prison camp, without hope or comfort. And when after six months the first letters brought us the news of conditions at home, we were made even more aware than before that none could help us but our Lord in the Blessed Sacrament. From the one or two who had received every morning, the number swelled to a hundred.

In time to come, we were to need this strength even more. After two years, the first real news of our Fatherland reached us. One man learned that a Russian tank had rolled over his wife and their four children. This was a man who had particularly loved his family, often showing around to the others the family portrait, his prized possession in camp. Now they were dead.

He left his room and could not be found, and I feared we would find yet another suicide in a corner, as so often happened after one of these letters was received.

I went to the chapel—and saw that the cross on the altar was missing. As my eyes grew accustomed to the darkness, I saw the missing man collapsed on the floor before the tabernacle, holding the crucifix in his hands. I tried to comfort him, but through his tears he stammered, "No, I need no word of comfort. Please help me pray what you preached yesterday."

I thought back; it was a sermon on the Our Father, emphasizing the part that says, "Thy will be done." We prayed the Our Father together, and as he said the words "Thy will be done!" the battle was won. I felt the tension and the grief go out of him like a physical thing, so great was it, and he walked out of the chapel shining with strength and the will to continue.

Such experiences were frequent; by the strength we found in prayer we obtained many graces—strength that I in particular was to need in days to come.

With the war over and lost, the Red Cross sent less and less; food became even more scarce. The French had learned about Dachau and some of the other German concentration camps, and the byword in the prison camps became "revenge is sweet". Ours was a Nazi camp, and we knew what was in store for us: penance. The only way of escape was to get out of the camp by joining a work group where we would not starve to death. Up to this point, the leader of the camp had passed the word along, "A German sergeant does not work, and especially, he does not work for the enemy." Only a few had dared to act otherwise. Now, however, hunger drove the men to volunteer.

Ministering to the work groups was a new assignment for me. I had already visited some groups about a hundred kilometers away, in that same filthy Midelt where we had stopped on the wild bus ride that brought me here two years before. Conditions there were shocking; the soldiers, some sixty of them, made it quite clear that they had no need of religion. They were satisfied with things as they were, having become quite stout. They were all trained craftsmen—a rare thing in the desert—and their wages were good. Arab girls crowded about the camp and sold themselves. It was a pool of corruption, utterly disgusting, where vice was taken for granted.

Sadly, I said my Mass all alone in a corner. There was a church in Midelt, with a sickly old Franciscan as pastor. This saintly old man had grown weak and ineffectual, heartbroken, over his long years of devotion and selflessness; I pitied him, yet felt humble before his example of peace and patience. He had to travel an hour's distance each morning to say Mass for some Franciscan Sisters and was glad when I volunteered to go. I had received a Franciscan habit at last and could now walk around freely and also visit the Sisters; but it was difficult for me, more difficult than I had anticipated, for I was but skin and bones. I arrived at the convent that first morning too weak to say Mass. After resting for a while, I managed to say it, and then I was surprised when the Sisters asked for a sermon. I managed, though imperfectly, to preach the word of God in French. The Sisters, Franciscan Missionaries of Mary, had their faces veiled; but after a few minutes their veils went up, handkerchiefs appeared, and they all began to cry as if on signal. That had never happened to me before, and I was quite bewildered, almost unnerved. At last, I could not go on and simply ended up by saying "Amen."

After Mass I asked the Superior over a welcome cup of good coffee what was the matter.

She said, "We have had no sermon for months; we wept because we could once again hear the word of God." She twinkled somewhat mischievously, "There was also another reason."

"What was that?"

"We had to cry because our beautiful French language was so mistreated. It was a martyrdom for tongue and ears." (That did not hinder them from asking me quite insistently every time I came for the same kind of martyrdom, however.)

That was my first meeting with the Franciscan Missionary Sisters, and it was to mean much to me, for these good Sisters sympathized with our poverty and started a wave of assistance; soon autos came, loaded with good food and clothing and other articles. This great and unexpected help from the "enemy"—for they were all French—this true love which the Sisters showed, was the best possible advertisement for our religion. I was aware that many of the men who lined up to receive some of these precious gifts were there only for what they could get; but we asked no questions, simply giving to all no matter what their religion or philosophy of life; that, too, won many hearts.

More important than these material gifts was the fact that these Sisters prayed for the conversion of the prisoners. Day and night, they prayed before the Blessed Sacrament for the conversion of the Nazis, not only the Sisters in Midelt, but also those in another convent. Soon we had a dozen convents in North Africa praying and making sacrifices for our camp. In the face of such storming of heaven, many men lost all resistance, expelled the unbelief and paganism of the Nazi credo from their hearts, and accepted belief in God; after some months of prodding they came to confession and received their second First Holy Communion.

There was one man in particular, a rabid Nazi, who was notorious even in Germany. His conversion was so exceptional that it is worthwhile to follow it in more detail.

It happened some months before this trip to Midelt that resulted in my meeting the Missionary Sisters. On one of my trips to another work group, I learned that in the valley of these mountains, known as the "Valley of Hell" because of its intense heat, a Sister was living all alone. I could not believe it at first, it was so unprecedented. When I had a chance to go there later on, I found Sister Jeanne living isolated from all Europeans in the beautiful mountain district of Khenifra, in solitude and penance. Having obtained special permission from the Pope, she had sought out this lonely spot, where she fasted with almost inhuman rigor. The three days I was there I suffered continuously from hunger—I, who thought I knew a great deal about privation! She cared for the native sick in the villages, going from early morning until late at night into the dirty huts to nurse their frightful wounds and festering sores. Then every night she knelt as motionless as a statue of stone before the Blessed Sacrament for three hours—I saw this with my own unbelieving eyes. By special papal permission, she was allowed to keep the Blessed Sacrament in her small chapel; every three or four months a priest-hermit came from still higher up the mountain to renew the Species. Then for months again she would be all alone with her work and with her Lord in the Blessed Sacrament. What I heard and saw there was unbelievable. Her bed was a board; her meal, thin soup; but she was happy as a child and physically much stronger and enduring than I.

The first time I came into her solitude—it was soon after I became chaplain in the Nazi camp—was at a time when I had lost all courage to go on because of the extreme opposition and persecution I suffered, while making no progress that I could see. When I told her that I was thinking of going to another camp where the work would be easier and more satisfying, she told me almost fiercely that I was to return to the Nazi camp.

"Sister Jeanne, I cannot. It is just too much for me. I have done everything I can, and still I have failed to bring that camp to Christ."

She amazed me by seizing my habit and looking me in the eyes, saying in a voice that pierced bone and marrow, "Father, in God's Name, you are going back to your camp at once!"

I recovered from my surprise at being so "commanded", since her order was given in such a way that I knew I dare not oppose her. At the same time, she made me write down the name of the worst enemy of the Church on a piece of paper. "Leave all the rest to me, Father", she said.

I did as she asked, giving her the name of Kroch, a fanatical Nazi, a terrible persecutor of the Church and her French people, and returned to camp. I really did not have too much time to think about Sister Jeanne after that, and when Kroch came to speak to me three months later, I was preoccupied. I was so angry at his continuous vituperation against me and his ugly remarks against God and the Church that I would not see him.

"If Kroch wants to speak to me, tell him to come in the morning when everybody can see him and not in the darkness of night!" It was an angry message, and I was sorry at once; but I let it stand as it was said.

The next morning as I stood in line for the small bread ration, he actually came up to me and asked, without trying to conceal his request from the others standing by us, if he could go to confession.

"I was a Catholic, Father. Once I was even a Mass server; my mother was a pious woman, who would be so happy if she could know that I had come back to the Church." I could hardly believe my ears, but it was really so. I knew something of his history; for many years, even before the war, he had been a leader of the youth against God and had played a leading role in Nazi Germany.

However touched, however moved I was by this request, his admittance back into the Church could not be a simple matter. He must do public penance for his many public wrongs. Every Sunday for months he had to stand before the altar, a poor penitent, an admitted sinner. Finally came the Sunday when he acknowledged publicly before many hundreds of men, who listened breathlessly to what he had to say, his guilt and his whole shameful history—from a pious lad to one of the most vicious haters of the Church. He recounted the story of his return to the Church and asked for pardon.

Then at last he received sacramental absolution and Holy Communion. The men stood around the altar with tears in their eyes, and later many of them stood waiting patiently before the confessional to end their lives of sin.

Good Sister Jeanne, in her solitude at Khenifra, had put the paper with this man's name before the tabernacle, and every night she spent six hours in prayer for his conversion.

Chapter 21

THE VERY MOUTH OF DEATH

And so the war was lost, and to escape the terrible hunger the prisoners in camp had to volunteer for the work crews. The number of those who did not want to go to distant places to work grew smaller and smaller, but many Catholics refused to go; they preferred the hunger in camp. Why?

One told me, "If we go to work out there, we will be without a priest, a hundred kilometers away. And without a priest, we have no Mass, no Communion. It is better to suffer from physical hunger than to be starved in one's soul. We have finally learned what daily Communion means; how then can we give it up? How could we exchange the bread of the soul for the bread of the body?" Truly, this was an amazing, a strong and genuine faith!

And as has been promised from the beginning, for those of faith in him, God gives all that is needed. He rewarded this sacrifice, made consciously in his name. Hundreds of men had left, all the best work crews were full, when suddenly the French Sisters came, wanting good Catholic men for their many convents. I recommended my men, who got the best work to be found in Africa; they had light garden duties, good food, new clothes, and Sundays free. They had daily Mass, and, to the edification of the Sisters, they were daily at the Communion railing, praising and thanking God for his great goodness. The Sisters reported to me that it was gratifying to see how these converts held to the faith when there was no one there to prod them on.

In late autumn of 1945, a chaplain from another camp, who had once been chaplain at Ksar-es-Souk, came to pay us a visit. He had tried in vain to build up a religious group here, finally being driven away by insult and mockery. He could hardly believe it when he saw so many receiving Communion every morning. He rejoiced sincerely with me, but as he was leaving he said, "Pray that the cross that surely will come to you will be bravely carried."

I answered that we already had many crosses to bear in this camp; but still he thought that I as a priest would have to carry a special cross, for so many blessings and graces would certainly have to be paid for by a special sacrifice.

He left the camp and returned again, and he asked me to prepare myself and the men by preaching on the Way of the Cross. In the evening sermon, I told the men about what he had said, and we determined to do as he asked. By January 17, 1946, I was preaching on the eleventh station during the evening Mass.

I had just finished a short trip to a work group. Returning to camp in the later afternoon of January 17, I was told that something was up, this time not from the Germans but from the French. They had been examining several good Catholic men and also many Protestants. The Protestant chaplain was also interrogated; it was all about me, but I was kept busy answering a number of trifling requests from the camp leaders and so had no time to speak quietly with anyone or to inquire what this might be about.

Mass began, and I spoke on the experiences of my last trip. Immediately after the Consecration, French soldiers with drawn swords plunged through the doors. I kept on with the Mass and was able to give out Holy Communion and put the remaining Hosts in my pocket before the soldiers took me from the altar and handcuffed me. I was led through the camp and found the Nazis and other enemies of the Church assembled at the gate, rejoicing that their enemy and the "Chief Nazi" of the camp, as they called me, was getting his comeuppance.

I could not imagine what was wrong. The next few hours brought no solution but revealed to me that some heavy charges had been brought against me. I was stripped and examined carefully and as humiliatingly as they could conceive. Above all, they were searching for the SS marks that had been tattooed on the left arm of the SS men; but I did not have them, for, at the time it was done, I had been in the hospital. About twenty soldiers visited me, but for the most part they were drunk, and I had great difficulty in keeping them from profaning the Sacred Species. One of them, a Catholic, finally took the golden pyx and later gave it to me unopened.

After some hours of none-too-reverent treatment, I was locked naked in a cold cell, with no covering on the cement floor but dirt and filth and without food. I thought of the priest's warning that a special cross would be the price for so many blessings. From one of the cells nearby, I heard the cries of a man being beaten, and from another cell, I heard a man praying aloud and singing the *Te Deum*.

The next morning, a closely guarded car took me for the last time over the high mountains to the north. I had made this trip more than twenty-five times on the top of the fantastic bus, uncomfortable, indeed, but protected by my Franciscan garb. Now I was tied face down on the floor of a car; a soldier with a gun stood guard, and I gathered from some of their remarks that they did not have the best opinion of me. I was starving. The summer before I had been deathly sick, and the Franciscan Fathers in Morocco succeeded in getting me to their beautiful monastery at Rabat Agudal, where I recovered in three weeks under the loving care of my brethren. But since this, many months of hunger had passed, and, after many difficult journeys, I was once again skin and bones. In autumn, I had contracted a lung infection from which I was not fully recovered. The night of lying naked on the cold cement brought on a heavy cough again, and I arrived in Meknès with a high fever. I was put into a dirty prison, with vermin and rats running around at night, with only one filthy covering.

For several days I lay in fever, provided with only the scantiest and most ill-smelling food; a guard was always at the door, and every few minutes he would look in to make sure that I wasn't up to some evil scheme. I could not stand up, and a few days later, they literally had to drag me before the court for examination.

There I heard the most unbelievable things being said about me. What it all came to was that I was an enemy to France, since I had spoken against the Red Cross in Rabat in regard to the management of their affairs, stating that the Commissions merely looked over the supplies. Furthermore, I was a Nazi, one of the worst, who was responsible for the death of many foreigners and especially many Frenchmen. I was considered to be a criminal, for I had even deceived the Pope and thus received an invalid ordination to the priesthood.

This was bad enough, but the worst was yet to come. In the final charge of the indictment, they stated that not only was I a killer of innocent people in battle—but I was the former commander of Dachau!

I was, of course, dumbfounded by such a litany of lies, but I could not help smiling and asked, somewhat amused, how they expected to prove such ridiculous accusations. But my smile vanished when the judges showed me a list of twenty-seven signatures of men from my camp who took an oath that I was one of the most dreaded and hated Nazis. I saw the names of men who had come daily to receive the articles the Sisters sent us, so much so, in fact, that often the Christians received nothing for themselves. These men were now walking around wearing clothes we had given them, their bellies enjoying food that someone else had sacrificed to send them; and all the while they had conspired and testified that I was the long-sought most infamous Nazi. They had reported under the expert guidance of the German Nazis that I knew the place and existing conditions in Dachau, and they gave names and dates and described under what circumstances I was seen to commit a crime. That was more than I had ever dreamed possible, and I saw clearly the gravity of the situation. Both judges told me plainly that I was in danger of losing my life.

I was imprisoned, and then a doctor came to see me. He in turn told Father Bonaventure Hermentier, the military chaplain of Meknès, where I was, and one morning I heard again that unforgettable, frightful cursing, to which I had become somewhat accustomed through my many visits and overnight lodgings with the warmhearted but rough-tongued fellow friar. Now he came again, the cussingest Franciscan in existence, but one who had the tender heart of a child. He simply pushed the soldiers aside, extended his hand to me, a starving skeleton, and dragged me onto his mighty shoulders. Amid continuous vituperation, he put me into his car, and I was soon lying comfortably in his own bed. He gave orders to his servants to allow no one to enter and drove off.

About half an hour later I heard the car return; he had a big pig in it. It ran around the yard as if realizing what was to come. Hearing the noise, I looked from my bed, which was set next to the window, and soon was so weak with laughter I had to lean my head on the windowsill. Of course the pig was to be slaughtered, but how and when? First it had to be caught, and this made a very good show. The good Father was not as quick as the pig, and for some time it eluded his grasp; it ran around the car, under the car, here and there and everywhere, with Father Hermentier in hot pursuit, his skirts flying, and cursing all the while, quite loudly, almost artistically. Finally, perspiring profusely, he took off his habit and continued the chase until he finally trapped the squealing victim under his car. Its last hour had come. Even the killing did not go off too easily, being rather a gruesome spectacle, and in the end it was difficult to tell which was the butcher and which the pig, since both were covered with scarlet. Finally the pig was hanging up in the yard, and a few hours later good-sized pork chops were being served me in my bed.

In the meantime, there was a heated debate at the door; the Father, clothed in his quaint butcher's garb, naked and gory to the waist, clutching the huge slaughtering knife in his right hand, in his quietly obscene way soothed the prison guards who had come to fetch me, assuring them that he would take responsibility. For he left them in no doubt that he would allow no priest, and above all no Franciscan, to be starved and killed, especially when he was convinced of my innocence. He returned and kept repeating the quieting word, *"Merde!"*

At one point I told him I thought perhaps that word was a little strong for a priest to use. The next day he brought along a dictionary and showed me that, since the word was found in the dictionary, he could use it with complete propriety. Against such logic I could say nothing; I simply collapsed in helpless laughter.

For two weeks I lay in his bed; he brought me Holy Communion in the morning, and three times a day he brought a huge pork chop with orders that I eat it all for myself, leaving not even enough for the dog or the cat. I obeyed, and after two weeks had recovered somewhat. He took me back to prison but first saw to it that it was cleaned up; he added some coverings from the Sisters, and even Sister Jeanne came down from her solitary cell to work with them. How she learned of it so quickly was beyond me; they worked together with Father Hermentier to make things easier for me. One of the priests connected with Father Hermentier's work wrote up the whole affair for the Sisters in Switzerland in the convent of Grimmenstein in Walzenhausen, and I soon felt the effects of their continuous prayers.

At 5:00 P.M. on February 27, 1946, a French officer with three corporals came to me to tell me that on the following night, by verdict of the war court, I was to be shot.

Father Hermentier was away on a trip, so there was no one I could call on for help. I lay on my plank bed, weak and miserable. Around me were some other prisoners who were criminals, not soldiers, and they asked me what was up. When I told them that my turn was coming before theirs, one of them wished me happiness on my quick journey to heaven.

The French officer wanted to know why the prisoner was laughing in such a friendly manner. I told him he was glad that I should get to heaven so quickly.

The Frenchman looked at me unbelievingly, "Heaven—do you think you'll get to heaven?"

"Yes, certainly. I hope to get in."

His astonishment grew, and he asked me, "Where is heaven? What kind of place is it?" and other questions. I could not answer all of them; he was a Frenchman living in the colony and, as I later learned, a physician.

I wanted to be free of him, and so I asked him to have a little patience—I would send him a picture postcard from heaven; but there would be some delay until I had served my time in Purgatory.

He shook his head and went away but returned very soon with some others, all black soldiers with many medals on their uniforms; he told them in my presence that I was going to heaven the next evening. He came back again, and yet again, still asking about heaven. That evening, I was given a good meal—a bad sign. It did begin to seem that things were in earnest.

At 2:30 A.M., ten soldiers came and took some of the other prisoners; they must have been given the death penalty. Around 3:00 A.M., my cell was unlocked and four men entered: the officer of yesterday afternoon with three others.

"Get up; the company is waiting for you in the courtyard."

I was not all that anxious to go to my execution; I was weak in body and soul and told them, "You will have to carry me, for I cannot walk."

At this, the officer showed some hesitance; he ordered the soldiers to get out and to bolt the heavy iron door from the outside. The astonished men did as they were told, and the strong officer, as big as I was when I was not skin and bones as I now was, remained. He put the torch he was holding into an iron ring on the wall and suddenly came at me with a sabre. I thought my hour had come, but no—not yet. He put the edge of the sword to my chest and asked in a choked voice, "Are you really going to heaven?"

I didn't dare to breathe heavily with that sharp, cold steel so close, and so I said, slowly and easily, "I hope so.

Then suddenly he removed the sword, took off his belt and put down his steel helmet, and grasped my hands with an iron grip as he blurted out, "Father, I want to go to confession!"

I was speechless, and I winced with pain from his tight, hard clasp. Was he crazy? He was almost wringing my hands off with his great strength. But again, he repeated, "Confession, now, please."

I said, "There are many priests in town; go to one of them."

"No, no, it must be you, you", he cried.

"Why me?"

"Because you will be going to heaven right away."

What could I do? I heard his confession; he wept as he made his confession, his first in many years, and then he kissed my hands. He was happy for the first time in years, and it hurt him that he now had to call his men for the execution. He was convinced of my innocence, but there was nothing he could do about it.

I said, "Would you like to receive Holy Communion? I still have two Hosts with me." He assented, and I gave him and myself the Bread of Life. He wept unabashed; things were getting to be a bit too much for me, too, when all of a sudden, there was a great noise from the outside. He quickly rose and armed himself, and now another officer entered the cell.

He held a piece of paper in his hand, and both men began to speak excitedly, too rapidly for my tired mind to translate. Then they left and locked the door. I heard several rifle shots from the courtyard. I heard the soldiers leave, and then quiet, a fearful stillness, settled over the compound.

What next?

Nothing. Nothing more happened, and I fell asleep, dead tired. After some days I learned that an order had come from Paris to reexamine my case, and, as I found out later, the Holy See had somehow got word of the whole affair and had intervened.

At any rate, I was saved, and that extraordinary confession,

which delayed the execution, conspired with the timely arrival of the order from Paris, which saved me once again from
the very mouth of death.

Chapter 22

A WOMAN WITH THE WAYS
OF A QUEEN

That uncanny experience, with its extraordinary outcome, did more to strengthen my belief in the rightness of my mission than had any other single event in my priestly life so far. It was not that it impressed me with my own impregnability; rather, it gave me a deeper humility, an even greater acceptance of the Divine Will of God in all things. I knew that whatever might happen to me, whatever might befall me for the rest of my lifetime, I was truly sealed to him I served; I felt that this strange occurrence had perhaps taken place to show me that I was on the right road, that all I had to do was to continue following where he led.

And so I was saved. Two days later I was taken to Ram-Ram, to the camp there south of Casablanca. I spent a wonderful day there with a good and pious fellow Franciscan. I was greatly surprised to learn that I was to be sent to Europe the next day, and, if all went well, I would be allowed to return to my home. That suited me fine, but I had had too many narrow escapes to trust this sudden good fortune. I received "new" old clothes, my luggage was checked, and everything was made ready for my departure; but things grew more mysterious as time passed. I was right in not rejoicing too early, for I was commanded now to go to a large prison where I celebrated Easter with men who were sick in body and in mind. Their pathetic condition troubled me, for it was difficult even to be sure that the message of hope could reach the depths of their terror-damaged minds.

One morning I was told that I would leave the next day, which I did, but not by ship, as promised, but by truck for a camp in the South Atlas, Ouarzazate. It was a camp for officers, and they had no chaplain. When I arrived, I was taken into a room full of young officers. The general called for me, stood up as I approached, and extended his hand. This had never happened to me before. When we were alone, he asked for my blessing; he was a Catholic, and I later learned that he was a noble man in body and soul. He promised me every possible help, but I was not to do too much as I was not the official chaplain. I had actually been sent there to have my case reexamined.

"Is there anything I can do for you, Father?" he asked.

"I would like to have my baggage and my Mass kit." But they were all there already, awaiting my arrival from Ksar-es-Souk. At least I could once more offer the Sacrifice of the Mass. At first, I did so in a small corner room. Then we felt that a chapel was needed, and so, after having been there fourteen days, and having recovered my strength somewhat, we began with zeal and the help of the general to build one. We finished in a short while since I had had experience before and could avoid some of the errors made back in Ksar-es-Souk. It looked beautiful. The officers, many of them outstanding Christians, worked harder than the non-coms had back in Ksar-es-Souk, for they did not believe, as the sergeants had, that it was beneath their dignity to dirty their hands with physical labor. With their aid, it turned out wonderfully well, and after it was blessed we knew great joy. I was

ABOVE: *Ouarzazate, an officers'*
camp, was a welcome contrast to
Ksar-es-Souk.

RIGHT: *The tenements of*
Ouarzazate.

BELOW: *Sent back to Europe,*
where the war prisoners were to be
given their freedom, Father Gereon
assisted at Mass celebrated at a
prisoners' camp in Chartres by the
Papal Nuncio, Cardinal
Roncalli—later Pope John XXIII.
This took place in 1947.

not allowed to preach "officially", but, if the general closed both eyes, all worked out well.

Unfortunately, the excitement and the many miles of travel proved too much for me. I became seriously ill, with my third attack of pleurisy in half a year. The general did all he could; his wife brought the best food to me in the French sick ward where he insisted I be cared for. After two weeks I was able to stand. Doctors had taken good care of me, and the general himself visited me every day. I was about to take my first walk out of the room when he called on me late one evening. He was sad, and he told me that I was to leave early the next morning.

"Where am I going this time?" I had no interest in yet another journey.

"I cannot tell you where; I am sorry. But do not lose courage. I know you are no Nazi. Everything will come out well, Father—even though you may have more rough days ahead." The good man was more perturbed than I was as I once again set out for an unknown destination.

Next day, at 2:00 A.M., an auto arrived with four men as guards for one weak, helpless priest. I was asked to promise that I would make no attempt to escape—what a ridiculous idea, in my weakened condition!—and my hands were left untied. We drove over the high Atlas until seven o'clock in a dizzy drive along sharp precipices and arrived in the town of the Franciscan Martyrs—Marrakech, where I had said Mass once before and been welcomed by my Franciscan brethren.

I asked the officer if he did not want to stop for a few hours; I would like to visit the Franciscans.

"Sorry, Father, I have orders to take you to Algiers by the shortest route."

I knew now where I was going. It was decided that we would board a waiting train in Marrakech, which would bring us to Casablanca in three hours. There, we would have a lay-over of seven hours.

"Where will we stay during that time?" I asked.

"Why, naturally you will be put into the prison there; we will find ways to amuse ourselves." And they smirked.

I knew this prison; it was a series of large boxes made of bars, a target for loafers with rotten tomatoes and other items of endearment. I thought, "This could turn out to be very interesting. But just wait and see." I had survived many a storm before now.

My companion had a basket of choice food from the general in the camp and invited me to help myself, but I refused for it was Thursday, the day of the institution of the Blessed Sacrament, and I wanted to say Mass if possible. Up until now I had managed to say Mass every Thursday. He laughed at this. It was impossible for me to visit a church; he showed me the order that I was to be taken to a camp in Algiers by the shortest way possible, without speaking to anyone on the way.

Now I knew for sure that I was regarded as dangerous, and I knew, too, why I had been put in a section by myself, though the train was very crowded. My companion, who otherwise was so pleasant, told me that from the papers he was reading it was evident that serious charges were outstanding against me.

We arrived in Casablanca; the station was crowded, and with the four guards we managed to push our way through the crowd. There I saw, on the opposite side, the prison where I was to be locked up to become the laughingstock of the town. But, as I emerged from the crowd, two or three Franciscan Sisters stood before me, seemingly out of nowhere, and with them the stately figure of Mère Monique, the Mother Provincial. I felt I must get in a few words with her.

I knew her from a year ago, when I received a letter at Ksar-es-Souk that read:

> Please come to see me as soon as possible.
> Mère Monique.

Her address was Casablanca. Since I had never been to Casablanca and didn't know Mère Monique, I went to the French general of the camp and asked him if he could explain this to me. I don't believe he really read the letter; he saw the signature "Monique" and at once became quite friendly, saying that I must go immediately to Casablanca.

"When this woman writes such a letter, there is only one thing to do—follow instructions." He would not explain who she was, simply told me to get started at once. Evidently this good general had great respect for—if not to say even fear of—this Mère Monique. With the general's aid and urging I left camp that night—it was always good to get away—and after two days came to Rabat, where I spent the night with the Franciscans.

When I showed Father Commissary, the holy Père Maurice, the letter, he who was peace and tranquility personified became excited and said I should go there at once; it was not good to keep this woman waiting.

Well, I had to see the bishop about some faculties for the camp and went to see him first, a little irritated by all this fuss and bother over a nun's command. In regard to the faculties, the bishop quieted my anxieties with a smile, saying, "You are the favorite child of the Holy Father and the Bishop of the Sahara; do as you think best." Then I showed him the nun's letter, and he said, "Go at once, and be very humble in her presence."

I sputtered, "Your Excellency, who is this Mère Monique? Everyone seems to respect her—many even to fear her!"

He laughed and said, "Go and see for yourself. But I will tell you this much, Father: if you do not succeed in winning the friendship of this woman, then I cannot help you either. You might as well prepare to leave Morocco at once."

These were strong words, and I was anxiously anticipating the outcome of the meeting in Casablanca, where Anfa is the Motherhouse for Morocco of the Franciscan Missionaries of Mary. I arrived and had hardly been seated in the parlor when Mère Monique came rushing in.

There is no other way of describing her entrance—she came in like a storm—and, before I could say a word, I was addressed and scolded in the same breath, "So you are the Father who is considered to be a Nazi, and who conducts himself too mildly with the Nazis in his camp! Why have you come to Morocco, if you wish to follow such wrong methods? I say to you that from now on you are to deal more severely with these persecutors of the Church—these murderers!"

Speech failed me; this was more than I had expected. A command from a woman! My reaction was one of anger, and I said harshly, "I am a German sergeant-major; do you think I take orders from a woman, a nun? I know from personal experience how Nazis are to be treated. Have you ever met one? I have lived among them for years; I was trained as a soldier among them, and my methods are correct, as the results obtained in camp have proven. If you wrote to me just to tell me this, I can return at once." I was terribly angry, and I was about to leave, but she rose and blocked the door. She became amiability personified, as if she had said nothing unpleasant. It seemed that my conduct pleased her not a little; this was what she admired in a chaplain of the Nazis.

"You must not take it ill, but I have heard so much about you from Mother Superior Agnes in Midelt, about your work and your excellent French that makes your listeners weep." How tactful and capable she was in humiliating me as she praised me! "You will please sit down. Now, Father Gold-mann, here is why I summoned you. I want to enter into an agreement with you."

"An agreement with a chaplain of prisoners?"

"Yes, for you know the suffering and sacrifice of prison life, and I want you to offer up all the trials of the prison for our convents. In turn, we will offer up our prayers and sacri-fices for the sake of the prisoners. From such an exchange, Father, nothing can come but blessings."

I was forced to admire her, for such a plan could come only from a heart full of faith—and for this she had had me come more than a thousand kilometers! She spoke so glowingly of the effects of such an arrangement, entered upon by mutual, heartfelt accord, that I could do nothing but agree heartily with her. We became good friends, and so I should have no need to pack my bags and slink out of Morocco.

It is hard to describe all the things that this woman, with the ways of a queen, did for us; how she had her Sisters pray for us continuously, how she helped us with material things, how she hired our Christians as gardeners for her convents, and how she cared for us with the heart of a mother and the generosity of a great lady. God will repay her all this, now that she has been called to her eternal reward.

Chapter 23

CAMP SEEDS

So that was Mère Monique, and now she was in Casablanca, like some energetic specter, absolutely the last person in the world I would have expected to see. Before I or the guards knew it, she had me in one auto and my guards in a second before they could make any resistance. We were on our way to Anfa, to the white convent of the Sisters, speeding like madmen. We were given water there for washing ourselves, and I was taken at once to the sacristy, where the vestments were laid out for Mass and where two of my men who were working here as members of the work crew were waiting for me. At first I didn't recognize them; a few months' time had served to make them fat and healthy, and they wore new clothes that made them look like lords, compared to the ragged skeletons they had once been.

The most important thing for the moment, to me, was that now I could say Mass, thanks to Mère Monique.

After Mass, I asked her how she knew I was coming, and how she knew it would be on that train. I had been taken out secretly, and no one was supposed to know that I was leaving or where I was going.

Smiling a secret kind of smile, she said, "It is really very simple, Father Goldmann. You yourself have often told the

Sisters of the power of prayer and of your own trust in the intercession of St. Thérèse of the Child Jesus. Three weeks ago, a Sister from Casablanca happened to be in Paris, working at the Central Bureau for prisoners. She was trying to negotiate workers for the convents. She was made to wait in the commandant's private office for quite a long time, and while waiting"—here she laughed—"her eyes fell, quite by accident, of course, on a paper that was lying on the table. It was stamped 'Strictly Secret' at the top, and again, quite accidentally, she happened to see your name on it. To her horror, she read that Father Goldmann, about whom she had heard so much, was to be brought from Ouarzazate to an evil camp in Algiers for punishment. Below the words 'Strictly Secret' was written 'Nazi-Priest'.

"She wrote to us immediately to tell us this distressing news. The letter arrived nine days ago and caused much consternation among the Sisters. One of them thought that you would have to pass through Casablanca on your way to Algiers, and so perhaps we could help you at the station."

"And so you went every day to the station to meet me?"

"No, no, it was much simpler than that. Sister Sacristan proposed to make a novena to St. Thérèse that you would come here after nine days, and behold—today is the ninth day, and since there is only one train daily from the south, you had to be on it. So we drove to the station, and there you were!"

I was dumbfounded by the faith of these Sisters. But they not only had the faith that is as simple as doves; they were also as wise as serpents. Not only did I get a princely meal, but my guards also got the best food. The leader of the group received a bottle of wine and instructions to let me off in Rabat at the Franciscan monastery.

In late afternoon, the wine-happy Frenchmen were driven with me to the station. We traveled in a first-class carriage, and, as we arrived in Rabat around nine o'clock that night, there stood some Sisters; they had been alerted by Mère Monique, and we were taken by auto to the Franciscans, where we all got a good room. My guards did not mind such a trip at all and were no longer in such a hurry, so we stayed in Rabat several days.

I went to the old Bishop of Vieille and told him what was awaiting me. He became all fire and flame, wrote it all up, and promised to write a protest to the General of the Prisons; this helped me considerably later. I visited some worthwhile sights in my Franciscan habit, and then we continued our journey to the punishment camp. We had an hour's wait in Meknès, and again some good Sisters stood waiting with a basket of food and two large blankets made of sheep's wool, which came in handy later on.

In Oujda, the station on the border, I was taken by auto to the Franciscan monastery where I had stayed three years ago on entering Morocco under such memorable circumstances. The same affable Superior welcomed me, and after a night's rest we continued our journey. My guards were always fortified with excellent wine, and at every station the good Sisters met us to hand over food baskets. It was a very pleasant trip, and I tried to keep my mind away from what waited at the end of it.

We went south from Algiers through the mountains and desert land and came at last to a place whose name I have forgotten but whose activities I shall ever remember. High up on a mountain there was a church and a settlement that could be seen for miles around; below in the valley lay the camp. In one corner of it was a special section for Nazis, with extra barbed-wire fencing, extra guards, and a special menu of thin soup. The small barracks were full of bugs, and contained fifty men listed as Nazis. What stupidity! These men were

Hungarians, Bessarabians, Poles, Russians, Italians, and Belgians, many of them good men who had committed no crime at all. True, some had done wrong, including a couple of murders, but Nazis these men were most decidedly not!

I was honorably received at the entrance to the camp. The French interpreter and other Frenchmen there were very polite when they saw a German prisoner with a chaplain's cross and a Red Cross band on his arm marching in. They were startled to see four guards for one man, and when they read the report, their attitude did a complete about-face. The interpreter roared at me, "Nazi, pig, criminal liar!"

They stood around regarding me as if I were the devil incarnate. Then of course came the examination in the nude, and the general disappointment in not finding the damning SS mark on my left arm. Among those who struck and reviled me was a young corporal, who approached me with angry words and came very close to me. Amid the worst scoldings, he suddenly said quietly a word that sounded like "seminary". I thought he was making fun of me, and when I did not answer he seemed to become even more angry. Finally I was led through the camp guarded by machine guns and was taken to the SS barracks.

Among the men already there, there existed much astonishment, much suspicion. How could I be a chaplain and an SS man both? Something was wrong; the men were reserved, no one trusting anyone else. I knew from bitter experience that in these camps men would turn in or inform on a man who had saved their lives for the sake of a temporary increase in their food allowance or some other form of preferment.

The barracks were narrow, hot, and dirty; the floor was clay, the bed-boards were full of bugs, and most were without any covering. My two snow-white, woollen, giant-sized covers immediately aroused suspicion—I must be some secret agent! On the first day no one spoke to me. We were given only soup, which smelled bad and tasted worse, but I had been eating well and so could stand it for a while.

The barracks roof was made of large palm leaves, which made things somewhat cooler but had other disadvantages. Soon the rains came, the first heavy rain in two years, and we had to seek shelter under our boards, sitting in the mud. Day after day we lived in the mud, drenched to the skin, cold. Many became terribly ill, but, after all, we were only Nazis, not human beings. Thick snakes crawled from the roof to be caught by the Hungarians, who ate them. I tried, but my aversion almost choked me, though really the taste was not bad at all. I preferred to go hungry. The Hungarians also roasted rats, which we caught in goodly numbers. A practical man eats anything when hungry. We learned to prepare a salad from roots and the bark of trees.

I spent two unforgettable months in this prison.

There was a narrow walk around the barracks, with a guard marching back and forth, watching us lest we disappear in the thick hedge. As soon as the sun came out, we sat in front of the crumbling building to dry our clothes and search for lice; but the worst thing, after the continuous pangs of hunger, was the swarms of flies. Thousands pestered us mercilessly, until many of the men became indifferent, and the flies settled on the many wounds of their bodies. Flies by day and bugs by night—that was our penance.

One day I heard a loud, angry voice calling for the Nazi chaplain. Outside stood the young corporal who bellowed at me the loudest when I had entered the camp. He had a whip in his hand, and I got ready for the worst. He seized me as I stepped up and pushed me, yelling and swinging his whip. Never once did he hit me. My comrades had told me that they were beaten often in the corner of the camp to make them tell secrets that they never knew. I was led to that corner, out of hearing and partially out of sight of the others. The corporal swung his lash, but it landed on the posts instead of me, while he kept on scolding; now and then, in whispers, he managed to get out bits of his story: he was a seminarian; I must pardon him for seeming so angry and for treating me so roughly, but this was the only way he could help me, lest the others become suspicious.

"Do you need anything?" I was taken completely by surprise, and I told him at once that I could use some bread and wine so that I could say Mass.

"That is impossible, Father", he whispered as the lash once more hit the post.

"I will manage, if you can get the bread and wine to me."

He returned me to the barracks, still scolding and shouting, and that night at ten he brought what I needed. He had gotten them from the priest on the mountain.

Now, I could say Mass—but where? Here in the barracks, if worse came to worst, but better yet would be the cleaner barn nearby. The question was, how were we to get to that barn? We were not permitted to take a step outside the prison limits; our latrine was a bucket at the entrance. The guard would shoot at once if anyone stepped out of bounds. We were counted once or twice a night because we were so dangerous, and yet some still managed to escape in spite of all the precautions. We had nothing to lose and everything to gain, and when I asked several fellow prisoners if they were willing to dare, after the second roll call, to crawl to the barn, they surprised me by agreeing at once.

After the 2:00 A.M. head count, with the guard back on his beat, we crawled the twenty meters to the barn. I lit the stump of a candle, and the two who were with me held a small board as an altar while I said Mass, with a small stole for a vestment, with the wine in a drinking glass, and with the help of a small English missal.

I had said Mass before in surroundings just as strange. In the prison at Meknès, a black man supplied me with the Mass kit of Father Hermentier. He said he "found" them in the sacristy, omitting that I had informed him of the entrance to the sacristy and where the key was. He went in when no one was around and borrowed them. At that time, two other men had to hold me up, I was so weak. One held the chalice so that it would not fall or slide down, and we celebrated Mass with the help of the guards.

Now we were in a barn; one of the men who held the board that served as an altar was a murderer, as I later learned. I said Mass in this way for fourteen days. In the end I said Mass early in the morning when we got up and were allowed to wash. It was not difficult to get to the barn, which I had cleaned up. I had placed a board on two pegs fastened in the walls and used this for my altar.

After two weeks things changed completely. I was not released from the barracks, but I was summoned by the general of the camp, who talked with me for a long time with no interpreter. Only the seminarian, the corporal, was there. I was given permission to go to the priest up the mountain for confession, which I did at once, and thereafter twice a week. Now I could procure for myself all the things needed for Mass, and I was allowed to say Mass in the camp chapel. The chaplain there was a German, but he did not trust me and kept me isolated. I learned from the seminarian that a note had come from France telling them to treat me kindly; word had been sent to Paris from the Holy Father, asking why I was treated like an evil SS man when permission for my ordination had come from him.

Many months before, I had smuggled a letter out of prison with the help of a guard, addressing it directly to the Holy Father; perhaps it was this letter that brought his intercession. In any case, I could now draw a deep breath, as could the other prisoners in that special section of the camp. I was able, without a guard, to go to the small settlement on the mountain to regain my strength in the home of the pious, poor, and loving priest and to help my starving comrades with gifts sent by the people of the settlement.

Unfortunately, this lasted only a few weeks. One morning there was great excitement; the camp was surrounded by soldiers. We learned that an entire company had succeeded in escaping, after months of preparation and with the help of many Arabs and Frenchmen who provided them with clothes and all that was needed for flight. With the German precision for details, the flight was planned carefully; they got away in a French military truck, whose absence was noticed only days later, as these daring men were reaching Spanish Morocco. Among those who escaped were two from our camp and one from the special section. It came out that I had known of the plan and by my knowledge of Morocco had helped them. I was German, even though perhaps not an SS man and a Nazi as the French understood it. Now things were happening again. Under heavy guard—in fact, a guard for every man—and with many machine guns, ten of us were taken from camp to the railroad station. There, in a truck with three times as many guards as prisoners, we went east—where, we did not know. The truck was kept darkened. We stopped for days at a time at some places we could not even see, but as we got enough food and were not molested, things were not as bad as they might have been.

After many days of travel, we reached Constantine, the easternmost large city of Algeria, and were taken to the camp. I was put in a barracks reserved for the Nazis. Everyone knew who we were, but we received no special ill treatment. We were, of course, confined to the camp, but that suited me. The commander examined me repeatedly, and I noticed that while he did not speak much in my favor, he let it be known that I had the best protection in the world—meaning the Pope. The only thing that interfered with my complete peace was the fact that the small church was locked; the chaplain was away on a trip.

I got a big surprise when he returned; Father Debatin was one of the best, most zealous, most pious, and gifted priests I ever saw in Africa. I knew him from the days of my ordination and felt privileged to be allowed to be with him. I was permitted to say Mass, and for many months I was with him, not indeed in the same barracks, yet together with him throughout the day when he was not, as was often the case, on a trip visiting detachments of soldiers. For me, these months were the best kind of retreat. I had before me the example of one whose life was one of prayer and the care of souls, who lived the life of an ideal priest. For me, a young priest, this was indeed a blessing.

For years now, I had been turned loose to function as a priest, and the longer I acted, the more I realized my deep ignorance and need of instruction. This was almost like days spent in a seminary, and I determined to make the most of it. I could perform no priestly duties until my case had been cleared, so I concentrated on helping Father wherever I could. The camp was dirty, so I cleaned things up a bit. I was glad to be of service to him and to learn how to serve others. It was something I had not known until now, and I gloried in the opportunity; besides, I learned to know practical men, men of faith and uprightness, who had become good Christians under the guidance of this chaplain. Here I saw what one good priest can accomplish, as he draws out the goodness of the human soul. Some of these men became priests; others, who had not been Catholics, embraced the faith. I spent many hours with these men, helping to plan every detail of Christian life in families and parishes. I have received many letters since then from the men who survived the camps in Constantine and elsewhere in Africa, testifying that their good resolutions held after the pressures that brought them forth had been removed. The sowing of the good seed in these camps brought many good results.

I was privileged to spend more than six months with Father Debatin, counting it a valuable part of my training and really not thinking of it as imprisonment at all. Then things began to happen quickly once more, and I was prepared for a change.

The general told me abruptly one day, with more kindness than he had so far shown, that my case was closed.

"You are not the one we thought you were."

"What do you mean by that?"

"You are not the Nazi we thought we had. We believed you were the commandant of Dachau, and that you had been masquerading as a priest to escape the consequences of your villainous acts." I was not beyond amazement after all; I had thought that those charges were long since disproved. "You may return to your home—you are to be released. However, we do know that you are no friend of France."

"I am no friend of injustice, General, and I saw much of it take place in many camps in the name of France; I saw crimes perpetrated on the persons of innocent people who had no more share in the crimes of the Nazis than I did. When I spoke to the authorities regarding the Red Cross, I did so as my duty dictated; I was a human being, a German, and a priest, and I could not fail to speak up about such terrible things.

"As for the rest, I will leave behind many friends in North Africa, from the circle of Frenchmen, and I will never be able to show my gratitude for the things Frenchmen have done to help me and those I served." I could not refrain from adding, "I will pray fervently that some day punishment will be meted out to those Europeans of whatever nationality living in Algiers and Morocco who are inflicting such oppression on the natives there. Their mistreatment cries to heaven for vengeance and inevitably will incite these natives to seek revenge. Heaven help all Europeans, oppressors and innocents alike, when that happens!"

The general shrugged his shoulders and replied, "You see, in a certain way you are also a Nazi." With that, he sent me on my way.

Chapter 24

THAT IS PRAYER

The dreary yet grace-laden years of imprisonment were slowly drawing to a close. Our ship landed at Marseilles, and after a few days I was in Paris. Of course, several days went by in investigations and searching the baggage. I was assigned to a camp near Chartres, of which I had heard much, but of which I could believe little. It was a camp for seminarians, with many hundreds of students and a real theological-philosophical school. The teachers were in part clerical prisoners, mostly professors of theology, who had volunteered to come so that they might teach the prisoners.

There I met my esteemed teacher Father Sebastian, lector of moral theology; I spent some happy weeks with him in the camp, and to my joy I was allowed to preach the word of God to these hundreds of men. There was a special ordination of two theologians in the imposing cathedral, and my joy knew no bounds when, as one like themselves who had received my orders very early in life, I was privileged to act as deacon; Holy Orders were given by the apostolic nuncio of Paris, Giuseppe Cardinal Roncalli, who later became Pope John XXIII. Our Easter celebration that year had in it so much of faith and glory that we thought our bursting hearts must make the whole world glad in the wonderful story of the Christ.

I was given permission by the French general of the camp to make many trips, as a kind of reparation for the injustices done to me during the last fourteen months. I visited all the beloved holy places, the cathedrals and the chapels where I had prayed for the grace of the priesthood, which had been a reality now for some time.

Naturally, I wanted to go to Lisieux to thank St. Thérèse, as I had promised, but my permission to travel did not extend that far. The only thing to do, then, was to obtain civilian clothes from my friends and try to get there secretly, though it would mean, perhaps, my being taken from the list of free men. My French was good enough that I was taken for a native of Alsace. I packed my vestments so that I could say Mass in Lisieux.

I arrived safely and found things better than I had expected. The seminary of the Mission of France took me in, and I spent several glorious days among the seminarians. The spirit of the house was one of love and joy, which impressed me deeply.

I was allowed to say Mass in the church of the tomb of the Little Flower, and I was even given a small relic of hers when I narrated the strange story of my ordination and the part played by St. Thérèse. It was a real pilgrimage, where I felt deeply the spirit of the little saint. I prayed at her grave, and then returned safely to Paris and Chartres, arriving just in time to get the news of my direct and imminent departure for home.

It was a strange feeling to travel once more as a free man without a soldier at my back and without the feeling of insecurity that plagues every prisoner.

After a brief stop at the convent in the mountains near Gengenbach to thank the Sisters for their many years of loyal, persevering prayer, I went on to Fulda, to the motherhouse

The cathedral of Lisieux. Here, at the tomb of St. Thérèse, Father Goldmann gave thanks for his safe return home.

Cardinal Roncalli (later Pope John XXIII) celebrating Mass. Father Gereon is third from the right—the tallest, as usual.

of the province, where joy and astonishment prevailed upon my arrival.

It did not last long. Within an hour I was called into the cell of the prefect of studies, who began at once, and with words that were none too friendly, to tell me that my way of achieving Holy Orders was not found in the Franciscan statutes. He felt duty bound to tell me that not all the friars agreed with my impetuous and vigorous ways. The unsuspecting man did not know how singularly forceful and stormy the events of my life had been to lead me to such an end.

To the professors and to all in the house I was merely a newly ordained priest; I could hear no confessions, preach no sermons, until I had finished my studies and passed the examinations. That was a cold bath, indeed. After four years of wide experience in the care of souls, to be treated as a newly ordained priest, one without experience, was indeed a humbling experience. Well, perhaps I needed it. I was to make up the whole course of theology and to take all the examinations. A few hours after receiving this news, I received still more: I was still to be allowed to say Mass, but that was absolutely all. I understood that it was right for them to do this, but it rankled a bit, at first. In addition, I could feel the envy on the part of some at my having been ordained so early.

Since the prefect of studies told me I would have to start at the beginning, the plan he gave me indicated that completion of my studies would require three years. Father Provincial said that I would have to take all the examinations at my own pace; now I wanted to prove to these men that my mind and reason had not been dulled by the war but, rather, that my necessarily catch-as-catch-can priesthood had sharpened and toughened me. I attended only those lectures I considered important, and rose at 2:50 A.M. every morning to be busy studying by 3:00. After a day or two of uninterrupted study, I

A photograph of Father Goldmann in 1948, two years after his return home.

mastered a section and took the exam in the room of the lector without saying anything to the prefect of studies. A few lectors were very obliging in this way and gave me all my examinations, which I passed successfully.

At the end of nine months, I had all the papers I needed, and I brought them to the prefect of studies, who was surprised and astounded. He did not trust his eyes, but everything was there in black and white, all in order. All of the exams had been passed successfully. There was nothing left for him to do but to admit me to the examination for pastoral theology, and the day before Ash Wednesday I took it successfully. I was given the faculties for the care of souls. During Lent I preached everywhere, spent many hours in the confessional, and was in heart and soul a pastor of souls.

I spent a happy year in Fulda serving as assistant to a wise old pastor who taught me much in the care of souls. Under his guidance, the parish was renewing itself from the ravages of the war, and I learned how truly immature I was. From this pastor I learned some caution and prudence, as well as many practical things that had had no place in my priestly life while I was a prisoner with others in the unreal circumstances of the prison camps. I had to learn to live in the civilized world all over again, and this gave me the opportunity to do so.

The Americans picked me up about a dozen times and took me to Wiesbaden for investigation as a possible Nazi criminal, sometimes in the middle of the night. They brought forth all the documents from the French prisons, including some of my sermons, which had been typed out. There must have been several hundred of them. I finally had to tell them of my involvement in the assassination attempt of July 20, and after they had investigated they decided on the basis of that that I could not be a Nazi.

I wanted to fulfill my dream of going to Japan and applied for a visa; but it was some years before it came through. In the meantime, I served as I was sent, working with young seminarians in Germany and Holland. One more unique experience deserves to be shared. In 1951, ten young men and I traveled by bicycle to Rome. After traveling for eight weeks, we arrived in Rome and were received in audience by the Holy Father in Castel Gandolfo; he gladly gave his blessing when he learned that the young men intended to become Franciscan priests, and he generously gave me a special blessing as the instructor of these young candidates.

During our eight-day stay in Rome I received a letter from an old priest who had been a friend for many years; he told me not to fail to call on a monastery in South Germany whose name I was familiar with because the beloved artist Berta Hümmel had been a Sister there. I had never been to the place before. The letter further informed me that a Sister Veronika, who had prayed for me, was expecting me.

I made the side trip to a small town called Saulgau, where there was a Franciscan friary, and then walked some thirty minutes through the beautiful countryside to the large convent and Motherhouse of Siessen. I had never been in this region in my life, much less at this convent.

I rang the bell and gave my name to the Sister Portress. She shouted for joy, left me standing open-mouthed in the open doorway, and went for the Superior. She came with beaming face and flying skirts (most unbecoming, I thought) and told me that the Sisters had been waiting for this visit for a long time.

"Sister, there must be some mistake—this is my first visit to this region, and I have absolutely no connection with this house."

She smiled. "Come, you will soon see that you are wrong."

I was taken to the building where the sick Sisters were housed and to a room with the name "Sister Veronika" on its door. I was ushered in and there saw lying in bed an old Sister with heavy lines of suffering on her face, which, however, reflected an inner joy and light and serenity. Another surprise was that there were about a dozen birds in the room, some on the bed, some on her hands. They flew out of the window to the neighboring trees but came in and settled down again when Sister called them by name.

I spoke softly, so as not to disturb the birds, and told her that I had been told to stop by here, but that I did not know why.

"If you will sit down, you will hear it all", she said. It seemed that years ago, Father Bernardine, whom I had first met as a lad, had taken an interest in a young boy who, having been removed from Fulda by his family, was forced to confront the temptations of the city and overcome them on his road to the priesthood. Father described to the good Sisters, there in the chapel, some of the trials that awaited a young man striving for ordination, so serious that the grace of vocation, which seemed very strong in the boy, might well be lost. He asked if some Sisters could be found who would pray and sacrifice in a special way for such a boy, that the Church might be blessed with another priest.

Sister Veronika received permission from her Superior and asked Father Bernardine what she should do. He took her to the chapel and there before the Blessed Sacrament she consecrated herself to the priestly Heart of Jesus and promised to offer up all her prayers and sacrifices each day for this boy. Thus began an uninterrupted prayer.

Soon afterward, she became terribly ill, and for twenty years she suffered in bed, having to undergo many operations. It was a life of suffering and pain.

"She never complained", Sister Superior told me afterward, "even when the nursing Sisters were harsh. When we wanted to console her, she smiled and said, 'I know for whom I am suffering; I have a boy whose vocation to the priesthood I must safeguard.'"

Now I sat on her bed, and she said with the greatest joy radiating from her ravaged face, "Now I see again how good God is; for twenty years I have prayed and suffered, and he has richly rewarded me."

I could say nothing! Now I knew yet another reason why I had become a priest in such singular fashion—God accepted the prayers and sufferings of this holy soul as he had accepted the prayers and supplications of Sister Solana May.

The power of prayer was brought home to me even more strongly in another instance. I was resting for a day in the monastery of Grimmenstein, near Walzenhausen, where for five hundred years Sisters of Perpetual Adoration had dwelt. The Superior, Sister Maria Theresia Jocham, had written that I should pay them a visit when I could, and this was my chance.

There, I heard the following story:

In the month when I was condemned to be shot by the military court in Africa, a Father from Switzerland had the opportunity, as a friend of a French officer and as a chaplain in Meknès, to see the papers relating to my case. He was convinced that it was nothing but lies and deceit. He also knew that the death sentence would be carried out in a short time, so he wrote hurriedly to the Sisters in Grimmenstein explaining the case and made an urgent appeal to them to storm heaven with prayers for the safety of the young German priest.

Day and night, the Sisters prayed in unbroken adoration for my safety, and the singular manner of my rescue has already been told.

"So you see, that is prayer; for months and years we prayed for you, and now we see you here present and know that our prayers were answered", said Sister Superior. She showed me the Chapel of Adoration; there on a card on the kneeler of the Sisters my name had been written, so that no Sister could forget the special prayer for the priest.

The words of Scripture had been fulfilled, that whoever prays to the Father in the name of the Son will be heard.

*After completing his studies, Father Gereon
served in parishes in Germany and the
Netherlands. Here he leads a band of pilgrims
to the Shrine of the Precious Blood at Waldurn.*

EPILOGUE

Full of joy and gratitude, I returned to Germany and spent some years working with candidates for the priesthood as a teacher of some two hundred youths who were so preparing themselves.

Finally came the long-awaited day when I received my visa for Japan, which I had been trying to secure for years. I gave my last sermon at a mission for many people in Germany on January 23, 1954, leaving the same day by plane for Tokyo. I was airsick again.

I arrived on the feast of the Conversion of St. Paul and saw a rare sight—snow and ice covering the city, a symbolic picture of human souls who were still in the winter of paganism and needed so badly to be warmed by the grace of God's Son and thawed by the flame of the Holy Spirit.

While my story must end, as stories do, it is necessary to bear in mind that the life of the Church goes on and on. Now, ten years later [1964], I am pastor of St. Elizabeth's in Tokyo-Itabashi, and the reality of God's tender care for his children has never been more real. One way and another, our labors are fruitful; we have a beautiful church and parish house, a retreat in the mountains where every summer hundreds of poor, Christians and non-Christians, find a welcome rest from the heat of the city. Baptisms are still not what one would hope for, but our plan for helping students to help themselves is flourishing. I still have an unhappy propensity for working to the point of debilitating fatigue, and I still seem to have some facility for drawing excitement into my area. But despite obstacles, despite heartbreak, despite occasional bouts of sickness and discouragement in this still-pagan land, we strive on in the unshakable confidence that, whatever happens to the men who follow the Way of the Cross, the unconquerable life of the Church continues—an unbroken thread weaving through and over and around the entire world, so that good men everywhere may someday experience the sweet and awesome reality of God's Love.

APPENDIX

But I preached daily twice, — and
the Nazis knew: the war is lost!!
In 1945 — I think as was March —
they got very radical. Every people
who would speak to me, would have
been beaten at night! So I was 2 weeks
alone! But one of the prisoners got
to the French, entered the Foreign Legion
ant told all the things to the French!

Appendix

THE RAGPICKER OF TOKYO

RELATED BY JOSEPH SEITZ

Early in 1954, Father Goldmann flew to Japan. In a letter of January 22, written while flying to Bangkok over India and Burma, he enthusiastically described this great adventure. "Forests, jungle, swamps. No settlement for miles and miles. In clear weather, from a height of twenty thousand feet, one can see large areas of mighty river valleys, a vast expanse. And then the inhabitants! Each people is different. And nearly all of them are pagan. Huge temples. What an immense mission field here! But that is what we are here for. I hope for the best." On the feast of the Conversion of St. Paul, January 25, Father Goldmann arrived in Tokyo: "The city is snow-covered and icebound, a rare spectacle, symbolic of the soul still held captive in the bonds of paganism, in dire need of being thawed out by the warmth of God's grace and illumined by the fire of the Holy Spirit."

On February 14, 1954, he wrote:

I am at school, studying hard. The language is unbelievably difficult, harder than any I have learned so far. . . . My bed is Asiatic, a few blankets on the floor. By evening I am worn out from the most intense study. Of thousands of written characters to be memorized, I know only 45, the easiest at that. . . . Our parish counts three hundred thousand pagans and one hundred Christians—no lack of work. These few Christians, however, are unbelievably zealous. As many as forty at a time squeeze into my thirteen-by-nineteen-foot room, which serves as a chapel as well. The people are exceedingly poor but most lovable. Then there is the vast distinction between classes— great opulence on the one hand and indigence on the other—a disheartening consequence of a way of life in which the concept of love of neighbor has no part. Those who think that Christianity has failed in Europe ought to live for a few weeks in the slums here, and they would soon learn to appreciate what a few hundred years of Christianity have accomplished.

Then, on July 10, 1954: "Paganism is terrible, especially in its immorality. The men generally do as they please, and the women are left to shoulder the burdens of the family. At any rate, I know what I shall have to do some day."

Similar thoughts are expressed in all his letters. On the one side, there is the ardent desire to work as a missionary; on the other, his inability to do so because of incredible language difficulties.

Finally, September 1, 1955, Father Goldmann took charge of the only Catholic parish in Tokyo, Itabashi. It had been founded by the Franciscans of Fulda in 1953. There was one small house with a garden. Upstairs were three tiny rooms. A grey-haired missionary once gave this advice, "Take good care, Father, not to sneeze, or else there'll be a little earthquake shaking the house."

Itabashi is a suburb where thousands upon thousands live from hand to mouth. There is no Sunday in their daily

A pagan festival in Tokyo.

The first chapel in Tokyo, Itabashi (13 x 20 feet).

A wooden church in Tokyo, Itabashi, under construction. To the right is seen the old mission station.

drudgery. How can one reach these people living without any knowledge of God? Let me quote from a book entitled *Es Fiel Mir Auf* (I noticed), a report of a trip around the world, by Francis Gypkens, 1957:

> For an adult to begin a new life is a rare accomplishment. By dint of incredibly hard training and work, Father Goldmann has achieved within two years what others never learn—to converse fluently in Japanese, to squat motionless for hours like a Buddhist monk, to eat foul-smelling fish without vomiting (the practical preparation for a pastor in Tokyo). . . .
>
> At a time when food was rationed, Father Goldmann made contacts with the rice and fish dealers by showing them a crucifix or picture of a saint, asking them if they had ever seen such articles. This is how he would discover a clue to their way of thinking. Some would stand with him at the railroad station from 5:00 until 10:00 in the morning, collecting alms for the tuberculosis fund of the city. This task brought thirty-eight applicants for Baptism. . . .
>
> This pastor lives like one of the poorest in Japan. For months he has not tasted meat or coffee or cigarettes. His day begins around 5:00 in the morning. By 7:00 he has visited a number of ill-smelling hospital wards. Then he offers Mass. After this he travels by bicycle twenty to thirty miles to make house calls. The short lunch break is followed by uninterrupted work until 11:00 P.M. He teaches religion to children—both Christians and pagans. He gives individual instruction to catechumens—poor and rich, clerks and doctors, students and workmen. On Sundays he celebrates Mass five times.
>
> Here, the early Church has again come to life.

Here is a living cell that promises to grow into a vast organism, the pulsating strength of which is, at the moment, concentrated in this unassuming man dressed in shabby clothes.

In contrast, we well-fed Europeans are small indeed; we who cry "apostolate" and mean "tom-tom noise", we who talk of work while being comfortably situated, we who call ourselves Christians but are not on fire with love for Christ! We had to come here in order to discover Christ in a single genuine Christian.

An American eyewitness reports:

Imagine a couple Japanese trucks with high side-boards, manned by a few strong men who, week after week, in pelting rain and burning heat, call at homes and fill the trucks with refuse—rags, paper, tin cans, bottles, etc. Then they carefully drive their precious burden downtown to the famous "Ragpicker Village", where they sell it for good yen. The sale will bring enough money to help the poor. Maybe, after some time, it will bring enough to build a church. And this is exactly what has happened. Let him who doubts drive three and one third blocks south of the Grant Heights military housing area to Itabashi, Ku, Saiwai Cho 8, and turn to the right. There is the evidence: the Catholic Church of St. Elizabeth.

Father Gereon Goldmann is a marvelous and extraordinary ragpicker. Besides financing a new church, he enables twelve young Japanese to study at the University of Tokyo by helping defray their tuition. For these talented but poor young people, he created a special student fund, called the *"Lumpensammlerstudienstiftung"*, the Ragpicker's Student Aid Fund.

In the mountains near the beautiful town of Karuizawa stands another "monument" of the work of this selfless priest—a home for widows and orphans. It is the first Catholic recreation center where these hard-working poor people may rest briefly during the hot summer days, often for the first time in their lives. The land for this mountain home was donated, quite unexpectedly, by a rich Japanese, a non-Christian.

The "ragpicker church" was planned and built before anyone—including Father Goldmann himself—had the slightest idea where the money was to come from. When the building was completed in December 1957, his superior could not believe that a church actually existed. So he came from Hokkaido (a 26-hour journey) in order to see for himself, for he had called it an impossible undertaking, an empty dream.

This Franciscan is never at rest. He himself makes all needed preparations in the tiny room of his small house beside the church. There all available space is usually occupied by sleeping or playing children. Besides the daily home visiting (either on foot or by bicycle), he prepares sermons, directs Sunday school classes, hears confessions, and gives regular Bible and catechetical instruction—often far into the night. To date, the number of those converted by him to the Christian faith is about five hundred. One look at the faces of his congregation during divine worship suffices to convince us of the sincerity of their faith.

With the help of American families who live in the Grant Heights housing area and in the nearby settlement of Mutsumi Dai, the ragpicking business was undertaken on a broader scale, although, to be quite honest, his Japanese "colleagues" were at first opposed to this inroad into their own business. However, once they realized that all the proceeds went to improve the lot of poor people and that he kept nothing for himself, they came to admire this zealous priest.

"People are very good to us", he remarked. "It is absolutely necessary to build another church." And to forestall our astonishment, he quickly added, "I am quite confident, we'll make it again. You will see" (Chief Master Sgt. Arthur Wilson DeBaun, U.S. Air Force, 1958).

Although these brief eyewitness reports can highlight only a few details of the richly patterned fabric of this missionary's life, they do give an idea of the tasks he undertakes and the methods he employs to achieve them.

Father Goldmann often makes surprisingly sudden decisions. As soon as he is convinced of the necessity or importance of a project, he pursues it without delay, using every means available—no matter how absurd it may appear. Useful as this talent of resolute decision-making is, the really decisive factors remain patience and perseverance. Father Goldmann allows nothing to dissuade him and sees his projects through to the end, without regard for his own person. The following episodes will make this clear.

A FEW YEARS ago the *Messenger of St. Anthony*, a periodical of the Franciscan Missions, published the following article by Father Goldmann under the title "My Secret":

One day a few gentlemen drove up to my house in an American limousine. They handed me their card, which said, among other things, "Ministry of Foreign Affairs, Department of Culture and Education". Soon they bombarded me with questions that at first made me rather

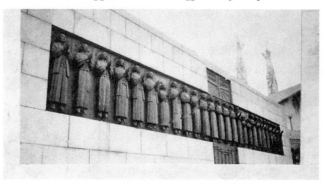

On February 5, 1577, twenty-six Christians were put to death by crucifixion on the "Holy Mountain", above Nagasaki. Among them were three Franciscan priests, three Brothers, and twelve Franciscan tertiaries. They were the first martyrs of the persecution of Christians in Japan, which lasted two hundred fifty years and is considered one of the more cruel martyrdoms in the history of the Church. Pope Pius IX declared on June 8, 1862: "Because these 26 martyrs died for their faith, they are solemnly canonized today. Let the faithful of all nations venerate them and call upon them for their intercession. February 5 is to be celebrated as their feast day." The monument was built after the dropping of the first atom bomb.

This church in Tokyo was built through the initiative of Father Gereon.

cautious, for one never knows what these officials may be up to. They told me, however, that I could speak quite freely, since they had come to thank me for all the help I was offering to Japanese students. I was surprised that the news of my hidden work had reached the highest authorities in the country.

A week later the Japanese state television telephoned me. After a little tug-of-war I consented to appear on the most popular program of the week, "My Secret", which is viewed by millions of interested people.

Thus it happened that one day I stood in my modest suit on the stage of the great TV studio—in the glaring light of the jupiter lamps and amid the buzzing of cameras. Four of the best-known reporters sat facing me, and thousands of spectators filled the hall to overflowing. The reporters' task was to discover my secret. Naturally, I tried to give the shortest possible answers, so as to leave the questioners in doubt. Their task was not easy, for my "secret" involved the coining of a hitherto non-existent Japanese word. All the same, those expert journalists came closer and closer to the solution, and in about ten minutes, amidst the applause of the audience, they had arrived at the conception of *"Kusu no shoogakushikin"*, the Japanese equivalent for "Ragpicker's Student Aid Fund". The next day the press reported it, with the result that millions of Japanese had learned of my "secret".

Father Goldmann tells us how the "Ragpicker's Student Aid Fund" came into existence:

A few years ago a young student came to me crying. He had just moved into my parish, and I knew only that he had four brothers and sisters and that his father operated a

Father Gereon saying Mass for his Japanese congregation.

When he was an altar boy, Father Gereon had dreamed of being a missionary in Japan. His dream came true in 1954, when he was sent to Tokyo.

small business. He himself was a second-year student of economics. Now he sat before me and could hardly control his sobs. When at last he was able to speak, he told me that his father, up to his ears in debt, had gone bankrupt and had been missing since yesterday. This morning he was found dead in a public bath—a suicide. What was to become of his family? Suddenly, in desperation the young man ran into the church, weeping without restraint. The family had no money. He was the oldest of five children. What would happen? Would he have to interrupt his studies or even drop out altogether? That would mean the loss of precious time; and no matter where he might knock, he would not find employment or earn enough to make ends meet in the home. Who would employ a student halfway through school in 1955 when the country was still bleeding from a thousand wounds caused by the war, and when endless lines waited daily outside the employment offices—among them many who were specialists. To the young man, everything seemed dark and hopeless. No wonder he cried. He told me, "Father, if I were not a Christian, I would follow my father's example."

This hour saw the birth of the Ragpicker's Student Aid Fund. Just the day before, I had made a good "catch". In my ragpicking excursions I had not only "fished" out of garbage barrels, bottles, paper, and tin cans, but I had also received two good refrigerators. Their American owners thought they were broken, whereas in reality they proved to be quite sound after they had been adapted for Japanese voltage. That was a matter of an hour's work, after which both were running perfectly. After another hour I had sold them for a good sum to a hotel. This was at a time when a refrigerator was still considered a fortune.

Suddenly it dawned on me that Providence had provided this money for the poor student. Hence, what else could I do but promise that he could continue his studies? "I shall pay your tuition," I told him, "and when you have finished, you will pay back everything in small installments, without interest."

He looked at me puzzled, not comprehending the import of my words until I laid a year's tuition on the table. Then he began to cry again, but this time for joy. In time he completed his university course, but even then he was far from finished. When he had received his degree, he came to me saying, "I am sorry, Father, but it will be a long time before I can pay you back."

Somewhat impatient, I was tempted to ask what had gotten into his head. Had he not promised to pay back everything? But he anticipated my thoughts, saying, "I have decided to study further, for I want to become a priest." I was speechless, but, true to his word, he entered the seminary. In the meantime, he has reached his goal, and as an ordination gift I absolved him from his debt.

That was the first case. Here is another: A young man worked day after day, from morning till night in a metal workshop. No other word but "slavery" is adequate to describe his labor. He told me that, according to a contract between his parents and the firm, he would have to stay on for five years. So he was working ten hours a day, often longer. His sleeping quarters and those of his companions were above the workshop. Their so-called "meals" defied all description—fit only for pigs! This young man came for a year for catechetical instruction—never before 10:00 P.M., for he could not get off work earlier. In time, he was baptized and was as zealous as he could be. Two free days a month did not allow him much time for going to church.

Then one day I realized that I had not seen him for several weeks. I inquired and learned that he had been removed to a tuberculosis sanatorium. His colleagues said they had noticed that one morning his bed was soaked with blood. It took weeks before I found him. He lay pale and spent on his hospital bed but happy that he was able to sleep and rest now. Almost two years passed before he was dismissed, after delicate lung surgery. That left him disqualified for his previous occupation. What was to be done now? His poor family with six other children could not afford to have him trained for different work. I took him into my house for a couple of weeks. There I noticed what I had also observed at the hospital, namely, that he was reading day and night. This, then, was the solution: he was cut out for study.

"But, Father, I am twenty-one! Besides, I lack the needed preparation."

"If you can muster enough courage, you will simply go to school with the fourteen-year-olds."

And he did have the courage. It was not easy, but he persevered, and after three years he passed his university entrance examination. By now he has obtained his degree, and as a lawyer he sends small monthly sums in payment of his debt—without interest, of course.

Such was the beginning of the Student Aid Fund, which enabled about a hundred young people to obtain a better education. But it is not a matter of merely caring for the poor and needy. Equally important is the fact that Christianity is gaining a foothold among the learned and upper strata of society. Seven of Father Goldmann's protégés have begun to

Children praying

RIGHT: *"Fifty baptisms in one year! For such a small parish in Japan, this is almost unbelievable."*

BELOW: *"The Japanese are—God be praised!—still Christians in their primitive fervor, not traditional or so-called 'cradle Christians'."*

study theology in preparation for the priesthood, while some forty girls have entered religious communities where they are active as teachers, nurses, social workers, and even foreign missionaries.

SOME YEARS before plunging into the student-aid program, Father Goldmann had launched another project—one that remains to this day unique within the Catholic Church in Japan, namely, the building of a center for mothers and children of his parish who cannot afford a vacation. Here is the story. For years Father Goldmann had dedicated all his strength to helping his parishioners and all those in any way near and dear to him. For, he reasoned, what is the use of preaching about love of neighbor when there are no deeds to show this love?

He saw what a heavy burden weighed upon the mothers in their struggle for daily bread, saw how tens of thousands of children were growing up in poverty and filth, and saw that most of them had never set foot outside this anthill city, had never feasted their eyes and hearts on God's free and beautiful creation. Their thoughts and actions centered on the basic necessities of life. In their daily routine there seemed to be neither time nor place for faith and religion. These mothers were hopelessly overburdened.

Father Goldmann racked his brain as to how he could best help. It would really be necessary to lift these tired mothers out of their work-a-day routine, take them somewhere into the mountains, where they could relax completely and settle down to think of higher things. But how and where? Since there was no money for such projects, this seemed simply impossible.

One day, however, Father Goldmann decided to visit a rich

Japanese landowner. This was like venturing into a lion's den for he knew that this man was notoriously stingy. His magnificent home stood in a spacious park surrounded by a high wall. When the politely formal servant asked Father Goldmann his business, he said that he wished to speak to the master in person; but the servant only showed him the door. Father Goldmann refused to move. Even the two big dogs could not frighten him. A stern look and the pretense of throwing a stone were sufficient to chase them away. The servant felt so embarrassed that he, too, turned on his heels and walked away. So Father Goldmann stood alone in the well-tended garden and waited.

After a considerable lapse of time a venerable looking gentleman appeared, who, with a ceremonious bow, introduced himself as the owner. At first he hesitated but finally invited his questionable visitor into his house. The solid furniture indicated at once that this wealthy lord belonged to the old upper aristocracy. Father Goldmann came to the point at once. He spoke of his work and of the mothers and children he wanted to help and of how urgently they needed a holiday. The man understood, but he asserted regretfully that it had always been like that and could hardly be changed.

"Why not?" asked Father Goldmann. "All I need is a piece of land somewhere in the mountains, and I shall see that these mothers get a holiday."

That was asking too much, and it was incomprehensible to the landowner. Quite beside himself but with a forced smile, this Japanese kept repeating, "You expect me to give you the ground for it? Never!"

All eloquence proved unavailing. The heart of this wealthy man, who possessed money like stones, was equally as hard as stone. Then something unforeseen happened. Father Goldmann relates it thus:

St. Anthony's Home, in the mountains, offers board and lodging to eighty people in need of a summer vacation.

Hundreds of mothers and their children vacation in St. Anthony's Home, free of charge. For many, it is their first vacation.

Japanese Christians take their Christmas gifts to a home for the aged.

I was just preparing to leave in disappointment when the man's wife came in. She looked amazed at the tall foreigner in her husband's private study and inquired what was going on. I daresay (but this is only a conjecture) she must have overheard much of the heated conversation before she betrayed her presence. Be that as it may, her angry husband was able at last to relieve his pent-up feelings, and he did so with gusto, making copious use of unsavory expressions that an educated Japanese normally tries to avoid. He had no way of knowing that a foreigner understood "technical" terms like these.

While his wife listened quietly and waited patiently for his agitation to die down, I spoke silently to my friend St. Anthony, promising him that I would give the new home his name if he assisted me this time. I had ample time to repeat the prayer many times.

At last the husband turned to me again and asked if the ground would really be used for building a vacation home for needy women and children. "Of course, what else would you expect me to use it for?" And I tried to explain once more, "For years now I have used all my strength and time to serve the Japanese people. For myself I want nothing at all."

At that moment a change came over his face and manner, and then he gave the answer I had no longer dared to expect. In a most conciliatory and even friendly tone he declared, "If you, a foreigner, are so much concerned for the welfare of our mothers and children, then I, a native Japanese, can hardly do less. I will donate the ground to you."

That word brought St. Anthony's Home in the Mountains to birth. The first houses and a little chapel, all of wood, were erected with the help of my friends in the archdiocese of Cologne. In due time, this holiday home was enlarged to include eighty beds, and it is equipped with recreational facilities to provide pleasure and diversion. These include a playground, a wading pool, swings, bicycles, etc.

For twelve years now, hundreds of mothers and children have spent their vacations there during the oppressively hot summer months. For them these weeks are the happiest of their burdensome year. Here, free from the trials and daily toil, their hearts and minds can open and expand in the magnificent new world of the mountains.

For Father Goldmann and his helpers, however, these days are not only the most strenuous of the year but also the richest in blessings. This becomes apparent from a letter:

> The burdens of my selfless "angels" grow steadily heavier. After four weeks they and I are dead tired. The mothers and children consider it paradise; for us these weeks are the hardest of the year. Thanks be to God that so far everything has gone well. The blessings that flow from here upon countless souls cannot be told in words. Once on our return from the mountains my four faithful assistants and I were caught in a storm. These women were trembling with fear, but I said to them, "What does it matter if you are struck by lightning now? After all the work you have done these last weeks, you are certain to be admitted up there" (letter of December 3, 1965).

ANOTHER IMPORTANT branch of Father Goldmann's social work is his aid to families. In a news letter dated December 8, 1964, he writes:

I must admit that I return from my parish visitations with an ever increasing sorrow. Not infrequently I find families of eight and more living in one small room. I have seen how youngsters are accommodated on bunks built into the walls, pressed against each other like sardines, among them teenage boys and girls in the same bed. There is simply not enough room.

That is why, along with the student-aid plan, I began a family housing project. So far I have provided five families with adequate living quarters. I had a house built for a family with nine children. I should like to help at least twenty more families toward better living conditions. Only then can they begin to breathe freely. Does not every plant need fresh air and space to expand? How much more so a human being?

When I discussed this project with one of my German friends, he was sceptical and thought it would be difficult to convince Europeans of such a necessity. To him it seemed a hopeless situation. May I, therefore, give an example: A family with three children lives within a space not worthy of the name "room". It is located in an old block of two-story flats occupied by thirty-eight other families. On each floor there is only one cooking niche and one primitive toilet shared by nineteen families. In such an "apartment" the above family of five is housed, together with a nineteen-year-old retarded sister of the mother, whom the parents in the country have cast off. Later, when the husband's sister died and no one wanted to take in the three children, this Christian woman took them also under her care. "Father," she said, "my pagan relatives cannot possibly know that the Bible says, 'He who receives one of these little ones receives Me.'"

"And where do you intend to put them all?" I asked

her. Pointing to a bunk on the wall, she said with real conviction, "Just look at these children. Through them the Lord himself looks straight at you." I was speechless. That same evening I signed the first contract for my family housing project.

This social work was sometimes delayed because of other pressing needs. Father Goldmann's Pentecost circular of 1968 reports:

According to the newspapers, Japan has outrun Western Germany economically. If this is true, has financial aid to St. Elizabeth's not become superfluous? Here is my answer: during the past few years many people from Germany have visited me here. They lodged in hotels in central Tokyo, and they, too, would question the necessity of continuing aid. In reply I usually take them for a tour through my parish and show them how my people live. Invariably, the visitors, deeply moved, were speechless. Many said they had never dreamed such poverty was possible. Let me add that even today more than 50 percent of the families in my parish are living in a single room, but this does not mean one small family, for the room is often shared by relatives up to four generations— from grandmother to grandchild. I, who enjoy the comfort of a five-story parish center, could never answer for such "luxury" unless I was really concerned for the living conditions of my people. Therefore, I have decided to build homes for them so that they will at least be able to live as befits human beings. These houses with four small rooms, kitchen, and bath are not a free gift. The owners will pay for the house in about twenty years. Up to now they had to pay $22 rent for a single room. Now they pay

The parish center, a "hospital for hearts". At lower left is the roof of the church.

The courtyard.

From old clothes, women make new ones for children.

This is for many people the only place where they can relax mentally and spiritually.

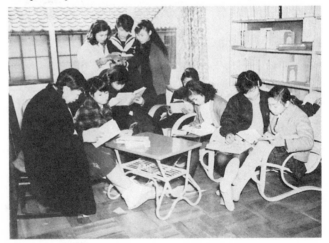

the same amount in monthly installments for a whole house, and they can take possession immediately. You cannot imagine how grateful these people are. This housing project is the great task awaiting me at the moment, and it will keep me busy for many years to come.

On account of other urgent involvements, the family housing project had to be dropped during 1970. But in his circular letter of May 1, 1971, Father Goldmann reported:

I built three more houses. I simply *had* to build them! These were special cases of need. I could not say "no". Let me tell you about one of them: a family of seven, the father a laborer, had been living for eighteen years in one room, without any daylight, only electric light. This building was to be torn down. Where should these people move to? They had no bank account, and no one was willing to lend them money. They would have had to move into a slum area with all the misery for body and soul that is prevalent there. Unexpectedly, a doctor who was moving to another city offered me a lovely house at a reasonable price. There were five rooms, kitchen, and bath. I bought it immediately, even though that depleted my bank account, leaving less than $2.50. The family moved into *their* house, which they will pay for in small installments during the next forty years. You cannot imagine the joy of these people! When I came to bless the home after a few weeks, I noticed they had taken in an eighteen-year-old young man. The woman explained, "This man, who is a deaf-mute, is the son of a divorced mother who had planned to put him in a mental institution, for she wanted to marry again. He is completely normal and a good tailor. No one wanted to take him in, but we have now a place for him. God certainly did not give us this house so that a room would be empty!" I must acknowledge in shame that this woman made me see that I had no right to have a comfortable vacant room in my house, and so I turned it over to a student.

There were two similar cases, and I simply could not say "no". To be truthful, I would have liked to say "no" in each case. Last year, for the first time in sixteen years I was free of debt, a very unusual, though far from unpleasant, experience. But now the debts are higher than ever! Nevertheless, I could not say "no".

This applies not only when it comes to providing housing for the poor but also in other cases. One night at 11 o'clock, I received a telephone call from the hospital. The mother of a family of five had been involved in a serious car accident. She was in the hospital with head injuries and the loss of one eye. Who will pay the admittance charge of $750? The amount needed may seem unbelievable, but it is a fact. Naturally, I paid it. Who else was there to pay it? If all goes well, I will get part of it back from the insurance company, which at this moment is fighting the case, for it does not want to pay. If all goes well, we'll get the money at the earliest after three or four months. Meanwhile, the woman is back on her feet. One eye could be saved. Such things have happened more than once.

As a rule, Father Goldmann does not calculate for long—he simply acts. Whenever he gets wind of a pressing need, he appears on the scene and tries to help. The following excerpts taken from various letters illustrate this fact:

Every week my young people and I visit a large home for the aged, where thousands of the very poorest are

Punctually, on October 16, 1969, Father Goldmann was able to send the promised $25,000 to help finance this mission station in Wakkanai.

Two of the acquired homes in Tokyo-Itabashi. Previously, these families had "vegetated" in one room. Now they have a house of their own—even if, by our standards, a very small one; and, of course, they are happy and grateful.

waiting for death. We have taken under our wing also a home of eighty-seven blind people. A number of patients in a mental hospital are among my best and most zealous helpers in prayer. This unity in prayer is my greatest daily joy and comfort in the midst of difficult situations. By and large the blessing of our work lies in prayer. Prayer is much more important than money. If we had enough people to pray, we should be able to supply all our wants.

November 19, 1965: This was the most successful year in the history of our parish—fifty baptisms (mostly adult converts). For a small parish in Japan this is almost unbelievable. If we had such exemplary Christians in Germany, there would soon be enough Sisters to staff every hospital, and no bishop would have to worry about a shortage of priests. The Japanese Christians are—God be praised!—still in their primitive fervor and not yet "traditionals".

IN ONE OF the above letters, Father Goldmann mentions his parish center, which has replaced the small house that in the beginning served both as chapel and living quarters. Father Goldmann launched this building project—the greatest he had yet undertaken—in 1961. Although he had been promised only a fraction of the required funds, he set about erecting a large modern earthquake-proof house in steel and concrete. On July 5, 1961, he wrote to me:

Without special and powerful assistance from Divine Providence, I might as well stop building. But our material needs are the least important. Incomparably more do we need prayer for the higher, the spiritual goods. My greatest concern by far is to find people who will remain faithful to prayer commitments. What profit is there in the noise and labor of building if prayer is lacking? At a given moment material gifts may cease, but prayer must never cease, or else the house I am building now will be left desolate.

A letter of October 11, 1961, reports, "I worked harder this past year than is possible to imagine—without taking off a single day. I really deserve a rest. Yet I must try to go to Germany as soon as I can, not primarily to recuperate but to preach and give lectures, so that at least part of my enormous debt be paid."

Thus Father Goldmann, after eight years of great deprivations, took his first vacation. During this "vacation" he preached 526 sermons and gave lectures in 192 different churches and halls. A free trip to the Holy Land and a month's stay in the hospital in Offenburg on account of total exhaustion took up the rest of the time. Nevertheless, all his debts were paid!

Today this center is truly a focal point for the entire parish. From early dawn till late at night it throbs with life. Here people learn, study, and make music. Here used articles and discarded clothes are sorted and made into "new" clothes. Here catechism classes and lectures are held. Here the people gather for recreational evening programs. Here the church choir holds its practices, and here, during their busy "feast-day season", some even spend the night. Above all, the young people feel at home here. With a thirst for knowledge and culture they bury themselves in the library, listen to good music (German classics preferred), or seek diversion from grinding routine in conversation and play.

According to Father Goldmann:

These Christians need a home for the heart. They cannot preserve their faith nor hold out against pagan immorality unless they have a home somewhere, from which they may draw strength and joy for a courageous witness against a godless and idolatrous world. For people who live with their families in a single room, this is the only place on earth where their souls can be at rest. How fully this Catholic center lives up to its purpose is apparent from the name the Japanese have given it—the hospital for hearts.

Such social work always has been and still is the key to Father Goldmann's mission endeavors. Every letter he writes voices the experience that one cannot convince another unless he is willing to live his Christian commitment to the full. In other words, love of neighbor not only stems from but also generates love of God.

"IT IS ABSOLUTELY necessary that we build another church. I have no doubt that we shall manage it again." This was Father Goldmann's prediction some years ago when, in spite of numerous difficulties, he had just completed his Church of St. Elizabeth. Shortly after, part of his district was assigned to a new parish of St. Andrew's. But even this did not solve the space problem for long, for in the spring of 1961 he wrote:

This fall we shall have to enlarge our church, which on Sundays is full to overflowing. Nearly everyone receives Holy Communion. Nor is there enough room in the small rectory. I have there twenty-five bed mats, and every night poor homeless people make use of them—free of charge, of course. I often have to sleep on the floor

PHOTO: *the Cathedral of Tokyo, consecrated by Cardinal Doy on December 8, 1964. The Catholics of the Archdiocese of Cologne contributed significantly toward the erection of this House of God.*

INSCRIPTION: *"To the parishioners of St. Elizabeth parish, we extend our cordial blessing and heartily thank all who in any way assisted them."*

The first Mass of Father Maximus in the cathedral church of St. Elizabeth. He was not the first one from this parish to be ordained, nor the last.

Not far from St. Anthony's Home, the vacationers assist at daily Mass and pray for their benefactors.

since someone has put his children in my bed. Everyone knows he is welcome to eat and sleep here. No room is locked, yet nothing is ever missing.

The enlargement of the church was financed by poor Japanese Christians, all of whom sacrificed one or more of their monthly pay checks for this cause. At Pentecost, 1964, I received an SOS from Father Goldmann addressed to all his friends and benefactors:

> I had hoped not to be obliged to start another project, but, at the request of the Cardinal of Tokyo, I accepted a burden greater than any I have hitherto known. To the five hundred thousand people living in my parish territory another two hundred thousand will soon be added. They are to be lodged in a housing addition four miles in length. It is impossible for the Catholics among them to fit into my already overcrowded, though enlarged, church. Unless I act at once, we shall witness another suburb mushrooming without God. I have found a site for the new parish buildings, and I have placed the project into the hands of St. Joseph. I made a pact with him: if you will send me half the money needed for the land, I'll take the inevitable plunge. In the meantime I received exactly one half, namely, $30,000, from a German diocese. I had to act quickly, for it is becoming increasingly difficult to obtain suitable land for building. Moreover, I am responsible for this huge parish. So I signed the contract on Ascension Day. The attractive price was offered on condition that the remaining sum be paid in August. My poor parishioners have offered to advance me their meager savings, but they constitute but a tiny fraction of what is needed.

Then the incredible happened. Without support from influential persons, without any publicity, the property was paid for within six weeks. One letter of appeal from Father Goldmann to his friends had sufficed. (Incidentally, the Pope's mission intention for June 1964 was the missions in Japan.) The press duly publicized this success, one headline reading, "German Record in Tokyo Even before the Olympics". Another article, on the front page of *Neue Bildpost* (the German equivalent of *Life*) on September 13, 1964, concluded with these lines, "Congratulations, Father Goldmann, on your first gold medal for Germany! The spiritual athletes who trust in Divine Providence remain undefeated. Even though your Olympic feat may not be beamed by television satellites, the transmission and performance were twice as good!" In another report we read, "This record will continue to result in gold and silver medals long after the 1964 Olympic games in Tokyo have ended and their victors have sunk into oblivion."

Thus a second parish came into being in this gigantic suburb—the parish of St. Joseph. Cardinal Doy of Tokyo was so touched by this spontaneous gesture of liberality that he presented each donor with a picture of himself.

Nevertheless, though the property had been purchased, new difficulties arose and delayed the building operations. To begin with, the Franciscan missionaries of Fulda were prohibited from establishing a second parish in Tokyo, for, according to an ordinance, foreign religious communities are not to administer more than one parish in the Japanese metropolis. Therefore, only a native priest was eligible as pastor of the new church of St. Joseph.

Another great difficulty was the poverty of the Church in Japan. Time and again Father Goldmann reported for an interview with the cardinal and his auxiliary bishop, only to be put off until another time. At last, on November 19, 1967, the project had become a reality. According to a letter of that date:

> The new parish of St. Joseph the Worker celebrated its first Mass today. You, too, must rejoice with us, for you worked hard to help us achieve this goal in the Olympic Year, 1964. What ready generosity was shown by your gifts! Without the $30,000 contributed within six weeks, this parish would never have come into being. Today such a site could not possibly be paid for. Since this parish owes its existence to your spontaneous generosity, our first expression of gratitude goes to you. Rest assured that all of you, together with your intentions, are included in the daily Mass offered here.
>
> That this parish of St. Joseph is administered not by my order but by the Japanese diocese does not matter. The important thing is that a new pastoral center now exists with a native pastor who can be more effective in his work. We missionaries, in spite of all our work and endeavor, remain foreigners and strangers and can never hope to influence people as powerfully as can a priest from their own ranks. Our task is to strive to fertilize the stony ground and to sow good seed. When and how the seed will germinate and whether it will produce abundant fruit, that is the Lord's concern.
>
> The rectory and the parish center of St. Joseph have been completed, but there is as yet no church. At the moment, the small parish hall has to serve as a temporary church, with a curtain to conceal the altar when not in use. The building site is there, but the funds are exhausted. One might ask why the parish hall was built before the church. The reason is that in Japan the Church and the state are entirely separated, and the latter gives no support

whatever to religious bodies. Besides, Christian communities as well as vocations to the priesthood come almost exclusively from the poorer classes, who live mostly from hand to mouth. How can a priest live under such conditions? Where should he lodge in order to carry out his work? He depends completely on the fee the state grants for the conducting of a kindergarten. If this kindergarten is equipped to care for 120 children, the income can be stretched to provide a modest livelihood. Not very many students—Tokyo counts 360,000 at present—would muster the courage needed to study theology under such a system. At the moment there are seventy-five theology students in the seminary of Yonbancho—a small but elite group.

The Japanese episcopate, too, is very poor. My bishop said to me, "Father, it is thanks to your initiative that St. Joseph parish is able to function. Your many contributors have made it possible. Could you not procure another $7,500?" (To beg is for a Japanese the greatest humiliation.) Sorry to say, I had to disappoint my bishop. "My lord," I answered, "there is only $75 in my account, whereas my debts are much higher. As much as I would like to, I simply cannot help you."

Father Goldmann's pockets are almost always empty. The more money he receives, the less he possesses. Mission aid is and will remain a bottomless pit. From a purely business angle, he should have long ago declared bankruptcy. His trust in God, supported by prayer a thousandfold, often surpasses every sober calculation. But for all that, Father Goldmann is no "dreamer". On the contrary, he has both feet firmly on the ground of reality. However, the needs of his fellow men are more essential and primary than all business calculations and considerations. In his semiannual report of May 1971, he writes:

> It was absolutely necessary to build a new parish church. The young Japanese pastor, living in two tiny rooms in a large block of flats, was able to accommodate only a small fraction of his parishioners. Mass had to be offered hurriedly and without singing. Eighty percent were not able to attend Mass because there was simply no room. I had promised him $12,500 to purchase the land for a new church. That was in December, and I needed the money on April 16. That day came and I still did not have the money. In the afternoon, however, one hour before the bank closed, I received a telephone call telling me that the money had arrived! Yes, we are still living in an age of miracles!

Already during his first missionary vacation, Father Goldmann preached, "Churches must be built where people pray." Even more important to him than churches, however, are priestly and religious vocations. In a recent circular letter he described briefly the special way of a candidate to the priesthood:

> The occasion of the First Mass of this newly ordained priest was a day of great joy. Twelve years ago Father Maximus came to me to be instructed and baptized. At that time he was a high-ranking student at one of the best academies in the state. For his excellent achievements in art, he was chosen to attend the French Academy of Art in Paris. For this reason I gave him regular private lessons in French. However, when he was ready to leave for France, he decided to return his scholarship to the state. I

was not exactly pleased with that decision, for I had hoped he would use the opportunity for higher studies. Then he told me, "Father, if I go to Paris, I will learn to create figures of bronze or stone. What remains of these, you can see from the ruins of Greek sculpture. I, however, would like to create something more permanent, something that neither men nor time can destroy. You mentioned in class that every soul was to become an image of God, according to the plan that God had conceived from all eternity. To sculpture this image surpasses all material creations. Therefore, I would like to become a priest." Now he has reached his goal. In spite of serious illness through a twice-repeated siege of tuberculosis, in spite of the two-year interruption of his studies, in spite of repeated illness during the entire time of his studies, so that doctors feared he could not make it—he never gave up. He always began again with new courage. And since we found a very good medicine—the German PK 7—he was helped in a wonderful way and was able to pursue his course. He now feels like a new person. His first Mass was a day of joy for God and for all of us, especially for me! It was the second ordination in one year, and a third will follow in the fall. Another student has begun his studies. Should we not, therefore, rejoice? Your prayers and sacrifices have not been in vain.

MORE THAN ONCE Father Goldmann had the opportunity to visit his brother Franciscans on the island of Hokkaido, the largest island in northern Japan. On several occasions he described conditions under which these Franciscan missionaries work. The first time he visited them was after his overseas vacation. In his circular of November 25, 1962, we read:

Before my return to Tokyo I stopped for ten days at our Hokkaido mission, where we have been laboring under the greatest financial difficulties. When I arrived on November 6, it was already snowing. By now the snow lies several feet deep. It was the first time I had seen some of these stations, and now I realize that my life in Tokyo is relatively easy, for there is simply no comparison with the privations our missionaries in the north have to undergo. I was really shocked and ashamed to see what sacrifices our men are making, often amid the deepest isolation and abandonment.

In the course of this tour I came also to Bibai, a mining region that extends deep into the mountains and primeval forests. There a fellow Franciscan is in charge of a small station. He comes from the Bohemian Forest, where his relatives live to this day. However, for a long time he has heard nothing from them. I had a chance to observe this priest's work and way of life under conditions that we cannot imagine. He has a room not worthy of the name; his bed is the bare floor. He has no cook, and his fare reminds me of my prisoner-of-war days. It does not seem possible for a man to be poorer and more selfless than he is. The astonishing thing, however, is that he is able to accommodate a number of boys in this tiny room. How he manages this is a puzzle to me.

Father Goldmann returns to this subject again in his circular of June 29, 1963:

On my long and strenuous journeys to the north and south of Japan the life of our missionaries never ceases to impress and touch me. I who live in the metropolis of Tokyo can henceforth only be ashamed when I consider under what incredible circumstances and difficulties these

Mission Station Bibai with kindergarten and Sisters' convent.

priests fulfill their duties. This is almost too much to expect of anybody. On lonely outposts, in regions that even today must be classified as wilderness, these missionaries spend themselves for their small flock, often scattered over large areas reaching far into the mountains. Were they not men imbued with deep faith, they could not endure this life for even a month—let alone for dozens of years. These messengers of the Good News deserve our admiration and our prayers.

Similar concerns are revealed in almost every letter. Yet Father Goldmann was not satisfied with feeling sorry for his confreres. To help these missionaries he now exhibited an even greater zeal than he had shown for his own parish. He knew, of course, the means would never suffice to help everywhere. Nevertheless, with the help of his friends in Germany, a new mission station was erected and an existing one enlarged. In August 1966, Father Nicholas Prescher, a missionary from the Sudetenland, was presented with a kindergarten for 180 children and a completely furnished convent for the Sisters. A month later, on September 18, 1966, a chapel with a rectory and a kindergarten for 160 children was dedicated at Shibetsu. This is the field of activity of a young Japanese priest, Father Antonius Akoi, to whom Father Goldmann had promised his help in the fall of 1965.

When in May 1969, I wrote to Father Goldmann's friends calling their attention to his approaching silver jubilee on June 24, I cited the following excerpts from the above 1963 letter, in which he expressed his emotions regarding the conditions of these exceedingly poor and shabby Franciscan mission stations in the northern part of Japan:

> Today I am standing on the coast of Hokkaido, outside the little town of Wakkanai, immediately opposite Sachalin,

Mission Station Shibetsu, consisting of a chapel, rectory, and kindergarten.

which was seized by the Russians at the end of World War II. In front of me lies the channel between the Pacific Ocean and the Sea of Japan. Here two worlds separate. With the naked eye one can barely make out the highest peaks of the unproductive Siberian island where forty years ago our German missionaries landed, took upon themselves the greatest privations, and founded churches, which were later "suffocated" in the blood of martyrs during the Red persecution. A vivid reminder of this gruesome period is a little crucifix that was rescued and is now kept by a Japanese Franciscan here in Wakkanai.

Directly behind me stands a tiny blockhouse leaning toward the coast, so small and humble that it can hardly put up resistance to the constant storms. I just came from this house, which is more like a wooden hut than a house. In it is a tiny room with a small altar on which the Blessed Sacrament is kept. And who guards and inhabits this little house? Four Sisters of Charles de Foucauld—a fraternity of the Little Sisters of Jesus—three of them natives and one French. They pray and work, laboring as housemaids in the hospital and as fish carvers in the ill-smelling fish cannery. And here in a godless country they pray for many hours of the day and night before the Blessed Sacrament exposed; they pray for Russia and for world peace. They have permission to open the tabernacle, for, during the eight months of winter and amid endless storms, the presence of a priest is rare.

When I visited them, the stove was red hot, for then the temperature was so low that one could not do without a fire. They served me a bowl of tea while they told of their lives. When I asked them if it was not too hard to live for so many years in dire poverty and solitude, the French sister smiled and said in broken Japanese, "We are

never alone. Isn't *He* with us all the time?" They said they
would never want to leave this place. My pagan companion and I felt very much ashamed, and the former remarked thoughtfully, "How brave women can be!"

To return now to the summer of 1969 and my letter, the
approaching jubilee of Father Goldmann prompted me to
write the following lines:

> I am convinced that nothing in the world would please
> Father Goldmann more than a donation toward the build-
> ing of a mission station at Wakkanai, one fit for human
> beings to live in. Perhaps you are shocked if I name the
> sum of $25,000. I do not know, of course, whether we
> shall ever see the realization of this project, but I know
> that even more daring plans have materialized and under
> seemingly even more hopeless conditions. I have long
> since learned that nothing is impossible. . . .
>
> Everywhere in the world misery and distress abound,
> and it is impossible to help every cause. Jesus himself re-
> fers to this: "The poor you have always with you." Some
> day he will ask us, not whom we have helped, but
> whether we have helped at all. The decision is your own.
> Of one thing I am certain, however, and I am ready to go
> through fire for this truth: Father Goldmann is a faithful
> servant and a just steward, who does not bury the offered
> gifts but uses them to the utmost.

The circular was mailed out. Weeks and months passed.
Much money was donated. Father Goldmann, however, had
financial burdens greater than ever before. As a result, in August his treasury was exhausted. It was, humanly speaking,
impossible for him to meet a deadline. The contractors, on

the other hand, expected prompt payments, since it was stipulated that the new mission be ready for occupancy in October.

At this point the unforeseen happened once again. A stranger, hitherto completely unknown, gave the required sum without any knowledge of what it would be used for. Faithful to his contract, Father Goldmann was able to make the payment promptly on October 6, 1969. This payment was one-third of the total cost.

When I mention that I am no longer surprised at anything, I must add that Father Goldmann himself was deeply moved by this turn of events. As he wrote on November 19, 1969, "The success of this project is just another tangible proof that hoping against hope is as valid today as ever." Meanwhile, the new mission station of Wakkanai has come into being. The selflessness of the four Little Sisters of Jesus has brought them unexpected improvement in their living quarters. They, too, were full of wonder and gratitude.

In the meantime, new tasks came to Father Goldmann. Excerpts from two letters give a brief picture of them:

> November 19, 1967: "As I have reported more than once, quite some time ago my parish adopted another parish in South India. The people there live in much greater poverty than do ours here. Father Jerome, the Carmelite missionary in charge, describes the terrible conditions there in a heart-rending letter: "The most devastating famine of the year has held up all our work and plans. At the moment one fears for the worst. If our people manage to scrape together one meal a day, this is considered good. The sobering fact is that they are actually starving. It is heartrending to see children in such want. . . ."
>
> Through special help from Germany and my parish

here, we have been able to provide one meal of rice each day for up to three hundred children, thus keeping them alive. According to your wishes, the bulk of your gifts this year was sent to India. Add to this the monthly collection in my parish, amounting to at least $125. Thus, our regular money gift, though far from adequate, serves to alleviate the minimal needs of these people.

In a letter during the summer of 1968, Father Goldmann wrote:

As you know, two years ago my parish pledged itself to act as "fairy godmother" to another parish in South India. The starting point for this was a sermon in which I expressed my fear that all the praying, all church attendance, etc., are not sufficient to earn eternal happiness. I told my people how Matthew in chapter 25 describes the Last Judgment and refers to acts of charity, of which I had little evidence up to now, and yet these works of mercy are mentioned by the Lord Jesus as the only criterion of the Last Judgment. I reminded them of how much we had received, that we had the most efficiently developed Catholic parish in Tokyo, with a most beautiful parish center, that we had the only parish vacation home for mothers and children in the whole of Japan. What, I asked, are we doing for others? As a result of this sermon, my parishioners decided to adopt Father Jerome's parish in South India. Divine Providence had called our attention to this parish, where people lived in untold poverty and where many, especially children, were dying of starvation. My parish council decided to start a monthly collection to be taken up the first Sunday of each month. This collection amounts to about twenty

One of the new churches under construction in India.

This church, named in honor of our Lady of Fatima, was dedicated in Manalikara, India, in 1969.

Father Goldmann blesses Indian women.

In 1969, Father Jerome became provincial of the Carmelites in Manalikara, India.

times the ordinary Sunday collection. Beyond that, we observe two mission Sundays a year, one in Advent and one in Lent—both for India. On Passion Sunday this year, each of my people gave an average of $2.50.

Thus, with your collaboration, we were able to alleviate the needs of our adopted parish. The Mass stipends you sent through my friend Father Ludwig Fischl in Lederdorn have not only provided the Carmelite Fathers in South India with the much needed financial assistance but also have actively helped Father Jerome's poor people.

You and I have thereby done a deed that counts among the most consoling in my priestly ministry. On my return flight, I shall visit this Carmelite community, in order to determine what we can do—now that our enormous debts are paid—to prevent a similar famine in the future.

Early in 1968, Father Goldmann's physical condition had reached an all-time low. X-rays and examinations by the best specialists in Tokyo revealed a very serious condition. An operation was urgently recommended, but nobody could promise alleviation of his malady. Father Goldmann hesitated to give his consent. Providentially, at that critical moment, Lufthansa Airline offered him a first-class ticket to Germany. They did this not because they were aware of his plight but because they wanted to reward him for having led a group of thirty people on an air pilgrimage the previous year. To Father Goldmann the ticket was a sign from God, and he flew to Germany. Here, in the hands of specialists, his health improved visibly without the need for surgery.

On his return trip, Father Goldmann visited his adopted community in India. What he saw and experienced moved him profoundly. Space forbids us to describe the incomprehensible poverty he encountered. (The daily wage of young people for eight hours of heavy physical labor, for example, is only twelve to fifteen cents.)

This visit to India spurred Father Goldmann on to even greater efforts on behalf of his adopted Christians. He described his experiences in a long letter, and the response of his friends was spontaneous. Within two years he was able to finance five churches with the gifts of his benefactors. Altogether, Father Jerome's Carmelite Province now serves ten parishes. During the same period, all these churches were supplied with liturgical vestments and altar vessels. Thousands of rosaries and tens of thousands of holy pictures were sent. These simple Christians in India could hardly contain themselves for joy.

In addition to the pastoral aid given to the churches in India, several schools were erected or enlarged and electricity was installed. Also, some necessary farm machinery could be purchased. Several technical schools with workshops were opened, and needy students are provided with free board and room. In this way those who want an education are given a chance to rise to higher levels and as a consequence can obtain better paying positions.

In a 1970 circular Father Goldmann announced a very extensive and expensive project, a modern hospital to serve an area in India with a population of more than sixty thousand. In 1971 he was able to report:

> The building is finished, at least in part—with forty beds at present, and the capacity to treat more than two hundred outpatients a day. The dedication took place in June 1971. I was urged to attend, but I could not manage— neither timewise or moneywise. So far the hospital is only 60 percent complete. . . . Since I had promised to finance the entire building, I had to pay another large amount.

The architect's drawing of the hospital in Manalikara, India, a section of which was completed in June 1971. This undertaking was made possible through the generosity of benefactors.

The foundation wall of the hospital, in 1969.

The hospital under construction, autumn 1970.

This, too, we were able to do. Hence, it is really *your* hospital, built with your donations, a hospital from which, since July 1, 1971, great blessings flow for sick bodies as well as souls. Six Sisters are there; they still live in huts, but a convent will be built for them later. The nursing staff is adequate. A second doctor is urgently needed. What a beautiful monument built by your charity! All the worries and anxieties connected with the building have become very fruitful.

Early in 1972 I was privileged to be an eyewitness to what has been accomplished in India through Father Goldmann. With the aid of donations and Mass stipends received and sent to the Carmelites in South India, the following accomplishments can be noted: a large seminary for theology students; another seminary for students of philosophy; a large orphanage; eight new churches, some of them very modern; renovation or enlargement of several schools; about fifty homes for poor families; and, last but not least, a modern hospital that is without its equal in South India. (This hospital is already being enlarged to include one hundred beds.)

A word about the Carmelites in South India: The community numbers ninety-two priests. More than one hundred fifty students are studying for the priesthood. Annually between ten and fourteen priests are ordained. There is no lack of vocations, nor is celibacy a problem. These Christians are deeply religious, very intelligent, and extremely studious.

While in India, I witnessed on one day 138 baptisms—thirty-three of them adults. To see the devotion and inner recollection of these people during the two-hour ceremony was quite an experience. They are among the poorest of the poor, whose average income is twenty-five to fifty cents a day. They often have to work ten to twelve hours a day, but this does not make them in any way rebellious. They live for another world. For them, eternity is the only lasting reality, and this earthly life is merely a transition from this world to the next, comparable to the ugly caterpillar that is changed into a beautiful butterfly.

To the people of Kerala, India, the wonderful assistance that has come their way since the great famine seems all but incomprehensible—even miraculous. The real key to the mystery is nothing less than a rightly understood and genuinely lived Christianity.

AGAIN AND AGAIN Father Goldmann finds new avenues for his apostolate. The most daring and perhaps a unique undertaking of this kind was undoubtedly the peace pilgrimage he undertook with thirty members of his flock from May 15 to July 1, 1967. Nothing has stirred hearts and minds more than this journey to places of pilgrimage in Germany, Austria, France, Italy, and the Holy Land. People could not understand how these predominantly poor people could shoulder such a financial burden. Some feared for Father Goldmann's health, on which seemed to hinge the realization of the enterprise. Others again tried to dissuade him, pleading that the responsibility and risk were far too great.

This is not the place to enumerate the countless problems that presented themselves before the journey or to set about describing the unforgettable impressions of the pilgrims on the way—their meeting the Holy Father and other Church dignitaries, the enduring and absorbing experiences of liturgical celebrations, or the unsurpassed hospitality of their German friends.

The pilgrimage was in many respects unique and singularly blessed. During the seven-week journey, there was not a single breakdown, accident, or casualty, sickness, disagreement, or failure. In spite of a few unforeseen difficulties, the itinerary could be followed exactly as planned, punctual almost to the minute. Contrary to all expectations, the Japanese pilgrims were the first foreigners permitted to enter the Holy Land after the 1967 Seven-Day War. They were allowed to visit even the holy places that formerly had been closed to pilgrims. Father Goldmann, the indispensable organizer, travel companion, and interpreter, was able to hold out despite the unusual physical and mental strain. What blessings resulted from this pilgrimage can hardly be described in words. The person-to-person contacts among people of different nationalities and cultures greatly strengthened the ties of friendship. What a thrill to experience this sense of worldwide community, this fraternal relationship with people from other parts of the world! The concept of "mission" took on new meaning and life. The Japanese formulated their impressions in the following pregnant words: "The pilgrimage through Germany was for us a daily new and blessed experience of what the Church stands for. As Christians of a mission country and a diaspora Church, we discovered facets of the Church hitherto strange to us. To witness these was an exhilarating experience that will remain with us for life."

Among the pilgrims were two pagans, one an employee and the other a student. The former was baptized in Bethlehem, and the latter was received into the Church after returning to Japan. But what was the effect of this pilgrimage on the Christians of the Church of St. Elizabeth in Tokyo-Itabashi? The 1967 Pentecost circular describes it this way:

> When I state that the activity of the pilgrim group during the past few months has transformed my entire parish like a leaven, I have not told the exact truth, for "activ-

ity" is not the right word. It is much more than activity; it is an inner renewal in my parish brought about by the pilgrim group. A flood of zeal and prayer has been released, an avalanche of dedication has swept from the small group through the whole parish, carrying everything before it. When I recently bade good-bye to my parish before embarking on another trip, I could say in all sincerity, "I wish to thank everybody for this past year, which has brought such a rich harvest after fourteen years of planting and cultivation. It is a harvest that has yielded fruit beyond my fondest dreams."

First of all, I must mention a deepening of the life of prayer and worship. Though I had tried for fourteen years to build up my parish from the altar, these last six months have shown me how much really can be done. This Lent we counted at least fifty Christians at daily Mass. In order to appreciate this fact, we must consider that, since the division of the parish, membership is only 620, including 250 who are sick, aged, or children. Nor can we overlook the fact that most of my people must spend about three hours daily traveling to and from work, with a nine- and even ten-hour workday for the majority. The other Lenten services—the Stations of the Cross three times a week and numerous other Lenten exercises—were also well attended. Holy Week—the annual climax of my priestly life—was an unforgettable event. During the Good Friday services the choir combined the reading of the Passion by four lectors with the singing of Bach's musical composition *Johannespassion*. Between the readings, by way of meditation, we sang all the chants *a capella*. Then came the Easter Vigil on Holy Saturday night, with nine adult baptisms. This surpassed all previous experiences. With unbounded zeal, the pilgrim group had set the whole community on fire. The church choir, under the direction of our singer Veronica, after many weeks of daily practice, topped all previous achievements.

When our bishop was here for administering the sacrament of Confirmation, he told the people that he had never experienced a church service of such caliber as at St. Elizabeth's. I can proudly say that because of the peace pilgrimage my flock has become more dedicated and their faith has deepened.

Participation in charitable works—the real test of a genuine Christian—has also greatly increased. In the course of our pilgrimage, Christian charity impressed us very much, sometimes with humiliating force. After our return, the pilgrims never grew tired of extolling the love lavished upon them. It constituted *the* theme of the numerous talks and illustrated lectures in which the experiences of the seven blessed weeks were shared with the entire parish. As a result, a powerful wave of charitable activity is at present sweeping through the parish. Our young people regularly visit homes for the aged, in which people are housed under conditions I cannot describe, nor would you believe me were I to attempt to do so. I must confess I had been unaware of this situation so prevalent in our neighborhood, but my young people discovered it, and they are now striving with great selflessness to bring about a change. The women care for literally hundreds of old and sick people; they sew and mend for them; and they visit them frequently, even though this may entail a train ride of four hours to reach some of the distant homes. Almost every month my parish is summoned for blood donations required for cancer patients, and each time so many volunteers come forward to offer blood that the Japanese

Red Cross has repeatedly expressed its admiration and astonishment.

In time our parish activities became known throughout Japan. This is not surprising, since I was called upon to speak about them on television and before the press. In response we received thousands of letters—almost exclusively from non-Christians. This was a dimension we had not anticipated. It shows how many hearts may be touched by the example of one small parish community. These news reports were instrumental in bringing a large number of pagans from various parts of Japan to take catechetical instruction. What more wonderful radiation from our Christian activity could we expect?

In this apostolate we must give due credit to our parish publication *St. Elizabeth*. We are the only Catholic parish in Japan to publish a monthly magazine. At first it contained thirty pages, but the pilgrim group has doubled that number. Since September 1967, eight special editions have reported the memorable pilgrimage. These articles are of such quality that notable journals of Japan have copied them. We had to reprint a number of them because of the many requests from every part of the country.

I am wholly astonished at the thoroughness with which the participants have assimilated their experiences. I was often speechless when I read of the feelings and impressions of these newly baptized Christians, and I marvel at the insight with which they responded and the conclusions they drew. If I ever wondered whether this pilgrimage was justified, I am now completely convinced that it was both a necessary and an efficacious grace.

While penning these lines, I have before me the report of something that occurred here in Tokyo during our absence. One of the most respected bishops of Japan, from a far distant northern diocese, came to celebrate Mass with the parishioners of St. Elizabeth and to obtain some personal insight into the parish of which he had read in the press and heard about elsewhere. Though I do not know this bishop personally, I am astonished and delighted that he should have singled us out. How can I ever adequately thank each of you for obtaining so many blessings for us, through your prayers!

In August 1969, Father Goldmann undertook another pilgrimage in connection with his home visit, to which he is entitled every eight years. He did this knowing full well what an enormous burden it would be. This time I joined him, and those weeks will forever remain imprinted on my memory. Every day I felt humbled at the genuine piety and fervor of these twenty-eight Japanese pilgrims. Early in the morning, on my way back from breakfast, I would meet them coming back from the Church of the Holy Sepulcher, where they had knelt in prayer for two hours. This happened to be the time when the world press reported the fire at the Mosque of El Aksa. We were the only pilgrims in Jerusalem at the time. We made the Way of the Cross several times, and on each occasion our pilgrims took turns carrying a heavy wooden cross through the narrow alleys of the ancient city. Most of these pilgrims were young men and women. They paid no attention to ridicule or other abuse.

I was not the only one impressed by these pilgrims. The manager of the largest pilgrim hotel (Casa Nova), who for several decades has served thousands of pilgrims, said very simply that he had never experienced such natural and genuine devotion in prayer and song, combined with such buoyant cheerfulness. He would have liked to keep us much longer than we were able to stay. (What is the matter with our Western Christians when young Asiatic converts, by their genuine Christian witness, put us to shame?)

The unforgettable climax was our audience with the Holy Father. Father Goldmann reports:

> When the Holy Father received us in private audience, we gathered about him like children around their father, and we were privileged to sing for him. He greeted each one, and he told me what a consolation in his suffering was this visit of new Christians. Then I realized that our pilgrimage was truly a good and holy undertaking, on which the Pope had bestowed his blessing, tracing the cross on the brow of each of us.

FATHER GOLDMANN's manifold social work could not remain hidden for long, not even in the metropolis of Tokyo with its twelve million inhabitants. Shortly before Christmas 1965, he was invested with the highest award bestowed by the state for social work, when he received the "Order of Good Deeds" in the official hall of decorations, the Temple of Meiji. The document read as follows:

> Father Gereon Goldmann: You have labored unceasingly for many years to improve every kind of social work in your district, and in this way you have contributed substantially toward better cordial relations between Germany and Japan. Therefore, we express our admiration for your outstanding work and grant you the "Medal for Good Deeds".
>
> (Signed) TADASHI ADACHI
President.

Father Goldmann adds, "The Board told me that in this decoration are included all those who have supported these good works. With great joy and satisfaction, therefore, I pass on this recognition to you, my friends and benefactors at home."

Such honors are bestowed only once a year. So far few foreigners have been considered eligible, and Father Goldmann was the first German to receive this honor.

Hardly had he returned to Japan from his pilgrimage when Father Goldmann was invited to the German Consulate, where he was awarded the First-Class West German Cross of Merit. "One more decoration in my drawer", was his simple comment. And he added, "This recognition, too, belongs in the first place to my friends, for without their prayer and other help I should not have been able to obtain it."

A German reporter described his visit with him as follows:

> We had hardly sat down when Father Goldmann sketched his plans for the next two weeks, and he did so with a dash and enthusiasm that reveals the secret of his success. With him you can go to the ends of the world! This Franciscan is unquestionably the most unique person I met in traveling the length and breadth of Asia. He is also a most admirable missionary, who built up a parish in the midst of greatest misery. He has the knack of making all his endeavors bear fruit. He himself has remained poor and simple, not even having a car. What strength, what courage, what tenacity of purpose such men must have to endure a life devoid of all external comfort and consolation! Father Goldmann does his utmost to help Christians redeemed by the blood of Christ. People like him live entirely for others and for

Pilgrim group in an audience with Pope Paul VI in Rome.

Christmas 1965: Father Goldmann received the highest decoration the state awards for social welfare work—the Order of Good Deeds—in the temple of Jeiji, Tokyo.

Blessing of the cemetery of urns, in the cathedral church of St. Elizabeth. Here Father Goldmann wishes to repose someday, in the midst of his parishioners.

another world. And seldom have I seen a person laugh as heartily as these Franciscans, and especially, Father Goldmann, the Ragpicker of Tokyo!

POSTSCRIPT

What is recorded here has actually happened, but it is only a fraction of the life of Father Gereon Goldmann. Part of it I have experienced personally, and much came from firsthand sources, attested by witnesses and confirmed in documents.

Hundreds of thousands have read this book, including men who during the war had striven to silence Father Goldmann. Among countless letters received, there is not one that calls into question any of the happenings related here. A few critical inquiries regarding the timing of certain war occurrences could always be explained satisfactorily. They even served to supplement and corroborate what has been related here.

If this book has by now [1971] reached a circulation of over two hundred thousand, this is a testimony to the following facts:

1. The experiences of Father Goldmann have a message not only for him but for all men without exception.

2. Even in our times a courageous Christian witness is effective.

No matter how terse these anecdotes may be, they nevertheless give an idea of Father Goldmann's strength of will and deep faith, together with a daring trust in God and complete selflessness. However, it is not our intention to invest a man with a halo. What Father Delp wrote in the face of death is valid here also: "Man alone cannot do it. Every attempt at self-sufficiency is self-deception, even suicide." Only with power from on high can man achieve his true greatness. This cannot be forced, it has to be humbly prayed for.

Father Goldmann testifies to what mighty forces can be set into motion by unceasing and fervent prayer. He swears to its efficacy with a trust that moves mountains. "Seek ye first the kingdom of God", is his motto. In his sermons he repeats, "Churches must be built where there will be prayer." Or again, "Your money would be a curse to us if you did not pray. You must pray more for the missions." Of his friends in East Germany he writes:

> Many thousands in East Germany are interceding on our behalf. God alone knows how many prayers they send up to heaven. Again and again promises of prayer come my way, ranging all the way from a fixed number of ejaculations to daily rosaries. We can never measure the help we receive from this wonderful army of intercessors. These friends cannot send material help, even if they so desired. But prayer is and remains the most important.

Not only in East Germany do people pray. Together with the many friends and benefactors elsewhere, I have a long list of convents and congregations whose members unite day by day in prayer with their Japanese friends.

Prayer was and still is the key to all the providential events and happenings in the life of Father Goldmann. To prayer he owes his vocation to the priesthood. Prayer was the secret of his repeated deliverance from imminent death. Prayer is the secret of all his missionary successes.

Even at the beginning of his military training all his decisions and actions were prompted by his Christian conscience, even if that entailed going "against the current". In spite of military engagements at the front in France, Russia, and Italy, he never harmed a single person, let alone killed anybody. On the contrary, as a medic he helped to relieve physical suffering, and as a priest he saved many from eternal damnation.

Ten Franciscan priests, including Father Goldmann, concelebrate Mass in the church on the "Frauenberg", Fulda, on the feast of Corpus Christi, 1967.

Father Gereon Goldmann is one of many missionaries. They all follow the call of Christ, "Go into the whole world." And in so doing they sacrifice everything they hold dear— family and friends, home and native land, and themselves. Often misunderstood—or even despised and hated—these heroes labor on foreign soil, among people with strange ideas and customs. Sometimes they live in almost complete isolation, abandoned by all, with unsavory food as their daily fare and an unwholesome climate in the bargain. We seldom hear of their work. Lonely and unnoticed, such missionaries seem to eke out a poor existence for an apparently lost cause—but only apparently!

It is true that living and working in foreign countries estranges such men and women from the land of their birth. Their one-time familiar ties are loosened and gradually lost altogether, especially with approaching old age. While one would consider an occasional vacation overseas to be a long-cherished dream, how often did I hear such missionaries say, "How happy I shall be to return to my Christians!" Here the parable of the sower is reality: "Some seed fell on rich soil and grew and produced a hundredfold yield" (Lk 8:8).

When Father Goldmann told me many years ago, at a time when he still lived in greatest poverty, that he wished to remain in Japan to the end of his life, I was at first very surprised at this. By now, however, I have come to understand this attitude, for the real home of a missionary can be only the place where he was put in the earth as the "seed" and where the seed has taken root. It is not surprising, then, that Father Goldmann has already chosen his final resting place in the heart of his parish, where he, together with his flock, may await in peace the final resurrection and join with them in the chorus of the eternal Alleluia.

If in this book I have tried to report on one of many missionaries, I did not intend to single him out for the spotlight. Such men do not want this. Nevertheless, should we on this account draw the cover of silence over the heroism of our missionary priests, Brothers, and Sisters? Whether this would be right, judge for yourselves. . . .

—Joseph Seitz

FOR TWENTY-TWO YEARS Fr. Goldmann continued his work as a parish priest in Tokyo, preaching, according to his own count, a total of forty thousand sermons throughout all of Japan. Seventeen times he led his Japanese Catholics on pilgrimages to the Holy Land, staying only in monasteries and following rigorous Spiritual Exercises. After founding two Carmelite monasteries in India and several more in Japan, he then founded the Academy of Ecclesiastical Music in Tokyo. For the first fifteen years he directed the school, whose graduates today work as musicians in Japanese churches and whose reputation has spread throughout Asia and the world.

Now in his eighties, after having suffered three heart attacks, Fr. Goldmann resides in his native Germany. Following the third attack, the doctors pronounced him dead, but God had further plans for him. He awoke from his coma and was taken by plane to Germany, where, except for some trips, including one to Japan, he has remained since 1994. After several months spent in and out of various hospitals, he is finally able to live in what he calls "absolute quiet". He begins his day at 5 A.M., studying, personally replying to the many thousands of letters and cards sent to him, and receiving numerous visitors from all over the world. Fr. Goldmann also spends five to six hours a day in prayer, never forgetting that it is God, not he, who has accomplished so much with one life. It was while on tour in America that the speeches he gave about his World War II experiences were recorded and compiled into a book that has now been translated into more than a dozen languages. It is evident that God is indeed in charge of Fr. Goldmann's life, a life that has touched so many others.

Now I am in peace and have only
the duty of praying.
Be sure I pray from heart for
you.

Fr. Goldmann